IRISH

HISTORIOGRAPHY

1970–79

IRISH HISTORIOGRAPHY
1970–79

edited by
JOSEPH LEE

CORK UNIVERSITY PRESS
1981

© 1981 Cork University Press

Gearóid Mac Niocaill, Art Cosgrove
Aidan Clarke, J. I. McGuire,
M. A. G. Ó Tuathaigh, David W. Harkness,
Patrick J. Corish, Joseph Lee

ISBN 0 902561 20 0

Printed in Ireland by Watermans, Cork

CONTENTS

		page	vii
	Preface		
I	Gaelic Ireland to 1603 by Gearóid MacNiocaill, *professor of history,* *University College, Galway*		1
II	Medieval Ireland, 1169–1534 by Art Cosgrove, *lecturer in medieval history,* *University College, Dublin*		13
III	Ireland, 1534–1660 by Aidan Clarke, *professor in modern history,* *Trinity College, Dublin*		34
IV	Ireland, 1660–1800 by J. I. McGuire, *lecturer in Irish history,* *University College, Dublin*		56
V	Ireland, 1800–1921 by M. A. G. Ó Tuathaigh, *lecturer in history,* *University College, Galway*		85
VI	Ireland since 1921 by David W. Harkness, *professor of Irish history,* *Queen's University, Belfast*		132
VII	Irish ecclesiastical history since 1500 by Mgr Patrick J. Corish, *professor of modern history* *St Patrick's College, Maynooth*		154
VIII	Irish economic history since 1500 by Joseph Lee, *professor of modern history,* *University College, Cork*		173
IX	Index to *Bulletin of the Irish Committee of* *Historical Sciences,* 1939–1974 by J. I. McGuire		225

Preface

The first survey of Irish historiography sponsored by the Irish Committee of Historical Sciences, the body responsible for representing Irish historical interests on the *Comitè International des Sciences Historiques,* dealt mainly with work published between 1936 and 1970[1]. The contributions were not intended as bibliographies 'but as individual essays in the assessment and interpretation of achievement in the field of Irish history'[2]. The present volume, based on the same general principle, and dealing mainly with work published between 1970 and 1979, follows a broadly similar organisation. It adopts, however, a slightly different chronological structure and includes, in addition, two thematic contributions, dealing respectively with ecclesiastical and economic history since about 1500, as well as an idex to the *Bulletin of the Irish Committee of Historical Sciences* from 1939 until 1974. The Committee wishes to thank Mr James McGuire for his painstaking work in compiling this index.

The editor is grateful to Mr Donal Counihan, Cork University Press, and Ms Charlotte Wiseman, History Office, University College, Cork, for their dedicated work in preparing the volume for publication.

Joseph Lee

[1] T. W. Moody (ed.), *Irish historiography, 1936–70* (Dublin, 1971).

[2] *ibid.*, viii.

Gaelic Ireland to 1603

Gearóid Mac Niocaill

The work of the past decade may conveniently be divided, for the most part, by the period with which it is concerned – pre-twelfth century, and post-twelfth century.

For the earlier period, the decade is distinguished by the almost simultaneous publication of surveys of parts of it, by Mac Niocaill[2], O Corráin[3], and Byrne[1]. While the first two appeared in a series designed as *haute vulgarisation,* the deficiencies of existing work meant that they were in a large degree based on the primary sources as is clear from the critical bibliographies in both. The same is largely true of Byrne's work, though of narrower scope; and in all three cases it might fairly be said that the sections devoted to matters other than politics are the more satisfactory. This is in the nature of the material, as may be verified from Hughes' excellent survey of the primary sources of the period[4]; this can be supplemented by Mac Niocaill's survey of the annalistic material[9], and by such individual studies as Smyth's[11]. To this should be added Ó Corráin's critical handlist of publications on early Irish history[5].

Publication of primary sources has been scanty: the only substantial text to appear is Radner's re-edition of the mixture of annals and saga known as the *Three Fragments*[10]; however, new and sorely needed re-editions of the *Annals of Ulster,* the *Annals of Tigernach* and the *Chronicum Scotorum* are in progress, and related texts such as synchronisms[6] and short discussions of individual problems in the texts have appeared[7–8].

Work on early Irish politics has focussed predominantly on political structures such as early Irish kingship and its correlative the 'tribe' or *tuath*[19–22, 24], while Ó Corráin has shown how the genealogical tracts may be exploited to reconstruct the political structure of a single, albeit minor, kingdom[23]. In the domain of *histoire événementielle,* work has been carried on in three fields. Firstly, the reconstruction of the history of individual dynasties, such as Kelleher's work on the Uí Maine[26] and Bannerman's on the Dál Riata[25]. This latter, consisting of a collection of studies previously published in journals, deals also with such topics as the Iona Chronicle which lies at the heart of the early Irish annals. Secondly, the relations between dynasties at specific periods, such as Smyth's work

1

on the relations of the Hui Néill, the Hui Failgi and the Leinstermen[29-30], or discussions of individual episodes (e.g. Mac Niocaill[27]). Thirdly, the critical analysis of primary narrative sources, such as Ó Corráin's study of the *Caithréim Chellacháin Chaisil*[8].

Without doubt the most important publication of the decade has been the six volumes of D. A. Binchy's *Corpus Iuris Hibernici*[18], containing semi-diplomatic texts of all Irish legal manuscripts down to the end of the sixteenth century, with abundant cross-references. It provides a basis for progress both in the field of law proper, and in the study of early Irish society and economy. Not unnaturally, since all those who are active in the field have long been following the painful progress of the *Corpus* into print, scholars, with one minor and temerarious exception[82], have preferred to defer publication of work on the stocks until its texts and cross-references could be taken into account; and publications in early Irish law have been almost all Binchy's own, both editions of texts[12, 14], and discussions of aspects of early Irish law[13, 15, 16] and of its value in a wider context[17].

The history of the Norse settlements in Ireland has been handled largely from the standpoint of linguistics – loanwords and placenames[39] – or from that of numismatics, in the context of the Norse introduction of coinage to Ireland[40-43]; the contribution of archaeology to our knowledge of these settlements must await a full publication of the excavations at present being carried out. On the strictly political side, Smyth has attempted to reconstruct the ninth-century history of the Scandinavian kingdoms both of the British Isles and Ireland[45], and while his hypotheses here and elsewhere[44] do not invariably command conviction, he has at least provided a stimulus to further work.

In church history, discussion of the problems and dating of St. Patrick's mission, which occupied so prominent a place in the work of the sixties, has moved to the background, and even here is concerned much more with textual problems[48-51] and pseudo-Patriciana[47, 52], although Bieler's edition of four Latin lives[46] should be noted. This diminution of interest is in some measure counterbalanced by work on the cult of St. Brigit[54-5] and other saints, although some doubt may well be felt about Bowen's use of dedications as evidence of the area of activity of some early saints[56-7]. Interest in Hiberno-Roman and Hiberno-British relations in the proto-historic period, a field in which there has been a fair amount of activity[31-4], is in some degree a spin-off from the earlier Patrician controversy.

On a more general level there is little to note save a study by the late Kathleen Hughes, lucid as always, of interaction between the church and the world in early Irish society[58], and Donnchadh Ó Corráin's analysis of the ecclesiastical politics of the Dál Cais dynasty from the 11th to the 13th century[59] – an example which other scholars might profitably imitate.

An extremely promising field of research is the exploitation of the early literature to cast light on the interactions between pagan tradition and Christianity. In this P. Mac Cana, but not only he, has been extremely active[74–8], and this work offers the best prospect before us of a fuller understanding of the transitional period from the fifth to the late seventh century. In this context, attention should be drawn also to Henry's ambitious study of the founding of the Old Irish literary tradition[72], which, while containing much that is contestable, yet contains also much that is useful for the historian in the narrow sense. So too do such publications and analyses of early texts as those by Kelly[73], Ó Cathasaigh[79] and Ó Coileáin[80]; while Ó hAodha's edition of the Irish version of Statius' *Achilleis* contributes to our knowledge of outside influences and borrowings in Ireland towards the end of the early period, and draws our attention back to another problem too long neglected.

There has also been activity in the field of early Irish Latin learning, with Herren's work on the *Hisperica Famina* and related texts[66–8], that of McNamara[69–70], Dumville[61–2] and Doyle[60] on the texts of the psalter, New Testament and apocrypha circulating in early medieval Ireland. These, and the work of Hennig on the texts and sources of the early Irish martyrologies[63–5], all conspire to cast light on the contacts between Ireland, England and the Continent, to which, although in a slightly different context, Hughes[37–8], Bieler[35], Charles-Edwards[36] and Sanderlin[71] have also contributed.

Work on early economy and society, apart from the general sketches in the surveys noted above[2,3], has been notable for its extreme scantiness. This, the poor relative of early and medieval Irish history, is a field in which the archaeologist and historian can collaborate to their mutual profit; but of the excavations or surveys in progress or completed during the decade and relevant to the early medieval period, only two have yet been published in a form that the historian can exploit[84–5], and much of the archeological literature has been devoted to the recording of individual finds. M. Ryan has however provided a useful survey, on the basis of such finds, of one aspect of the material economy[83]. Again, only one text of direct relevance to the economy has been published[82]; but for the paucity of text-editions – which means mainly law-texts – the reasons mentioned above in the context of law apply, and we may perhaps anticipate a more abundant harvest in the 1980's.

The period from the 12th century onwards is much less satisfactory. The main reason for this is that 'Gaelic' Ireland is less clearly defined and definable, shifting with the political changes of the period and with the standpoint of the observer, as appears from Nicholl's survey[86]. In this latter the account of political change is by far the least satisfactory, while the discussion of economy and society, as in the earlier period, has by far the most meat in it. Here too the way forward would seem to be by painstaking analysis of individual dynastic histories and polities, as has been done by Ó Doibhlin, Ó Dufaigh, Ó Mórdha, Ó Fiaich and Simms[94–100]. Publication of primary sources has been well-nigh absent, although a deserved exception should be made for Nicholls' re-edition of the fragments of the Register of Clogher[87], and specific studies of primary sources hardly go beyond the work of Mac Niocaill[9] and O'Dwyer[88].

As far as the church is concerned the position is much the same, again prescinding from the problem of defining what is 'Gaelic' and what is not. We have studies of individual prelates such as Tomaltach Ó Conchobhair[102] and Nioclás Mac Maoilíosa[103], or of particular ecclesiastical units such as deaneries[105] or parishes[107–8]. Nicholls has however published a useful analysis of the emergence of the parochial system in the west of the country[104]. Work on the religious orders has been equally limited, and has focussed on the problems of the Cistercians in the 13th century[106].

Law and society has been opened up to some extent by Nicholls[92], Simms[93] and Mac Niocaill[89–91], but an enormous amount remains to be done before we can have any real grasp of the structure of late-medieval Irish society. There are however abundant indications that the distinction between 'Gaelic' and non-'Gaelic' Irish society is a conceptual tool that the historian can profitably abandon. As for the economy, it remains as near a *tabula rasa* as makes no difference, with only the work of Dolley[114] to suggest the possible scope of trade along and across the internal frontier.

For the study of mentalities, at least in the upper classes who paid for it, the literature of the period is indispensable. There can obviously be no question of surveying the publications of the decade in detail, but for poetry of the period the work of Ó Cuív[110] and of Williams[112] is of great value, while that of Risk[111] casts light on the extent to which the society in which it was produced was open to outside influences. To this work should be added the recent translation of Williams' history of the Irish literary tradition[113], which makes this necessary background more readily available to the Irish historian than does the Welsh original. A beginning has been made, by Bradshaw[101], in exploiting the literature of the end of this period for its ideological content.

Finally in the plastic arts, with their implications for patronage, both secular and ecclesiastical, and for the economy, attention should be drawn to the work of Stalley[116-7] and of Fanning[115]. It is only proper to point out, however, that these implications remain to be followed up, and are as yet a virgin field.

SELECT BIBLIOGRAPHY

(A) To The Twelfth Century

(a) General and bibliographical

1 Byrne, F. J. *Irish kings and high-kings* (London, 1973)
2 Mac Niocaill, G. *Ireland before the Vikings* (Dublin, 1972)
3 Ó Corráin, D. *Ireland before the Normans* (Dublin, 1972)
4 Hughes, K. *Early Christian Ireland: introduction to the sources* (London, 1972)
5 Ó Corráin, D. 'A handlist of publications on early Irish history' *Historical Studies* X, ed. G. A. Hayes-McCoy (Indreabhán, 1976) 172–303

(b) Annals and related texts

6 Boyle, A. 'The Edinburgh synchronisms of Irish kings' *Celtica* 9 (1971) 169–79
7 Harrison, K. 'Epacts in Irish chronicles' *Studia Celtica* 12–13 (1977–8) 17–32
8 Kelleher, J. V. 'The Táin and the annals' *Ériu* 22 (1971) 107–27
9 Mac Niocaill, G. *The medieval Irish annals* (Dublin, 1975)
10 Radner, J. N. *Fragmentary annals of Ireland* (Dublin, 1978)
11 Smyth, A. P. 'The earliest Irish annals: their first contemporary entries, and the earliest centres of recording' *ProcRIA* 72 C (1972) 1–48

(c) Law, society and kingship

12 Binchy, D. A. 'An archaic legal poem' *Celtica* 9 (1971) 152–68
13 — 'Distraint in Irish law' *Celtica* 10 (1973) 22–71
14 — 'A text on the forms of distraint' *ibid.* 72–86
15 — 'The pseudo-historical prologue to the *Senchas Már*' *Studia Celtica* 10–11 (1975–6) 15–28
16 — 'Féchem, fethem, aigne' *Celtica* 11 (1976) 18–23
17 — 'Irish history and Irish law' *Studia Hibernica* 15 (1975) 7–36, 16 (1976) 7–45
18 — *Corpus Iuris Hibernici* vols. i–vi (Dublin, 1979)
19 Byrne, F. J. 'Tribes and tribalism in early Ireland' *Ériu* 22 (1971) 128–66
20 Charles-Edwards, T. M. 'The heir-apparent in Irish and Welsh law' *Celtica* 9 (1971) 180–89
21 Dillon, M. 'The consecration of Irish kings' *Celtica* 10 (1973) 1–8

22 Ó Corráin, D. 'Irish regnal succession: a reappraisal' *Studia Hibernica* 11 (1971) 7–39

23 — 'The families of Corcumroe' *North Munster Antiquarian Journal* 17 (1976[7]) 21–30

24 — 'Nationality and kingship in pre-Norman Ireland' *Nationality and the pursuit of national independence,* ed. T. W. Moody (Belfast, 1978) 1–35

(d) Political

25 Bannerman, J. *Studies in the history of Dál Riada* (Edinburgh, 1974)

26 Kelleher, J. V. 'Uí Maine in the annals and genealogies to 1225' *Celtica* 9 (1971) 61–112

27 Mac Niocaill, G. 'The background of the battle of Tarbga' *Celtica* 11 (1976) 133–40

28 Ó Corráin, D. '*Caithréim Chellacháin Chaisil:* history or propaganda?' *Ériu* 25 (1974) 1–69

29 Smyth, A. P. 'The Huí Néill and the Leinstermen in the Annals of Ulster (431–516)' *Études Celtiques* 14.1 (1974) 121–44

30 — 'Huí Failgi relations with the Huí Néill in the century after the loss of the plain of Mide' *Études Celtiques* 14.2 (1975) 503–23

(e) External connexions

31 *Colloquium on Hiberno-Roman relations and material remains.* *ProcRIA* 76 C (1976) 171–292

32 Bateson, J. D. 'Roman material from Ireland: a re-consideration' *ProcRIA* 73 C (1973) 21–97

33 Carson, R. A. G. & O'Kelly, C. 'A catalogue of the Roman coins from Newgrange, Co. Meath, and notes on the coins and related finds' *ProcRIA* 77 C (1977) 35–55

34 Dillon, M. 'The Irish settlements in Wales' *Celtica* 12 (1977) 1–11

35 Bieler, L. 'Ireland's contribution to the culture of Northumbria' *Famulus Christi,* ed. G. Bonner (London, 1976) 210–28

36 Charles-Edwards, T. M. 'The social background to Irish *peregrinatio*' *Celtica* 11 (1976) 43–59

37 Hughes, K. 'Some aspects of Irish influence on early English private prayer' *Studia Celtica* 5 (1970) 48–61

38 — 'Evidence for contacts between the churches of the Irish and English from the Synod of Whitby to the Viking Age' *England before the Conquest* ed. P. Clemoes and K. Hughes (Cambridge, 1971) 49–69

[39] Almquist, B. & Greene, D. (edd.) *Proceedings of the 7th Viking-Congress, Dublin 15—21 August 1973* (London, 1976) [includes L. dePaor, 'The Viking towns of Ireland' pp. 29–37; J. A. Graham-Campbell, 'The Viking-age silver hoards of Ireland' pp. 39–74; D.Greene, 'The influence of Scandinavian on Irish' pp. 75–82; M. Oftedal, 'Scandinavian place-names in Ireland' pp. 125–33; B. Ó Ríordáin, 'The High Street excavations' pp. 135–40]

[40] Blackburn, M. 'Hiberno-Norse imitations of Watcht *Long cross* coins' *Numismatic Chronicle* 7S 15 (1975) 195–7

[41] Biggs, C. S. & Graham-Campbell, J. A. 'A lost hoard of Viking-age silver from Magheralagan, Co. Down' *Ulster Journal of Archaeology* 3S 39 (1976) 20–24

[42] Dolley, M. 'Some further light on the 1891 Viking-age coin-hoard from Ballycastle' *Ulster Journal of Archaeology* 3S 36–7 (1973–4) 87–9

[43] Hall, R. 'A check-list of Viking-age coin finds from Ireland' *ibid.* 71–86

[44] Smyth, A. P. 'The Black Foreigners of York and the White Foreigners of Dublin' *Saga-Book of the Viking Society for Northern Research* 19 (1975–6) 101–17

[45] — *Scandinavian kings in the British Isles 850—880* (Oxford, 1978)

(f) Ecclesiastical

[46] Bieler, L. *Four Latin lives of St. Patrick: Colgan's Vita Secunda, Quarta, Tertia & Quinta.* Scriptores Latini Hiberniae VIII (Dublin, 1971)

[47] Gwynn, A. 'The problem of the "Dicta Patricii" ' *Seanchas Ardmhacha* 8.1. (1975–6) 69–80

[48] Hanson, R. P. C. 'The omissions in the text of the Confession of St. Patrick in the Book of Armagh' *Studia Patristica* 12, ed. E. A. Livingstone (Berlin, 1975) 92–5

[49] — 'The D-text of Patrick's Confession: original or reduction?' *ProcRIA* 77 C (1977) 251–6

[50] — 'The date of St. Patrick' *Bulletin of John Rylands Library* 61 (1978) 60–77

[51] Hood, A. B. E. (ed.) *St. Patrick: his writings and Muirchú's "Life"* (London, 1978)

[52] Hughes, K. 'Synodus II S. Patricii' *Latin script and letters A.D. 400—900* ed. J. J. O'Meara & B. Naumann (Leiden, 1976) 141—7

[53] Powell, D. 'St. Patrick's Confession and the Book of Armagh' *Analecta Bollandiana* 90 (1974) 371–85

54 Bowen, E. G. 'The cult of St. Brigit' *Studia Celtica* 8–9 (1973–4) 33–47

55 Kissane, D. N. '*Uita Metrica Sanctae Brigidae:* a critical edition with introduction, commentary and indexes' *ProcRIA* 77 C (1977) 57–192

56 Bowen, E. G. 'The geography of early monasticism in Ireland' *Studia Celtica* 7 (1972) 30–44

57 — *Britain and the western seaways* (London, 1972)

58 Hughes, K. 'Sanctity and secularity in the early Irish church' *Sanctity and secularity:* studies in church history vol. 10, ed. D. Baker (Oxford, 1973) 21–37

59 Ó Corráin, D. 'Dál Cais – church and dynasty' *Ériu* 24 (1973) 52–63

(g) Literature and learning

60 Doyle, P. 'The text of St. Luke's Gospel in the Book of Mulling' *ProcRIA* 73 C (1973) 177–200

61 Dumville, D. N. 'Biblical apocrypha and the early Irish: a preliminary investigation' *ProcRIA* 73 C (1973) 299–338

62 — 'Towards an interpretation of *Fís Adamnán*' *Studia Celtica* 12–13 (1977–8) 62–77

63 Hennig, J. 'Studies in Latin texts of the *Martyrology of Tallaght,* of *Félire Oengussa* and of *Félire Húi Gormáin*' *ProcRIA* 69 C (1970) 45–112

64 — 'The sources of the martyrological tradition of non-Irish saints in medieval Ireland' *Sacris Erudiri* 21 (1972–3) 407–34

65 — 'The notes on non-Irish saints in the manuscripts of *Félire Oengusso*' *ProcRIA* 75 C (1975) 119–59

66 Herren, M. 'The authorship, date of composition and provenance of the so-called *Lorica Gildae*' *Ériu* 24 (1973) 35–51

67 — *Hisperica Famina. I: the A-text* (Toronto, 1974)

68 — 'Some conjectures on the origins and tradition of the Hisperic poem *Rubisca*' *Ériu* 25 (1974) 70–87

69 McNamara, M. 'Psalter text and psalter study in the early Irish church (A.D. 600–1200)' *ProcRIA* 73 C (1973) 201–98

70 — *The apocrypha in the early Irish church* (Dublin, 1975)

71 Sanderlin, S. 'The date and provenance of the "Litany of Irish Saints – II" (The Irish litany of pilgrim saints)' *ProcRIA* 75 C (1975) 251–62

72 Henry, P. L. *Saoithiúlacht na Sean-Ghaeilge — bunú an traidisiúin* (Dublin, 1978).

73 Kelly, F. *Audacht Morainn* (Dublin, 1976)

74 Mac Cana, P. 'The three languages and the three laws' *Studia Celtica* 5 (1970) 62–78

[75] — 'Conservation and innovation in early Celtic literature' *Études Celtiques* 13.1 (1972) 61–118
[76] — 'Mongán mac Fiachna and *Immram Brain*' *Ériu* 23 (1972) 102–42
[77] — 'The rise of the later schools of *filidheacht*' *Ériu* 25 (1974) 126–46
[78] — 'On the "prehistory" of *Immram Brain*' *Ériu* 26 (1975) 33–52
[79] Ó Cathasaigh, T. *The heroic biography of Cormac mac Airt* (Dublin, 1977)
[80] Ó Coileáin, S. 'The structure of a literary cycle' *Ériu* 25 (1974) 88–125
[81] Ó hAodha, D. 'The Irish version of Statius' *Achilleid*' *ProcRIA* 79 C (1979) 83–137

(h) Material economy
[82] Mac Niocaill, G. 'Tír Cumaile' *Ériu* 22 (1971) 81–6
[83] Ryan, M. 'Native pottery in early historic Ireland' *ProcRIA* 73 C (1973) 619–45
[84] Waddell, J. 'An archaeological survey of Temple Brecan, Aran' *Galway Archaeological and Historical Society Journal* 33 (1972–3) 7–27
[85] Warner, R. B. 'The excavations at Clogher and their context' *Clogher Record* 8.1 (1973) 5–12

B. FROM THE TWELFTH CENTURY

(a) General
[86] Nicholls, K. *Gaelic and Gaelicised Ireland in the Middle Ages* (Dublin, 1972)

(b) Annals and other primary sources
[87] Nicholls, K. 'The Register of Clogher' *Clogher Record* 7.3 (1971–2) 361–431
[88] O'Dwyer, B. 'The Annals of Connacht and Loch Cé and the monasteries of Boyle and Holy Trinity' *ProcRIA* 72 C (1972) 83–101

(c) Law and society
[89] Mac Niocaill, G. 'A propos du vocabulaire social irlandais du bas moyen âge' *Études Celtiques* 12.2 (1970–71) 512–46
[90] — 'Aspects of Irish law in the late thirteenth century' *Historical Studies* X, ed. G. A. Hayes-McCoy (Indreabhán, 1976) 25–42

91 — 'Land-transfer in sixteenth-century Thomond: the case of Domhnall Óg Ó Cearnaigh' *North Munster Antiquarian Journal* 17 (1975[7]) 43–5

92 Nicholls, K. *Land, law and society in 16th-century Ireland* (Dublin, 1976)

93 Simms, K. 'The legal position of Irishwomen in the late Middle Ages' *Irish Jurist* NS 10 (1975) 96–111

(d) **Political**

94 Ó Doibhlin, E. 'O'Neill's "own country" and its families' *Seanchas Ardmhacha* 6.1 (1971) 3–23

95 Ó Dufaigh, S. 'Notes on the MacKennas of Truagh' *Clogher Record* 8.2 (1974) 221–7

96 Ó Mordha, P. 'The medieval kingdom of Mugdorna' *Clogher Record* 7.3 (1971–2) 432–46

97 Ó Fiaich, T. 'The O'Neills of the Fews' *Seanchas Ardmhacha* 7.1 (1973) 1–64

98 Simms, K. 'Warfare in the medieval Gaelic lordships' *Irish Sword* 12 (1976) 98–108

99 — 'The medieval kingdom of Lough Erne' *Clogher Record* 9.2 (1977) 126–41

100 —'Niall Garbh II O'Donnell, king of Tír Conaill' *Donegal Annual* 12 (1977) 7–21

101 Bradshaw, B. 'Native reaction to the westward enterprise: a case-study in Gaelic ideology' *The westward enterprise*, ed. K. R. Andrews *et al.*, (Liverpool, 1978) 66–80

(e) **Ecclesiastical**

102 Gwynn, A. 'Tomaltach Ua Conchobair, coarb of Patrick' *Seanchas Ardmhacha* 8.2. (1977) 231–74

103 Mac Íomhair, D. 'Primate Mac Maoilíosa and county Louth' *Seanchas Ardmhacha* 6.1 (1971) 70–90

104 Nicholls, K. 'Rectory, vicarage and parish in the western Irish dioceses' *Journal of the Royal Society of Antiquaries of Ireland* 101 (1971) 53–84

105 Ó Doibhlin, E. 'The deanery of Tulach Óg' *Seanchas Ardmhacha* 6.1 (1971) 141–82

106 O'Dwyer, B. W. 'The crisis in the Cistercian monasteries in Ireland in the early 13th century' *Analecta Cisterciensia* 31.2 (1975[6]) 267–304, 32.1–2 (1976[7]) 3–112

[107] Ó Gallachair, P. 'The parish of Donaghcavey' *Clogher Record* 7.2 (1970) 251–320

[108] — 'The parish of Carn' ibid 8.3 (1975) 301–80

[109] Simms, K. 'The archbishops of Armagh and the O'Neills 1347–1471' *Irish Historical Studies* 19 (1974) 38–58

(f) Literature and learning

[110] Ó Cuív, B. 'The linguistic training of the medieval Irish poet' *Celtica* 10 (1973) 114–40

[111] Risk, H. 'French loan-words in Irish' *Études Celtiques* 12.2 (1970–71) 585–655, 14.1 (1974) 67–98

[112] Williams, J. E. Caerwyn, 'The court poet in medieval Ireland' *Proc. British Acad.* 57 (1971) 85–135

[113] — & M. Ní Mhuiríosa, *Traidisiún Liteartha na nGael* (Dublin, 1979)

(g) Material economy and art

[114] Dolley, M. 'Medieval coin-hoards from the Ulster mearing' *Clogher Record* 7.2 (1970) 204–20

[115] Fanning, T. 'Excavations at Clontuskert Priory, Co. Galway' *ProcRIA* 76 C (1976) 97–169

[116] Stalley, R. A. *Architecture and sculpture in Ireland 1150—1350* (Dublin, 1971)

[117] 'Corcomroe abbey: some observations on its architectural history' *Journal of the Royal Society of Antiquaries* of Ireland 105 (1975[7]) 21–46

Medieval Ireland 1169 – 1534

Art Cosgrove

(a) SOURCES

Since 1971 there have been few additions to the published sources for the history of medieval Ireland. The destruction of most of the records of the central administration in 1922 has been partially alleviated by the survival of much of this material either in transcript or among the original records in the English Public Record Office. Hopefully, the *Guide to the sources of medieval Irish history* being prepared for the Irish Manuscripts Commission will delineate the full extent of that survival. Illustrations of what can be achieved are provided by G. Hand, 'Two hitherto unpublished membranes of Irish petitions, presented at the midsummer parliament of 1302 and the Lent parliament of 1305' in *R.I.A. Proc.*, lxxi, sect. C, pp 1–18 and K.W. Nicholls, 'Inquisitions of 1224 from the miscellanea of the exchequer' in *Anal. Hib.*, xxvii (1972), 103–12.

In areas outside the records of the administration, three important publications should be noted. *Expugnatio Hibernica: the conquest of Ireland by Giraldus Cambrensis*, ed. with transl. and historical notes by A. B. Scott and F. X. Martin (Dublin, 1978) provides us with a modern critical edition of the most valuable source for the coming of the Normans to Ireland. Michael Haren has continued the series of calendars of papal letters and his edition of *Calendar of Papal Letters relating to Great Britain and Ireland vol. XV: Innocent VIII* (Dublin 1978) contains much of value for British as well as Irish medieval history. Armagh is the only Irish diocese to have preserved a series of episcopal registers in any way comparable to those possessed by most English sees, and *Registrum Johannis Mey: the register of John May, archbishop of Armagh 1443–56*, ed. W. G. H. Quigley and E. F. D. Roberts (Belfast 1972) is the first of the series to be published *in toto*. The editors are currently engaged on a similar edition of the register of Archbishop John Prene (1439–43) and it is to be hoped that the whole series will eventually appear in editions of this standard, thus making readily available 'the most important single source of original material, still surviving in Ireland, for its medieval past'.[1]

Other material of ecclesiastical provenance has been published by K. W. Nicholls, 'The register of Clogher' in *Clogher Rec.* vii (1971),

361–431, and Maurice P. Sheehy, 'The Registrum Novum: a manuscript of Holy Trinity Cathedral' in *Repertorium Novum* iii (1964), 249–81, iv (1971), 101–33. Those making use of the Ormond material preserved in the National Library should consult the notes by C. A. Empey and K. W. Nicholls in *Butler Soc. Jn.* i, 519–26. An indispensable introduction to the annals is provided by Gearóid Mac Niocaill, *The medieval Irish annals* (Dublin Historical Association, Medieval Irish History series, 3, 1975), wherein it is noted that a new edition of the chronicle of Henry Marlborough is in preparation. The burdens of the researcher should also be eased by the updated lists, tables and maps in *A new history of Ireland*, ix (to be published in 1981).

(b) SECONDARY WORKS

Any discussion of the secondary works must begin by acknowledging the sparsity of general text-books on the period. For almost fifty years, the standard, indeed the only text-book, was E. Curtis's *History of Medieval Ireland* (1st ed. 1923, 2nd ed. 1938) and, perforce, it continued to be used long after some of its facts and conclusions had been overthrown by more recent research. A new departure, therefore, was created by the appearance of A. J. Otway-Ruthven's *History of medieval Ireland* (London and New York, 1968). In her foreword, the author modestly described the book as 'no more than an interim report', but, although she deliberately eschewed any treatment of Gaelic Ireland or the Irish economy, she did produce a continuous and coherent political narrative for the period up to 1495 and she also succeeded in establishing for the later middle ages a sound chronology of events, a secure foundation on which others can build. These factors, taken in conjunction with the author's unrivalled knowledge of the medieval institutions of government, will ensure that the book will long remain an indispensable aid to all those engaged in the study of the middle ages in Ireland.[2]

A second significant advance was the publication of P. W. A. Asplin's *Medieval Ireland c. 1170—1495: a bibliography of secondary works* (Dublin 1971), which made a comprehensive survey of the secondary literature and thus allowed the progress made in particular areas to be accurately charted. The attached bibliography is intended as a supplement to Asplin's work, though it covers a slightly longer period.

Of the text books to appear since 1971, the only one to deal with the period as a whole is J. F. Lydon, *The Lordship of Ireland in the middle ages* (Dublin 1972). The book's minor defects, in particular its lack of an index and footnotes, should not be allowed to obscure its very considerable merits. The author set out 'to interpret rather than merely describe events' and drawing on a wide range of sources, both Gaelic and Anglo-Irish, he imposed upon events a coherent pattern which did not neglect Gaelic Ireland or, indeed, the social and economic history of the period. One reviewer commented that he knew 'of no book on medieval Ireland of comparable width and scope'[3] and, as an introduction to the middle ages, it has the additional advantage of inspiring in the reader a desire to know more about the subject.

The same author's *Ireland in the later middle ages* (Dublin 1973) covers a shorter period and deals more specifically with Anglo-Ireland. Again evident is the desire to interpret as well as recount and, although some of the attempts to generalise – particularly about society and the economy – may be over-ambitious, given the dearth of work in these areas, the advantages of this approach are readily apparent if one compares it with the over-reliance on narrative in Michael Dolley, *Anglo-Norman Ireland c. 1100 — 1318* (Dublin 1972).

A number of authors have cooperated in the survey of the whole period which will appear as *A new history of Ireland,* vol. ii (scheduled for publication by the Clarendon Press immediately after vol. ix).

Turning to particular periods, it should be noted that F. X. Martin has contributed a valuable series of historical notes to the new edition of the *Expugnatio Hibernica* and, in his 1975 O'Donnell Lecture, he attempted to rehabilitate the reputation of Dermot McMurrough after centuries of historical obloquy. W. L. Warren has continued to illuminate various aspects of twelfth-century Ireland. His witty and engaging essay on the historian 'as private eye' contains a salutary warning against the dangers of imposing artificial limitations, such as national boundaries, on historical inquiry. The specific example he adduces is the failure of Irish history books to take account of the loss of Normandy in 1204, but his warning has a relevance for the whole medieval period and not only for historians of medieval Ireland. Insularity has also had deleterious effects on the historiography of England, Scotland and Wales, and a widening of the context to comprehend the British Isles as a whole might lead to interesting revisions in the histories of all four countries.

On the other hand, within Ireland itself, there is much to be said for narrowing the focus. Since the island was never a political or administrative unit during the medieval period,[4] local studies have much to contribute to the advancement of our knowledge. On the Anglo-Irish side, a good example is C. A. Empey's study of the Butler lordship, which deserves to be more widely known and read, and there are valuable studies of Gaelic localities by Tomás Ó Fiach and Katharine Simms. The latter has also assessed the impact of the Anglo-Norman invasion on the Gaelic polity and, in her study of the relationship between the O'Hanlons, the O'Neills and the invaders in the thirteenth century, has reached the interesting conclusion that 'outside the areas which had been fully conquered and colonised, the Norman invaders only served to put the clock back by smashing the power of the Irish provincial kings, without being in a position to impose a stable alternative government'.[5]

The most notable recent contributions to the history of the fourteenth century have come from Robin Frame. His article on the Bruces in Ireland is a valuable re-examination of the attitudes and objectives of the Scots, the Gaelic Irish and the Anglo-Irish during the period of the invasion. In his studies of one chief governor, Ralph Ufford, and, later, of the difficulties which faced English officials generally in their dealings with Irish chiefs, particularly in Leinster, he has made skilful use of the surviving materials in the Public Record Offices of London and Dublin to produce a more realistic picture of the limited objectives towards which policy was directed. This enables us to perceive a *rationale* behind the recurrent campaigns and tortuous diplomacy of various chief governors in the first half of the fourteenth century. But Dr Frame is also aware of the limitations of the records of both the Dublin and London administrations in providing an accurate assessment of a highly localised society. In a more recent stimulating essay in *Past and Present* 76 (1977), he has suggested that a change in perspective, a concentration on the localities rather than the centre, would produce modifications in the generally accepted picture of a colony in continuous decline from c. 1300 onwards.

Revision of some traditional views is also a theme in Dorothy Johnston's paper, 'Richard II and the submissions of Gaelic Ireland'. In particular, she has argued forcefully that Richard II never intended that Art McMurrough and his followers should be removed from Leinster to another part of the island in 1395, and acceptance of this view means that the king should be spared the censures of historians for the impracticality of his approach. In her interpretation, the indenture with McMurrough involved simply an agreement by the Irish chieftain to surrender lands which had been seized by himself and his followers within Leinster and to abandon any claim to the title of king of Leinster. She has also reexamined the king's categorisation of the population of ireland: *En notre terre Dirland sont trois maneres de gentz, cestassavoir Irrois savages nos enemis Irrois rebelx et Engleis obeissantz.*[6] Her view that the terms 'wild Irish' and 'obedient English' were simply used as extremes to point up the importance of the 'rebel Irish' is not entirely convincing, but it is difficult to suggest any alternative explanation of this puzzling tripartite division.

The fifteenth century remains a comparatively neglected area. In part, this neglect reflects gaps in the source material and the scattered nature of that which does survive. For example, the absence, after 1377, of the issue rolls of the Irish exchequer makes it difficult to establish such basic information as the dates of chief governors' terms of office. A further handicap is the lack of any adequate Anglo-Irish annals after 1421 when Marlborough's chronicle ends. Exploration of the transcripts of the memoranda rolls of the Irish exchequer could compensate for some of these deficiencies, as can surviving private collections such as the *Dowdall Deeds* and the *Ormond Deeds*. The latter have been used effectively by C. A. Empey and Katharine Simms in their examination of the widespread and much-criticised system of billeting troops on the countryside, known as coign and livery, and of the ordinances which regulated the system in the Butler lordship in the fifteenth century.

I have attempted a reassessment of one of the most dramatic events of the century, the execution of the earl of Desmond in 1468, but overall the student of this period must rely on the text-book accounts by Otway-Ruthven and Lydon. Therein will be found interesting differences in interpretation. In her treatment of the 'declaration of 1460', Professor Otway-Ruthven, following Richardson and Sayles, dismissed the claims to independence made by the 1460 parliament as having no validity in law or custom. Professor Lydon, on the other hand, has stated that there 'was some historical justification for the 1460 claim' and has further argued that the declaration was an expression of Anglo-Irish separatist feeling.[7]

Conflict on this specific issue raises wider questions. To what extent had the Anglo-Irish become Gaelicised? Were they 'more Irish than the Irish themselves'[8] as has so often been claimed? And did Gaelicisation lead to the development of a 'separatist' political stance by the Anglo-Irish?

Any investigation of these problems will have to take account of the career of one of the central figures of the later fifteenth and early sixteenth centuries, Garret More Fitzgerald, the Great Earl of Kildare. Almost thirty years ago, G. O. Sayles expressed the view 'that the documents which explain the actions of the eight earl of Kildare . . . . . still await a scientific and objective examination; the interpretation of them has, so far, been too much the result of an attitude of *parti pris* and has made the earl's relations with the English government unintelligible'.[9] This challenge to produce a new biography to replace Donough Bryan,

Gerald Fitzgerald, the Great Earl of Kildare (1456 — 1513), (Dublin and Cork 1933), has not yet been accepted, but Steven Ellis has made important revisions in our understanding of Anglo-Irish relations in the period 1496 – 1534 and, at the end of the period, the traditional interpretations of the rebellion of Silken Thomas have been radically altered by the contributions of both Ellis and Brendan Bradshaw.

Ecclesiastical history continues to be well served. John A. Watt, *The church in medieval Ireland* is a survey of the whole period which can be read with profit by the specialist and non-specialist alike. One of his conclusions is:-

'It was the medieval church which refused Protestantism and remained Catholic at the Reformation. In the long perspective of Irish history, that decision must surely rank as the most important contribution of the middle ages to the shaping of modern Ireland.' (p. 216). Why the medieval church, both Gaelic and Anglo-Irish, should have done so is a question which further exploration of the late medieval period might help to answer.[10]

As the list below indicates, the emphasis in ecclesiastical studies continues be on government and organisation. Much less is known about the activities of the laity and the sources allow only an occasional glimpse of the popular practice of religion. One area of lay behaviour, marriage, particularly in Gaelic Ireland, has been the subject of differing judgements. Kenneth Nicholls took the view that throughout the medieval period 'what could be called Celtic secular marriage remained the norm in Ireland and Christian matrimony was no more than the rare exception grafted on to this system'.[115] On the other hand, Professor Watt's researches led him to conclude 'that generalisations about marriage in Gaelic Ireland remaining a purely secular concern should be treated with caution'.[12] More recently, the subject has been touched upon by Katharine Simms in her pioneering studies on the position of women in medieval Ireland. Clearly, the issue needs further investigation, but it may be worth noting that informality in marital arrangements was not confined to Ireland,[13] and comparisons should be made with contemporary European practices rather than with the much different post-Tridentine situation.

The starting point in this debate, as in nearly all matters concerning Gaelic Ireland, is Kenneth Nicholls, *Gaelic and gaelicised Ireland in the middle ages,* the first text-book to deal with this neglected area. His major contribution was the production of a coherent picture of the society, laws and institutions of the increasing portion of the country which lay outside the ambit of the Dublin administration, drawn in the main from unpublished sources. Too little space was allowed him in the second section of the work to deal with the labyrinthine complexities of local Irish politics, but even here he provides a starting-point for further investigations. His work has been supplemented by Katharine Simms in her studies of warfare in the Gaelic lordships and of particular localities, and much progress has now been made towards filling one of the two major gaps in the historiography of the period delineated by Professor Otway-Ruthven in 1971.[14]

The other neglected area, economic history, has been less well served. No survey has yet been attempted, though the contributions by Kevin Down and Kenneth Nicholls to *A new history of Ireland*, vol. ii, should go some way towards filling this void. The difficulties facing the economic historian are formidable. It is not possible, for example, to gain an accurate estimate of the population of Ireland at any point throughout this period, though Kenneth Nicholls has at least advanced the hypothesis that late medieval Ireland 'remained severely under-populated by contemporary European standards'.[15] Nevertheless, advances can be made. Philomena Connolly has demonstrated how the neglected memoranda rolls of the Irish exchequer can be made to yield valuable information for social and economic history,[16] and the renewed interest in Irish urban history, reflected in the choice of 'The town in Ireland' as the theme of the 1979 Irish Conference of Historians, has benefited the medieval period along with others. Here the main contributions have been made by Brian Graham, who has attempted to define what constituted a borough in medieval Ireland, and to draw up a comprehensive list of those which fall within the criteria adopted. Included are those 'rural-boroughs', which possessed urban characteristics but which never progressed beyond agricultural functions and thus failed to develop into true towns. Professor Geoffrey Martin has suggested a number of additions to Graham's list,[17] and Graham himself has recently put forward a model of how urbanization evolved in medieval Ireland. The groundwork on Irish medieval towns has now been done and the most obvious need in this area is research into Irish trade.[18]

Graham's interest in urbanization sprang from his more general investigation of Anglo-Norman settlement patterns, specifically in the Meath area. Cooperation between historians and geographers has proved fruitful in the advancement of our knowledge of the settlement process, and Glassock's surveys of deserted villages and mottes have been supplemented by Terence Barry's study of moated sites in south-east Ireland. The interdisciplinary approach involved in these studies promises further results.

Michael Dolley has continued his outstanding work on the Irish medieval coinage and Irish medieval architecture has found its historian in Roger Stalley. Much, as always, remains to be done; but, as the attached bibliography indicates, the achievements of the past eight years have not been inconsiderable

In compiling the bibliography, I have attempted to follow the categories adopted by P. W. A. Asplin in 1971.

My thanks to Dr. Terence Barry, Dr. Howard Clarke, Prof. J. F. Lydon and Prof. F. X. Martin, who suggested a number of additions and amendments to the list of secondary works.

1 G. O. Sayles in his review of Aubrey Gwynn, *The Medieval Province of Armagh, 1470—1545* in *IHS* vi (1948-9) 151.

2 A lengthy review of the book was published by F. X. Martin in *Studia Hibernica*, xiv (1974).

3 G. J. Hand in *Studia Hibernica*, xiii (1973), 179.

4 Cf. Robin Frame's comment that Ireland was 'less a lordship than a patchwork of lordships', in *Past and Present*, 76 (1977), 3.

5 *Seanchas Ardmhacha*, 9 (1978), 92.

6 *Proc. privy council, 1386—1410*, pp 55-7.

7 See Richardson and Sayles, *Ir. parl. in middle ages*, pp 92-3, 260, 263; Otway-Ruthven, *Med. Ire.*, pp 190, 387 n. 19; J. F. Lydon, *The lordship of Ireland*, pp 263-6; *Ireland in the later middle ages*, pp 144-5.

8 For attempts to trace the origin of the phrase, see my 'Hiberniores ipsis Hibernis' in *Studies . . . . to R. D. Edwards*, pp 1-14. For a discussion of the extent of Gaelicisation or 'degeneracy' among the Anglo-Irish, see Robin Frame, 'Power and society in the lordship of Ireland 1272-1377' in *Past and Present* 76 (1977) esp. pp 25-32.

9 'The vindication of the earl of Kildare from treason in 1496', *IHS* viii (1951), 39.

10 Cf. Brendan Bradshaw, 'Sword, word and strategy in the Reformation in Ireland' *The Historical Journal* 21 (1978), 475-502, and N. Canny, 'Why the Reformation failed in Ireland: une question mal posée', *Journ. Eccl. Hist.* 30 (1979), 1-28.

11 *Gaelic and gaelicised Ireland in the middle ages*, p. 73.

12 *The church in medieval Ireland*, p. 207.

13 Cf., e.g. Michael M. Sheehan, 'The formation and stability of marriage in fourteenth-century England: evidence of an Ely Register' in *Medieval Studies* 33 (1971), 228-63.

14 *Irish historiography, 1936- 70*, p.22.

15 K. W. Nicholls, *Land, law and society in sixteenth-century Ireland* (O'Donnell Lecture, 1976), p.9.

16 *Ir. Econ. and Soc. Hist.*, iii (1976), 66-74.

17 In his paper to the Irish Conference of Historians in Belfast, 31 May 1979.

18 See, however, Timothy O'Neill, 'Irish Trade in the later Middle Ages: a Survey', unpublished M. A. thesis, U.C.D., 1979.

SECONDARY WORKS 1971-9

Bibliographies and Guides

ASPLIN (P.W.A.) *Medieval Ireland c. 1170—1495: a bibliography of secondary works* (Dublin 1971).
EDWARDS (Ruth Dudley) *An Atlas of Irish history* (London 1973).
HAUGHTON (J.P.) et al (eds) *Atlas of Ireland* (Dublin 1979).

Historical Geography

AALEN (F.H.A.) *Man and the landscape in Ireland* (London 1978)
BARRY (Terence) *Medieval moated sites of S. E. Ireland: Counties Carlow, Kilkenny, Tipperary and Wexford* (Oxford 1977).
'The medieval moated sites of County Wexford' in *Journal of the Old Wexford Society,* vi (1976-77), 5-17.
'Moated sites in Ireland' in *Medieval Moated Sites,* ed. F.A. Aberg (London 1978), pp 56-59.
'The moated sites of county Waterford' in *Decies* x (1979), 32-36.
EVANS (E. Estyn) *The personality of Ireland* (Cambridge 1973).
GLASSOCK (R.E.) 'Mottes in Ireland' in *Chateau-Gaillard* vii (1975).
GLASSOCK (R.E.) and McNEILL (T.) 'Mottes in Ireland: a draft list' in *Bulletin of the Group for the Study of Irish Historic Settlement* iii (1972), 27-51.
GRAHAM (Brian) 'Medieval settlements in County Meath' in *Riocht na Midhe,* v (1974) no. 4, pp 40-59.
'Anglo-Norman settlement in County Meath' 'in *RIA Proc.,* 1xxv (1975), sect. C, pp 223-48.
'The evolution of the settlement pattern of Anglo-Norman Eastmeath' in *Fields, farms and settlements in Europe,* ed. R. H. Buchanan, R.A. Butler and D. McCourt (Belfast 1976), pp 38-47.
'Clachan continuity and distribution in Medieval

	Ireland' in *Paysages ruraux européens,* ed. Pierre Flatrès (Rennes 1979), pp 147–157.
McCOURT (Desmond)	'The dynamic quality of Irish rural settlement' in *Man and his habitat: essays presented to Emyr Estyn Evans,* ed. R. H. Buchanan, Emrys Jones and Desmond McCourt (London 1971), pp 126–64.
MITCHELL (Frank)	*The Irish landscape* (London 1976).
ORME (A.R.)	*Ireland* (London 1970).
SIMMS (Anngret)	'Settlement patterns and medieval colonization in Ireland: the example of Duleek in County Meath' in *Paysages ruraux européens* ed. Pierre Flatrès (Rennes 1979), pp 159–77.
	'Irland: Überformung eines keltischen Siedlungsraumes am Rande Europas durch externe Kolonisationsbewegungen' in *Gefügemuster der Erodoberfläche: Festschrift zum 42. deutschen Geographentag* (Göttingen 1979), pp 261–308.

Place Names

NICHOLLS (K.W.)	'Some place names from *Pontificia Hibernica*' in *Dinnseanchas,* iii (1969), 85–98.

General History

(a) General Histories

EDWARDS (Robin Dudley)	*A new history of Ireland* (Dublin 1972).

(b) Medieval Period

DOLLEY (Michael)	*Anglo-Norman Ireland c. 1100—1318* (Dublin 1972).

LYDON (JAMES F.)	*The lordship of Ireland in the middle ages* (Dublin 1972).
	Ireland in the later middle ages (Dublin 1973).
NICHOLLS (K.W.)	*Gaelic and gaelicised Ireland in the middle ages* (Dublin 1972).
RICHTER (Michael)	'The first century of Anglo-Irish relations' in *History* lix (1974), 194–210.
SIMMS (Katharine)	'The medieval kingdom of Lough Erne' in *Clogher Rec.* ix (1977), 126–41.

(c) Anglo-Norman invasion and settlement, 1170–1216

LONG (Joseph)	'Dermot and the earl: who wrote "The Song"?' in *RIA Proc.* lxxv (1975) sect. C, pp 263–72.
MARTIN (F.X.)	*No hero in the house: Diarmait Mac Murchada and the coming of the Normans to Ireland* (O'Donnell Lecture, 1975).
	'The first Normans in Munster', in *Cork Hist. Soc. Jn.*, lxxiv (1971), 48–71.
SHEEHY (Maurice)	*When the Normans came to Ireland* (Cork 1975).
WARREN (W.L.)	'John in Ireland, 1185' in *Essays presented to Michael Roberts,* ed. John Bossy and Peter Jupp (Belfast 1976), pp 11–23.
	'The historian as "private eye" ' in *Historical Studies,* ix (1974), 1–18.
	Henry II (London 1973).

(d) The Thirteenth Century, 1216–1315

FRAME (Robin)	'The justiciar and the murder of the McMurroughs in 1282' in *IHS* xviii (1972), 223–30.
SIMMS (Katharine)	'The O'Hanlons, the O'Neills and the Anglo-Normans in the thirteenth century' in *Seanchas Ardmhacha* 9 (1978), 70–94.

(e) The Bruce Invasion

FRAME (Robin)	'The Bruces in Ireland, 1315–18' in *IHS* xix (1974), 3–37.

Mac IOMHAIR (Diarmuid) 'Bruce's invasion of Ireland and first campaign in County Louth' in *Ir. Sword,* x (1972), 188–212.
PHILLIPS (J.R.S.) 'Documents on the early stages of the Bruce invasion of Ireland, 1315–1316' in *RIA Proc.* lxxix (1979) sect. C. pp 247–70.

(f) The Fourteenth Century, 1316–99
FRAME (Robin) 'The justiciarship of Ralph Ufford: war and politics in fourteenth-century Ireland' in *Studia Hib.,* xiii (1973), 7–47.
'English officials and Irish chiefs in the fourteenth century' in *EHR* lxxx (1975), 748–77.
'Power and society in the lordship of Ireland, 1272–1377' in *Past and Present* 76 (1977), 3–33.
JOHNSTON (Dorothy) 'Richard II and the submissions of Gaelic Ireland' in *IHS* (forthcoming).
LYDON (James F.) 'The Braganstown massacre, 1329' in *Louth Arch. Soc. Jn.,* xix (1977), 5–16.

(g) The Fifteenth Century, 1400–95
COSGROVE (Art) 'The execution of the earl of Desmond, 1468' in *Kerry Arch. Soc. Jn.,* viii (1975), 11–27.
EMPEY (C.A.) and SIMMS (Katharine) 'The ordinances of the White Earl and the problem of coign in the later middle ages' in *RIA Proc.* lxxv (1975) sect. C, pp 161–87.
SIMMS (Katharine) 'Nill Garbh II O'Donnell, king of Tír Conaill, 1422–39' in *Donegal Annual* xii (1977), 7–21.

(h) 1495–1534
BRADSHAW (Brendan) 'Cromwellian reform and the origins of the Kildare rebellion, 1533–34' in *R. Hist. Soc. Trans.,* xxvii (1977), 69–93.

ELLIS
(Steven)
The Irish constitutional revolution of the sixteenth century (Cambridge 1979).
'The Kildare rebellion and the early Henrician reformation' in *Hist. Journal,* xix (1976), 807–30.
'Tudor policy and the Kildare ascendancy in the lordship of Ireland, 1496–1534' in *IHS* xx (1977), 235–71.

Military History

ELLIS
(Steven)
'Taxation and defence in late medieval Ireland: the survival of scutage' in *RSAI* Jn., cvii (1977), 5–28.

HARBISON
(Peter)
'Native Irish arms and armour in medieval Gaelic literature, 1170–1600' in *Ir. Sword,* xii (1976), 173–99, 240–80.

SIMMS
(Katharine)
'Warfare in the medieval Gaelic lordships' in *Ir. Sword,* xii (1976), 98–108.

Constitutional and Administrative History

(a) Council and Parliament

FARRELL
(Brian) (ed.)
The Irish Parliamentary Tradition (Dublin 1973). (Includes:

MARTIN (F.X.)
'The coming of parliament' pp 37–56

COSGROVE
(Art)
'A century of decline', pp 57–67

BRADSHAW
(Brendan)
'The beginnings of modern Ireland', pp 68–87)

HAND
(G.J.)
'Two hitherto unpublished membranes of Irish petitions presented at the midsummer parliament of 1302 and the lent parliament of 1305' in *RIA Proc.* lxxi (1971), sect. C. pp 1–18.

(c) Central Government
(iii) *Exchequer*

CONNOLLY
(Philomena)
'The Irish memoranda rolls: some unexplored aspects' in *Ir. Econ. and Soc. Hist.,* iii (1976), 66–74.

NICHOLLS (K.W.)	'Inquisitions of 1224 from the Miscellanea of the exchequer' in *Anal. Hib.*, xxvii (1972), 103–12.
(iv) *Judiciary* HAND (G.J.)	'English law in Ireland, 1172–1351' in *N.I. Legal Quart.*, xxiii (1972), 393–422. 'Aspects of alien status in medieval English law, with special reference to Ireland' in *Legal history studies, 1972: papers presented at the Legal History Conference, Aberystwyth, 18—21 July 1972* ed. D. Jenkins (Cardiff 1972), pp 129–35.

(d) Local government

EMPEY (C.A.)	'The cantreds of medieval Tipperary' in *N. Munster antiq. Jn.* xiii (1970), 22–9. 'The Butler lordship' in *Butler Soc. Jn.* i (1971), 174–87. 'The cantreds of the medieval county of Kilkenny' in *RSAI Jn.* ci (1971), 128–134.

Ecclesiastical History

(a) General

BOLSTER (Sr M. Angela)	*A history of the diocese of Cork from the earliest times to the Reformation* (Shannon, 1972).
WATT (John A.)	*The church in medieval Ireland* (Dublin 1972).

(b) Government and organisation

BETHELL (Denis)	'Dublin's two cathedrals' in *Focus on Medieval Dublin*, ed. Howard Clarke (Dublin 1978), pp 27–34.
COSGROVE (Art)	'Irish episcopal temporalities in the thirteenth century' in *Archiv. Hib.* xxxii (1974), 63–71.
EDWARDS (Ruth Dudley)	'Ecclesiastical appointments in the province of Tuam, 1399–1477' in *Archiv. Hib.*, xxxiii (1975), 91–100.

LOGAN (Donald) — 'The visitation of the archishop of Cashel to Waterford and Limerick, 1374–5' in *Archiv. Hib.*, xxxiv (1976), 50–54.

Mac ÍOMHAIR (Diarmaid) — 'Primate Mac Maolíosa and County Louth' in *Seanchas Ardmhacha* vi (1971), 70–93.

McROBERTS (David) — 'The Greek bishop of Dromore' in *Innes Rev.*, xxviii (1977), 22–38.

NICHOLLS (K.W.) — 'Medieval Irish cathedral chapters' in *Archiv. Hib.*, xxxi (1973), 102–11.

'Rectory, vicarage and parish in the western Irish dioceses' in *RSAI Jn.*, ci (1971), 53–84.

O'BRIEN (A.F.) — 'Episcopal elections in Ireland c. 1254–72' in *RIA Proc.* lxxiii (1973) sect. C. pp 129–76.

SIMMS (Katharine) — 'The archbishops of Armagh and the O'Neills, 1347–1471' in *IHS* xix (1974), 38–58.

'The concordat between primate John Mey and Henry O'Neill (1455)' in *Archiv. Hib.*, xxxiv (1976), 71–82.

(c) Relations with the papacy

FLANAGAN (Marie-Thérèse) — 'Hiberno-papal relations in the late twelfth century' in *Archiv. Hib.*, xxxiv (1976), 55–70.

WALSH (Katherine) — 'The beginnings of a national protectorate; curial cardinals and the Irish church in the fifteenth century' in *Archiv. Hib.*, xxxii (1974), 72–80.

WILKIE (William E.) — *The Cardinal Protectors of England: Rome and the Tudors before the Reformation* (Cambridge 1974).

(d) Religious orders

CARVILLE (G.) — 'The Cistercian settlement of Ireland' in *Studia Monastica*, xv (1973), 23–41.

MARTIN (F.X.) — 'An Irish Augustinian disputes at Oxford: Adam Payn, 1402' in *Scientia Augustiniana: Studien über Augustinus, den Augustinismus und den Augustinorden: Festschrift für Adolar Zumkeller zum 60 Geburtstag*, ed. C.P. Mayer and W. Eckermann, (Würzburg 1975), pp 289–322.

WALSH (Katherine)	'Franciscan friaries in pre-Reformation Kerry' in *Kerry Arch. Soc. Jn.* ix (1976), 16–31.

Social and Economic History

(a) General

SIMMS (Katharine)	'The legal position of Irishwomen in the late middle ages' in *Ir. Jurist* n.s. x (1975), 96–111. 'Women in Norman Ireland' in *Women in Irish Society*, ed. Margaret MacCurtain and Donncha O'Corráin (Dublin 1978), pp 14–25.

(b) Gaelic Society

Mac NIOCAILL (Gearóid)	'Aspects of Irish law in the late thirteenth century' in *Hist. Studies* x (1976), 25–42.

(c) Anglo-Irish Relations

COSGROVE (Art)	'Hiberniores ipsis Hibernis' in *Studies in Irish history, presented to R. Dudley Edwards*, ed. Art Cosgrove and Donal McCartney (Dublin 1979), pp 1–14.
FRAME (Robin)	'The immediate effect and interpretation of the 1331 ordinance "Una et eadem lex": some new evidence' in *Ir. Jurist*, n.s. vii (1972), 109–14.
JONES (W.R.)	'England against the Celtic fringe: a study in cultural stereotypes' in *Jn. World Hist.* xiii (1971), 155–71.
Mac NIOCAILL (Gearóid)	'The contact of Irish and common law' in *N.I. Legal Quart.* xxiii (1972), 16–23.

(d) Agriculture

BUCHANAN (R.)	'Norman and native: the medieval period and the dark ages' in *Studies of field systems in the British Isles*, ed. A.R.H. Baker and R.A. Butlin (Cambridge 1973), pp 608–16.

BUTLIN (R.A.) — 'Some observations on the field systems of medieval Ireland' in *Geographia Polonia,* xxxviii (1978), 31–6.

LEISTER (I.) — *Peasant openfield farming and its territorial organisation in Co. Tipperary* (Marburg/Lahn 1976).

(e) Towns and Trade

BRADLEY (John) — 'The town wall of Kilkenny' in *Old Kilkenny Rev.,* n.s. i(1975), 85–103, (1976), 209–18.

CLARKE (H.B.) — *Dublin c. 840 to c. 1540: the medieval town in the modern city* (Dublin 1978).

COSGROVE (Art) — 'Dublin in the Later Middle Ages' in *Focus on Medieval Dublin* ed. Howard Clarke (Dublin 1978) pp 35–8.

GRAHAM (Brian) — 'The towns of medieval Ireland' in *The Development of the Irish Town,* ed. R.A. Butlin (London and Totowa 1977), pp 28–60.
'The evolution of urbanization in medieval Ireland' in *Jn. of Hist. Geog.,* 5 (1979), 111–25.
'The documentation of medieval Irish boroughs' in *Bulletin G.S.I.H.S.* iv (1977), 9–20 and v (1979), 41–45.

HEALY (Patrick) — 'The town walls of Dublin' in *The Liberties of Dublin,* ed. Elgy Gillespie (Dublin 1973), pp 16–23.

LYDON (James F.) — 'The city of Waterford in the later middle ages' in *Decies* xii (1979), 5–15.

McENEANEY (Eamonn) — 'Waterford and New Ross trade competition, c. 1300' in *Decies* xii (1979), 16–24.

RUSSELL (J.C.) — *Medieval regions and their cities* (Newton Abbot 1971).

SHIELDS (Hugh)	'The walling of New Ross: a thirteenth-century poem in French' in *Long Room* nos 12/13 (1976), pp 24–33.
SIMMS (Anngret)	'The topography of medieval Dublin' in *Focus on Medieval Dublin* ed. Howard Clarke (Dublin, 1978), pp 7–14.

History of Literature

(a) Gaelic

Mac NIOCAILL (Gearóid)	*The medieval Irish annals* (Dublin 1975).
O'DWYER (B.W.)	'The annals of Connacht and Loch Cé and the monasteries of Boyle and Holy Trinity' in *RIA Proc.* lxxii (1972), sect. C, pp 83–101.
OSKAMP (H.P.A.)	'The yellow book of Lecan proper' in *Ériu* xxvi (1975), 102–21.

(b) Anglo-Irish

HENRY (P.L.)	'The land of Cokaygne: cultures in contact in medieval Ireland' in *Studia Hib.*, xii (1972), 120–41.

History of Fine Art

HUNT (John)	*Irish medieval figure sculpture, 1200–1600: a study of Irish tombs with notes on costume and armour: with assistance and contributions by Peter Harbison*, 2 vols (Dublin 1974).
HUNT (John) and HARBISON (Peter)	'Medieval English alabasters in Ireland' in *Studies* lxv (1976), 310–21.
STALLEY (R.A.)	'Irish art in the Romanesque and Gothic periods' in *Treasures of early Irish art,* ed. G. F. Mitchell (New York 1977), pp 187–220. 'The medieval sculpture of Christ Church Cathedral Dublin', in *Archaeologia* cvi (1979), 107–122.

History of Architecture

STALLEY (R.A.) — *Architecture and sculpture in Ireland, 1150–1350* (Dublin 1971)
'Mellifont Abbey: some observations on its architectural history' in *Studies*, lxiv (1975), 347–67.
'The long middle ages: from the twelfth-century to the Reformation' in *The Irish World: the history and cultural achievements of the Irish people*, ed. Brian de Breffny (London 1977).
'Corcomroe Abbey: some observations on its architectural history' in *RSAI Jn.* cv (1975), 21–46.
'William of Prene and the royal works in Ireland' in *Journal of the British Archaeological Association* cxxxi (1978), 30–49 and Plate xvi.

Numismatics

DOLLEY (Michael) — *Medieval Anglo-Irish coins* (London 1972) 'An Edward III hoard, found in the Victorian epoch, from Scarden, Corbetstown, Co. Westmeath' in *Riocht na Midhe* v no. 4 (1973), 79–86.

DOLLEY (Michael) and LANE (Stuart N.) — 'A find of fifteenth-century English groats from Co. Dublin' in *RSAI Jn.*, cii (1972), 143–50.

DOLLEY (Michael) and SEABY (A.W.) — 'The thirteenth-century Anglo-Irish coins in the Kirial find from Denmark', in *RSAI Jn.*, ciii (1973), 86–92.
'A find of thirteenth-century pewter tokens from the National Museum excavations at Winetavern Street, Dublin' in *Spinks Numismatic Circular*, (1971), 446–8.

ELLIS (Steven) — 'The struggle for control of the Irish mint, 1460–c. 1506' in *RIA Proc.* lxxviii (1978) sect. C pp 17–36.

Genealogy

(a) General

NICHOLLS (K.W.) — 'The Irish genealogies: their value and defects' in *Ir. Geneal.* v (1975), 256–61.

(b) Individual Families

NICHOLLS (K.W.)	'The Butlers of Aherlow and Owles' in *Butler Soc. Jn.*, i (1967), 123–8. 'The Geraldines of Allen' in *Ir. Geneal.* iv (1969–70), 93–109, 194–200. 'The descendants of Margaret Dartas', in *Ir. Geneal.* iv (1972), 392–6.
Ó DOIBHLIN (Eamonn)	'O'Neill's own country and its families' in *Seanchas Ardmhaca* vi (1971), 3–23.
Ó FIACH (Tomás)	'The O'Neills of the Fews' in *Seanchas Ardmhaca* vii (1973), 1–64.
SIMMS (Katharine)	'The O'Reillys and the kingdom of East Breifne' in *Breifne* v (1979), 305–17.

Ireland, 1534 – 1660

Aidan Clarke

The decision to produce a cooperative, multi-volume *New History of Ireland* was a bold one. But the initiation of the series in 1976 with the publication of the third volume,[1] in which sixteen scholars combined to deal with the period from 1534 to 1691 under the editorial direction of T. W. Moody, confirmed the editors' belief that the state of the art favoured the enterprise, for its tone strikingly illustrated the effectiveness with which passion was exorcised from historical inquiry by the generation of scholars who began work in the 1930s. The tale that the volume has to tell is, in plain terms, one of domination, expropriation and degradation: but the objectivity of the presentation is unfaltering. Indeed, it has been left to an English reviewer to protest mildly that an element of judgement is not inadmissable in the writing of history.[2] Yet it would be wrong to think that the impartiality of *A New History of Ireland* proceeds merely from too literal a respect for the canons of the discipline: more significantly, it reflects a growing appreciation among historians of the ways in which the community of Ireland is, both collectively and severally, heir to the whole past rather than to selected parts of it.

It is the state of knowledge that gives rise to the difficulties of preparing a comprehensive history. Given the patchwork maldistribution of previous scholarly interest between different periods and themes, it was evident from the outset that the intended 'synthesis in the light of existing knowledge' could not aim to achieve an even treatment, either across the centuries or within them. There was, however, the consolation that the composition of a coherent synopsis of what is known would also produce systematic information as to what needs to be known, so that the undertaking has assumed in part the form of an historiographical stock-taking, at once a conspectus of work to date and a guide to future research. It is thus appropriate that the publication of the third volume prompted a number of reflective reviews which conjoined a generous acknowledgement of what the work had achieved with constructively expressed dissatisfaction about the state of the subject which it had exposed. In each case, the leading critical emphasis was placed upon inadequacies relating to themes of such comparatively recent interest as demography, mentalities, cultural modes and social mechanisms. Thus Nicholas Canny hailed the decision to entitle the volume *Early Modern Ireland* as an important advance in itself, observing that the use of a label now generally accepted as specifying a distinctive stage in Western European development implied a readiness to concede that some of the salient characteristics of Irish history in the Tudor and Stuart centuries were particular to the period rather than to the place; but he went on to show that the promise of the title was not fulfilled in the text, in which none of the themes which preoccupy 'early modernists' elsewhere received systematic treatment.[3] This was fair and useful comment, and Donal Cregan[4] and Raymond Gillespie[5] wrote persuasively to similar effect. But it would be wrong to conclude that since the work of the past has demonstrably failed to answer the questions of the present a new set of priorities has been established and the ground been cleared for a fresh phase of historical investigation.

The timeliness of replacing traditional approaches with new ones is far from being the plain lesson of *A New History of Ireland*. Indeed, the converse might be argued with greater force, for the shortcomings of the volume provide ample reason to believe that it must be premature to think in terms of any radical change of direction in a disciplinary situation in which it proved impossible to deal with Tudor economic history at all, and feasible to treat the early seventeenth century economy only in an exploratory, and at times impressionistic, essay. It may be questioned whether anything constructive is likely to be gained from following sophisticated continental fashion before the more prosaic task of laying a systematic foundation of mainstream economic history has been undertaken. Moreover, although the economy is the lacuna most relevant to emerging interests, it is by no means the only one. Thus, while *A New History of Ireland* is naturally strongest in its treatment of the political and constitutional themes which have traditionally claimed most of the attention of Irish historians, there are marked differences in the treatment of the Tudor and Stuart periods which arise from the firmer groundwork in seventeenth century studies provided by easier access to sources and a larger body of good research. The hints contained in the space allocation, which assigned three chapters and one author to the period from 1534 to 1603 as against eight chapters and three authors to the years between 1603 and 1660, are confirmed by the text, which observably changes intellectual gear at the turn of the century: the conceptual level becomes more sophisticated, straightforward narrative is replaced by explanatory exposition, and the treatment both broadens to take in a greater range of contributory elements and deepens in its consideration of their interactions. The Tudor chapters, in fact, represent a valiant attempt on the part of the late G. A. Hayes–McCoy to construct a coherent account from unpromising materials. He was successful in the sense that he produced a better ordered and more lucid treatment than any of his predecessors. But the controlled flow of his narrative disguises its narrowness, and his failure to engage a number of central themes, such as the progress of the reformation and the shifting character of colonialism, gives an impression of discontinuity that helps to make the new reign and the new century seem more decisive turning points in the history of conquest than perhaps they were.[6] His contribution, indeed, exposes a contradiction in the original brief which, when 'the light of existing knowledge' seemed dim, encouraged professional synthesizing skill to overcome the hesitancy of the scholar. And if Hayes-McCoy was the most beguiling contributor, there were others who wrote with an authority and assurance which at times concealed the thinness of the research base from which they were working. The volume benefits from this technical proficiency, but its value as an aid to taking stock is affected by a tendency to circumvent areas of ignorance rather than to signpost them. Thus the blunt truth, that there are still large tracts of political and constitutional history which need to be reconstructed from the original sources, does not emerge with sufficient force. By contrast, *Ireland in the age of the Tudors,* by R. D. Edwards,[7] revealed the incomplete and unsatisfactory nature of sixteenth century studies through a wayward determination to allow the record to speak for itself: it proved, if not mute, at best Delphic, for the resulting chronicle bore bleak witness to the need for more information as well as for some commentary. In fact, like Hayes-McCoy before him, Edwards was unlucky in writing a little too soon to benefit from the revival of interest in the sixteenth century which has been the outstanding feature of the last few years.

It has been evident for some time that the necessary preconditions to progress in Tudor studies must be to discard the simplistic interpretations of the past in favour of a fresh start and to forswear the use of the calendared state papers in favour of the original documents. In the seventies, a number of scholars have set to work along these lines. Brendan Bradshaw and Nicholas Canny have been notably energetic, prolific and quick to derive stimulating conclusions from their research, and others are at work. The process of inquiry has included a concentration of critical attention upon the events of the year 1534, which recommended itself as a dividing point within the scheme of *A New History of Ireland* because it 'opened an era of direct rule that was to last till 1921'.[8]

Inevitably perhaps, the result of new research has been to dispel the impression of discontinuity, while amending the familiar tragi-romantic story of the noble House of Kildare destroyed by the impulsive action of a headstrong youth, which was first promoted by the Geraldine apologist Richard Stanyhurst and was echoed down the centuries in the words of Hayes-McCoy[9] ('Enraged at the treatment of his father, whom he mistakenly believed to have been executed . . '). Bradshaw[10] and Stephen Ellis[11] have independently concluded that the rebellion of Silken Thomas, far from having been the occasion of the introduction of centralizing policies, was actually a premeditated response to such policies. Thomas Cromwell emerges as central, Silken Thomas appears as the executor of a preconceived contingency plan, and the rebellion takes its place convincingly in the more subtle and complex context of political designs which envisaged the assimilation of a scaled-down Kildare lordship into a new political order. These plans attracted influential local support, and were resisted by force because they were recognized for what they were: in Bradshaw's words, 'the FitzGeralds were victims, therefore, not of their enemies, but of their own refusal to adapt to a new political era'. Ellis ascribes more importance to both religion and the continental dimension than does Bradshaw, but what is in question between them is rather the way in which the rebellion developed than the reasons why it began: these now seem firmly established, and are corroborated by the unpublished work of Laurence Corristine.[12]

The emphasis placed by Bradshaw upon the support that Cromwell received from within the colonial community in Ireland is part of a larger re-interpretation of the political dynamics of the early period of direct rule. A full explication awaits the publication of his Cambridge doctoral dissertation on 'The Irish constitutional revolution, 1515–57', but he has already sketched the argument in several pieces.[13] The essence of the case would appear to be that for some time after 1534 policy initiatives were principally generated within Ireland itself. Political innovation reflected the interests of an influential section of non-magnatial colonists rather than the imperatives of an anglocentric policy of control and conquest. The 'revolution' involved the conjunction of the Kingship Act of 1541, which altered the juridical relationship between the king and his subjects in Ireland and implied larger responsibilities than Henry was anxious to assume, with the adoption of the policy of accommodation with established authorities in the areas beyond the pale that has been familiarly known as 'surrender and regrant'. The effects were to enhance colonial status, procure more settled conditions and commit the crown to an implicit obligation to extend its jurisdiction over the whole country. Students of colonialism will recognize this pattern: the search for a system of collaboration with the indigenes, the assumption that it was merely transitional, and the settler effort to ensure that imperial policy subserved local purposes. In the Henrician case, the mediating agent was the English lord deputy, St Leger, who sought to unify Ireland under the crown by cooperating with the colonists and conciliating the Irish. Much of Bradshaw's detail is supported by the work of Kenneth Nicholls,[14] who has not only similarly disclosed the colonial origins of conciliation, but demonstrated that the practice of surrender and regrant pragmatically incorporated local arrangements with so little regard for the doctrinaire letter of English property law as to leave no doubt that the object was stabilization rather than anglicization. Although Bradshaw's characterization perhaps needs to be modified to take account of the operation of both factional and spoils systems (a qualification which applies to almost all treatments of politics in sixteenth century Ireland), his reconstruction of the political interplay of the early years of direct rule involves an important revision of the long term trend of settler alienation. This no longer appears as a simple linear progression commencing in the 1530s and steadily growing thereafter: instead, it assumes the more complex pattern of an initially close and beneficial involvement with government followed by a quite abrupt disengagement in Elizabeth's reign. Thus Bradshaw's work leads neatly into the period and problems which have engaged Nicholas Canny, and the resulting disagreements have opened up a wide range of important themes. In *The Elizabethan conquest of Ireland: a pattern established, 1565—1576*,[15] Canny argued that the viceroyalty of Sir Henry Sidney marked a major and lasting departure based, for the first time, on an integrated national policy which took well judged account of the way in which situations varied in different parts of the country and aimed, most significantly, to increase control by decentralizing authority through the institution of provincial presidencies.[16] The traditional obligation to defend the pale was now seen to be most effectively performed by a general extension of jurisdiction which would bring both the required stabilization and access to resources which might make the programme self-sustaining. And once the government was committed to a vigorous assertion of authority and to direct responsibility for the administration of outlying areas, the suppression of resistance and the completion of conquest inexorably followed. Like many another thesis, Canny's seems weakest at the edges, for its comparative thrust lacks verification: not enough work has been done on the preceding viceroyalty of Sussex to underpin a firm judgement of the novelty of Sidney's approach, and the investigation of the situation seems likely to reveal (as Bernadette Cunningham's research suggests,[17] and Canny has elsewhere acknowledged)[18] that Lord Deputy Perrott reverted in some respects to the earlier practice of conciliating the Irish and cooperating with the established settler community. But the value of the book is unaffected by these doubts, for it is brimming with new information and fresh ideas. These are, perhaps, most valuably linked in a survey of social and economic conditions which challengingly emphasizes the similarities which lay beneath the more visible cultural differences between the various zones into which Ireland was divided, a point further developed and sharpened in a subsequent O'Donnell lecture on the emergence of the Old English elite.[19]

In *The Elizabethan conquest,* Canny associated the new directions of policy with the influence of new attitudes. He argued that the conciliatory approach of the colonists, prevalent before Sidney, was grounded in the belief that Gaelic society was susceptible to peaceful penetration and transformation: the severity practised by newcomers reflected the novel assumption that the barbarity and paganism of the natives, which they related to the evolving concept of anthropological inferiority, called for extreme measures of coercion and validated courses of action which disregarded normal moral scruples. This hypothesis, which accepted the distinction between 'hard' and 'soft' policies drawn by D.B. Quinn and sought to establish the contrasting ideological contexts, has already prompted a ramifying debate about the philosophic bases of Tudor policies and the alternative strategies deriving from different intellectual positions. The initial point at issue was drawn by Brendan Bradshaw in a review article in which he contraverted Canny's direct association between humanist renaissance thought and severity of approach, and argued that the ideological origins of policies of rigorous coercion are to be found in protestantism, which held that ignorance was wilful rather than circumstantial and concluded that it must be overcome by force rather than by persuasion: the humanist approach was the converse.[20] Bradshaw had already demonstrated, in his monograph on *The dissolution of the religious orders in Ireland under Henry VIII* and in two earlier articles,[21] that the colonial opposition to official policy in the Reformation Parliament can be explained in terms of vested interest, that the acceptance of Henry VIII as Supreme Head seems not to have raised serious problems, and that protestantism was more actively promoted in Edward's reign than has been supposed. Integrating these various strands into a coherent thesis on 'Sword, word and strategy in the reformation in Ireland',[22] Bradshaw charted the polarization between the alternative strategies of persuasion and coercion and argued, in effect, that the failure to resolve the contradiction which they presented resulted in the forfeiture of local support and was responsible for the lack of success of the reformation effort in Ireland. Thus, while the initial reaction to Henrician reform was neither favourable nor unfavourable, but non-committal, the preferences formed in the 1550s conditioned later choices, resistance to political aggression and religious coercion were conjoined, and the success of the counter-reformation was assured. In a reply entitled, in evocation of Lucien Febvre, 'Why the reformation failed in Ireland: *une question mal posee*',[23] Canny conceded the point originally in dispute, but extended the scope of the debate by constructing a counter-thesis. He argued that the propensity to conform was greater than is normally assumed, adducing a good deal of evidence to support the view that outward conformity to the reformation was not uncommon, particularly in the towns, for much of Elizabeth's reign. And he contended that the debate on strategy, continuing through the century, was conducted between protestants of local provenance, who supported modes of persuasion, and protestants from England, who believed that coercion was required. On this reading, the fate of protestantism, which Bradshaw regards as having been settled by the early 1570s, was still open in the 1590s and the sources of its failure, though rooted in the first Elizabethan generation, must be discovered at work in the second.

The work of Colm Lennon,[24] who has noted the tendency of palesmen to conform and speculated on the acceptability of an Erasmian 'middle way' in the 1560s, seems to support Canny's impression that reactions to the Elizabethan phase of the reformation were initially ambivalent rather than pre-set by earlier experience. But a certain reserve seems appropriate at the present stage of the debate: the batteries of contemporary quotations deployed by Canny and Bradshaw reveal, when aggregated and collated, a degree of inconsistency and ambiguity which suggests that the categories being used are more analytically useful than descriptively valid. To witness a debate on sixteenth century intellectual history in Ireland is so refreshing that it is tempting to welcome it for its own sake. But the reality is that however coherent and discrete a system of ideas may be in conception, it does not remain so in diffusion, and the intellectual furniture of both old and new settlers in Ireland shows too many signs of eclecticism and confusion to encourage confidence in so simple a sorting. The questions posed are worthwhile ones, and two positive advances may be recorded: first, the willingness to accept that the failure of protestantism to secure adherents in Ireland was not inevitable, and, second, the discovery that its rejection was not instant and absolute. Failure had, no doubt, something to do with strategic considerations and with the receptivity of the community, but a satisfactory reconstruction is unlikely to emerge until the logistics of protestant reform have been explored and the contribution of such factors as resource problems, lay influence, crypto-catholic personnel, lack of zeal and sheer incompetence have been assessed, for failure was surely related to a condition of organizational disfunction so pronounced in the early years that no strategy could possibly have been implemented effectively. The situation changed after the first generation, and it is necessary to remember that what the Elizabethan settlement tried and failed to do was to take over a going concern, rather than to create a new church *de novo*, which is what it succeeded in doing. Philomena Kilroy's work confirms the impression that in the early seventeenth century the Church of Ireland was intellectually vital, constructively overhauling itself, and consolidating its position, less ambitious but perhaps more congenial, as the church of the new colonists.[25]

While the Canny-Bradshaw debate has moved firmly into the religious sphere, Canny's original contention that the altered conduct of the English in Ireland was rooted in, and legitimated by, the putative paganism of the Irish has been subjected to a severely secular critique by Helga Robinson-Hammerstein.[26] Suggesting that the allegations of paganism cited by Canny were no more than local expressions of a rhetoric of abuse employed throughout Europe, in which the terms pagan and catholic were synonymous, and capping the argument with a Scottish allusion to 'the Pope, that pagan full of pride', she contended that disregard for behavioural norms in dealing with the Irish can be explained in juridical terms. For Tudor Englishmen, the constraints imposed by law and by law-determined processes were mandatory only in dealing with those who acknowledged their validity: they did not, in short, think it obligatory to treat outlaws lawfully. There may be an intermediate position here: what Canny's evidence seems to show is not that the English in Ireland believed the Irish to be pagan, but that they ascribed to them the special, and more culpable, condition of being lapsed Christians. But the point raised by Robinson-Hammerstein is central to the whole question of Tudor objectives in Ireland. It seems obvious that, while most governmental decisions were short term and pragmatic and most governors conceived their function as problem solving rather than policy making, choices were nonetheless made within a framework of long term assumptions which require clarification if the overall thrust is to be understood. It was doubtless complex enough to accommodate both the presumption of inferiority and the assumption of assimilability: the former, after all, may be applied to the present and the latter relegated to the future. Clearly, the connection between what people said and what they did was mediated in some measure by unstated assumptions and unconscious habits of thought which have yet to be reconstructed.

The irony of the position of the established colonists, urging the incorporation of the Irish into the community from which they were themselves being gradually excluded, is manifest. Bradshaw has portrayed their response as the development of a form of colonial nationalism, based on the constitutional integrity of the kingdom of Ireland, which not only embraced the Irish but, seemingly, transcended religious divisions, since the principal public spokesmen were conformable in religion.[27] Canny, on the other hand, has argued more elaborately that while the ideological position of the English evolved, the established colonists held fast to their original belief in the efficacy of 'amiable means of favourable reconcilement' to deal with the Irish, and developed what was in effect a counter-ideology which repudiated the revised premises of official policy and justified their own self-assigned role as mediators. Their withdrawal from the familiar philosophical ambience of England was associated with a transfer of intellectual allegiance to the continent, where they found, in post-tridentine catholicism, a system of belief that accommodated and supported their social and political attitudes.[28] This view of the established settlers, as briefly poised between catholicism and protestantism and basing their choice on compatibility with their existing philosophical outlook and situational needs, coincides interestingly with the emergence of fresh views on the counter-reformation itself.

Scholars elsewhere have been aware for some time of a pronounced discontinuity between the new catholicism generated by the Council of Trent and the old religion which it sought to supersede, and have drawn attention to the untidy and confused nature of the transition from one to the other, during which traditional and innovatory practices competed for some time in some places. One of those places, it has been argued by John Bossy[29] and Aidan Clarke,[30] was Gaelic Ireland, where the need to harmonize religious regulations derived from one culture with the highly distinctive social institutions of another had produced modifications of formal catholicism which went far beyond token concessions to local oddities. Deviance was particularly marked in the area of marriage customs: canonical impediments were ignored (at least on the female side), no distinction was made between legitimate and illegitimate offspring, divorce was permitted, and clerical marriage was accepted as a matter of course; and each of these practices was integrally related to the central mechanisms of a patrilinear lineage society in which the application of the tridentine decrees would have had a revolutionary effect. Organizationally, too, the Irish had for long been accustomed to entrust routine spiritual provision to the regular clergy, who could adapt to community divisions, rather than to the secular clergy, whose parochial structure cut across the lineage boundaries. Thus, the prevailing mode of catholicism in Gaelic Ireland was a survivalist resistance to the counter-reformation, which was, by contrast, congenial to the established colonists as a vehicle of civility. Clarke has argued that this interpretation provides an important clue to the elusive process by which the Anglo-Irish of the sixteenth century evolved into the Old English of the seventeenth, suggesting that the reason why the alienation of the settlers from both secular and religious establishments resulted in their emergence as a resolutely separate group, rather than in the association with their Irish fellow catholics that protestant observers predicted, was precisely because the forms of catholicism to which Irish and Old English were attached were themselves wholly distinctive. The beginnings of an answer to the obvious deficiencies of this statement – that many Irish were manifestly committed to the counter-reformation, however unsuccessful they may have been in introducing it to Ireland – is suggested by the work of Gerard Rice:[31] his investigation of the activities of one of the most prominent of the tridentine reformers indicates that the qualification for episcopal favour in the Old English diocese of Meath was not to be Old English rather than Irish, but to have been educated in France rather than in Spain. Similarly, Conor Ryan[32] detected clear signs of Gallican influence at work a generation or two later, in the 'loyal remonstrance' prepared for submission to Charles II in the 1660's which he presented as a logical outcome of the central position that the colonial political tradition assigned to the king. The Gallican attitude to the relationship between temporal and spiritual authority was by no means unlike that of the Old English, and it seems probable that the observable divisions and antagonisms within catholicism in Ireland were associated with differences within the counter-reformation church itself as well as with the more straight forward local struggle between survivalism and reform. Unfortunately, recent work on the educational institutions which were the springboards of missionary activity has been confined to information retrieval and has lacked any developed sense of the problems that need to be resolved.[33] Only Helga Robinson-Hammerstein has addressed the question of what was actually taught,[34] and there has been no systematic investigation of specific preparation for missionary work, nor any objective analysis of the mental attitudes and formation of those involved. The career of the Jesuit, James Archer, has been informatively sketched by Thomas Morrissey,[35] but the study of the exceptional adds little to the synoptic knowledge that is required. In 'The Irish Peter Lombard' John J. Silke[36] provided, despite his chosen title, a valuable reminder of the Irish primate's prominence in the church on the continent where, among other distinctions, he played a leading role in the condemnation of Galileo. There are so many other talented and successful Irishmen who deserve to be similarly presented in their European setting as to suggest, perversely, that it might be worth following up the implications of the unsatisfactory report on Archer submitted to the General of the order in 1587, which concluded that he was suitable only to serve as a preacher in Ireland.

The fragmentation of catholicism in Ireland, and the variety of influences that might affect the particular form to which an individual chose to subscribe, may contain a valuable hint of the appropriate approach to the consideration of the nature of social groupings. It has been clear for some time that the determinants of group membership were multiple, conforming to no simple correlation of ethnic origins and beliefs, and containing an element of choice. The identification of some Irish with the Old English, and of others with the New English, is well known, if insufficiently understood. Donald Jackson[37] has drawn attention to the reverse flow in a brief case study of the divergent histories of the descendents of pre-1570 colonists in Leinster, some of whom were assimilated, and some not. He suggested that the key to the difference may lie in 'the history of violence between colonist and colonized', arguing that it was the settlers who suffered violence who preserved their separateness, while those who inflicted it were inexorably drawn into relationships of both feud and alliance with their Gaelic neighbours which prepared the way for assimilation. Canny[38] has essayed a collective description of the Tudor New English in which he has examined the composition of the group, analysed the ways in which their views differed from those of the English in England (chiefly in the direction of fewer anxieties and greater confidence), and argued that while protestant settlers were dismissive of the Irish they looked upon the 'English of Irish birth' as effective and entrenched rivals and regarded them with active distrust: on the evidence, they seem to have viewed civility as a greater threat than barbarity. In a related essay,[39] however, Canny has presented the same topic from the bottom up: exploring the failure of colonizing schemes to work out according to plan, and focussing on the unsuitability of grantees and settlers alike, he has drawn a rather highly coloured picture of a colonial society with, at its edges, a marked propensity to defect. The piece raises the intriguing possibility that lower class settlers, whose worth was indubitably a matter of widespread concern, may often have been hostile or indifferent towards the dominant culture in whose name they came to Ireland, and correspondingly prone to abandon it, or at least, and more significantly, to have been so ill-equipped to represent it at its best that the process of planting centres of supposedly exemplary civility may have helped to defeat itself.

The emphasis on socio-political groupings, and particularly on the emergence of the articulate and influential Old English group, has already helped to clarify issues and to identify the pressure points in the society: the investigation needs to be extended by a closer attention to their structures, and by a consideration of the profile of non-elite groups. But it also needs to be balanced by the systematic examination of inter-group mobility: the indications are that this would help to show that conflict and rivalry were far from being the only modes of response to the realities of pluralism, and that the options open to individuals were, or could be, quite open, for the principles of association were cultural rather than ethnic. Moreover, the impulse to devise strategies of accommodation was strong, and intermarriage was certainly one of the mechanisms used. Jackson[40] has shown, in a rather impressionistic way, the existence of apparent patterns of variation in the prevalence and function of intermarriage in different groups and in different parts of the country. But firm generalization must await more information, and may require a more sophisticated approach: for instance, given the male-centred customs of each of the groups concerned, which ensured the cultural subordination of the wife and her offspring, it may be necessary to be alert to differences of practice between sons and daughters. Canny's assumption that immigrants were typically young males has introduced an entirely new perspective.

It is considerations of this kind that seem to be the most striking thematic omissions in the recent spurt of interest in the plantation in Ulster. Thus, for example, the welcome and illuminating perspective on the Scots as emigrants in Michael Maxwell's *The Scottish migration to Ulster in the reign of James I*[41] was gained in some degree at the expense of their Irish role as immigrants, and his authoritative reconstruction of the course of their settlement did not extend to a detailed analysis of their relationship with the local community. Philip Robinson,[42] applying sophisticated techniques to unusually good evidence, has produced important insights into the settlement process by disclosing a pattern of post-plantation redistribution, as settlers departed from the original deployment to take more informed advantage of the resources and opportunities on offer. His findings elucidate the 'economic sorting out' that pushed the Irish on to inferior land, and make good sense of the local demography, but they reduce people to statistical entities. Robert Hunter's work on towns has shown how the original scheme to introduce a distinctive urban component was largely defeated by practical difficulties, infirmity of purpose and landlord interests; J. H. Andrews has unravelled the complex details of the inadequate surveying that so greatly affected the character of the plantation by producing grant units too large to be colonized to the intended density;[44] and Peter Roebuck has reconstructed the managerial policy and fortunes of the Chichesters, who pursued development rather than profit, but lacked the resources to support both the cost of constructive estate building and the expense of the public role to which Sir Arthur was committed through his enjoyment of royal munificence.[45]

Other plantations have attracted less attention, but D. B. Quinn assembled his ideas on a theme that has preoccupied him for some time in an essay that makes 'Renaissance influences in English colonization'[46] clearer, though hardly more important, than before. A conference paper by Michael MacCarthy-Morrogh[47] confirmed Quinn's earlier demonstration that the Munster plantation went through a second phase of consolidation and supplementation in the early seventeenth century in the course of which it appears to have come close to developing into an economic appendage of south-west England. The point reinforces the conclusion that emerges strongly from the contrast between the informally settled counties of Antrim and Down and the officially planted escheated counties noted in Maxwell's book – that the conditions for colonizing success included not only resolute entrepreneurial activity, but also systematic linkages with an economically more advanced region. The contrast between colonies of settlement and colonies of exploitation seems not to have been as clear in practice as it is in theory. Fundamental to most recent studies of plantation has been an increased awareness of the delicate interplay between public and private interest which converged in the initial planning stages, but diverged thereafter as settlers reappraised their own circumstances. There is still some way to go before the history of colonization can be satisfactorily presented in terms of process rather than in terms of schemes and blueprints, with the emphasis on colonists rather than policy makers, but an organic approach is slowly replacing the older static treatment. What is chiefly lacking is any systematic examination of colonial economic practice: the argument presented in *A New History of Ireland,* that the planted areas witnessed a more intensive exploitation of resources without any substantial change in the character of economic activity,[48] remains unproven.

Economic history of late has been largely confined to external trade. Donald Woodward[49] and Victor Treadwell,[50] working on aspects of sixteenth century commercial activity and regulation, have extended knowledge of a subject on which the only substantial contribution is now fifty years old: Woodward has also written informatively on the livestock trade in the seventeenth century,[51] while D. R. Hainsworth[52] presented a uniquely detailed account of commercial practices in the 1630s, using a rich body of untapped material which he subsequently edited for the Surtees Society.[53] But these are contributions to a subject of which not even the general configuration has yet been satisfactorily established. Although it seems likely that market forces and the lines of communication opened up by migration led to a steady increase in the proportion of Irish trade that was conducted with England, it is scarcely possible to reach convincing conclusions without a systematic examination of continental sources of evidence. The inferences which may be drawn from what is known of the wine trade are an inadequate substitute for precise information. Similarly, the Irish setting, in terms of markets and consumption as well as in terms of the organization of production for local and international distribution, is most imperfectly known. Canny's description of the situation in the 1560s was a major advance in the coherent ordering of the evidence, and included a useful brief discussion of urban-rural links.[54] For the most part, however, although the outlines of the history of particular towns are fairly well known, neither economic treatments nor generalization have been forthcoming. The parallels between the rural and urban colonial experience in which, in the same sequence if at different intervals, conciliation was succeeded by the exertion of unfriendly control, and the planting of favoured new towns was followed by the confiscation and colonization of the old ones in the 1650s, remain undeveloped. T. C. Barnard[55] has examined the last phase closely, but the only general treatment of the urban theme, by R. A. Butlin,[56] is thin in its coverage of the established towns. Butlin stressed the mid-sixteenth century decline, but disregarded the official efforts to promote revival, which can be disclosed through the examination of the revised charters of the period as well as through the parliamentary legislation elucidated by Victor Treadwell. Similarly, although the importance of the introduction of the custom farm in the early seventeenth century is well understood in fiscal terms, its economic effects, as trade restrictions deriving from municipal privilege were forcibly relaxed in the interests of maximizing turnover and profit, have not been looked into.[57] The problems involved in the reconstruction of the economic history of early modern Ireland are admittedly large, and there is force in the cautious view that much more detailed information must be accumulated before a synthesis can be produced, but it is difficult to see how significant progress can be made in the absence of contextual awareness. Research on specific topics needs to be informed by some sense of the reciprocating mechanisms within the economy, so that some notion of the relationships between the parts and the whole can be gleaned. If it is too early for a synthesis, an integrated hypothesis is surely long overdue.

A useful example of the constructive value of attempting to produce a synthetic treatment on the basis of incomplete information was provided by Louis Cullen's discussion of seventeenth century population trends.[58] A systematic review of the unsatisfactory evidence in the light of recognized demographic principles enabled Cullen to demonstrate the probability that earlier, impressionistic estimates of population in the first part of the century had been unrealistically low: it also allowed him to isolate the level of mortality in the plague visitation of the early 1650s as the specific area of investigation which would contribute most effectively to a resolution of the remaining difficulties. Cullen's revised estimates have clear implications for sixteenth century studies. If at first sight they seem difficult to reconcile with existing assumptions, second thoughts suggest that the distinctive social and economic practices of Gaelic Ireland were conducive to a high birth rate and may even have reduced death rates below European norms, since the effects of crop failure and epidemics may have been mitigated by pastoralism and low density. But the arguments are scarcely susceptible to proof, for the institutions themselves are not well enough known.

There is a marked difference between the ways in which the respective histories of colonial Ireland and Gaelic Ireland are written. The former is concerned with the reconstruction of change and the explanation of its dynamics. The latter has yet to contrive a marriage between events and their context – indeed, has yet to arrive at a satisfactory measure of the significance of events. The dichotomy is exemplified in *Gaelic and Gaelicized Ireland in the later middle ages,* by Kenneth Nicholls,[59] in which a pioneering and extremely valuable attempt to construct a coherent account of Gaelic institutions, by bringing together an impressive range of evidence from four centuries, was followed by a group of histories of individual lordships which were little more than animated succession lists. The fault does not lie with Nicholls, as the treatment of the Gaelic Irish in *A New History of Ireland* indicates. In the narrative sections of the third volume they appear, for the most part, only when interaction with the government or colonists brings them into the mainstream. The editors have referred a detailed treatment of their institutions to the second volume. Thus the central process of societal change has been obscured by the absence of systematic information about the character of the society that changed. Moreover, since the editors have also referred the treatment of legal history, to the fourth volume, and since the interaction of English law and Gaelic institutions was one of the chief mechanisms of change throughout the period, a vital strand has been withdrawn from the story told in the third volume. At bottom, the difficulty of satisfactorily integrating the histories of the different communities in Ireland lies not simply in the complexity of their interactions, but in the fact that understanding of Gaelic society, though greatly advanced by Nicholls's willingness to synthesize, is conflationary. It has no certain application to specific times and particular places: how institutions changed through time and varied between places has still to be reconstructed in detail. And until this has been done, the difficulty of relating events to setting and writing Gaelic history of adequate sociopolitical depth are likely to defy solution. Valuable work, however, has been done. Mary O'Dowd's unpublished investigation of interest areas, group relations and the effects of colonial intrusion in Sligo is a good example of the kind of case study on which a better understanding of how change occurred in the early modern period must depend.[60] The work of Katherine Simms, who has displayed both a capacity for careful particularization in her unpublished research on the Ulster lordships[61] and a capacity for equally careful generalization in her essays on war and women,[62] offers hope of insights to come, not least because she is alert to the fact that the hibernicization of the settlers was only one element in a process of social change that affected Gaelic society also.

Katherine Simms's essay on war in Gaelic society, which neatly related the techniques and conventions of warfare to its political objectives, and argued that its destructiveness was limited by the need to preserve the human resources whose exploitation was its aim, has been the most ambitious contribution to military history in recent years. The discipline has suffered the loss of its two leading practitioners, Hayes-McCoy and Gerald Simms, and what slight attention it has received has been of extreme specificity. Amos Miller's research on Sir Richard Grenville yielded a modest addition to knowledge of the events of the 1640s, and the meticulous reconstruction of 'Cromwell at Drogheda', by Gerald Simms,[64] was a necessary, but characteristically courteous, corrective to plentiful inaccuracies of the account given in Antonia Fraser's biography of Cromwell.[65] Much of Irish military history was, of course, made outside Ireland, and Jerrold Casway's work in continental archives has produced two informative articles.[66] More generally, John J. Silke assembled a great deal of material about Irish people abroad in Chapter XVIII of the third volume of *A New History of Ireland*. What is missing is an aggregated treatment: a study of the composition, structure, life style and leadership patterns of the expatriate communities would not only be of intrinsic interest, but would also contribute importantly to the understanding of the 1641 rebellion, for it is clear that exilic intransigence both affected its plotting and confused its development in ways that have yet to be disentangled.

Significant elements in the local background to the rebellion have been treated in Clarke's study of Poynings' Law,[67] which helps to elucidate the ineffectuality of parliamentary means of protest, and in Maxwell's examination of Strafford's treatment of the Ulster Scots,[68] but the delicate balance of Irish, cross-channel and continental influences remains elusive. Clarke's characterization of the rebellion in its early stages, as an attempt to preserve the status quo rather than to undo it,[69] which received support from Maxwell's valuable reconstruction of the course of the outbreak in mid-Ulster,[70] offered a revised frame of reference for the investigation of the tensions that emerged as the situation changed and the exiles returned. In fact, however, while Karl Bottigheimer[71] and John A. Murphy[72] have disclosed the complexity of motivation and flexibility of response among protestants in Ireland in the 1640s, no comparable effort has been made to explore the diversity of attitudes and interests that lay beneath the superficial polarity on the Confederate side, though Donal Cregan's concise description of the Confederation as a constitutional system has cleared some of the ground.[73] The sustained coherence of Patrick Corish's narrative of the period in *A New History of Ireland* was a major advance, but the movement that brought colonial and native catholics precariously together was at one and the same time a revolt within the colonial system and a rebellion against it, and the analysis of its internal dynamics perhaps requires a more conceptual approach.

The aftermath has fared better than the struggle. Bottigheimer dealt with a central aspect of the expropriation which followed the rebellion in *English money and Irish land*,[74] marshalling the evidence concerning the 'adventurers' clearly and effectively to reach conclusions that contained no surprises, but are now thoroughly established on a firm quantitative base. By contrast, T. C. Barnard opened up an entirely novel, indeed almost unsuspected subject in *Cromwellian Ireland*,[75] in which he investigated the constructive aspects of English policy in Ireland in the 1650s. Apart from the freshness of much of the information, Barnard's work was interpretatively important, for it disclosed a calculated responsiveness to local protestant interests, on the part of Henry Cromwell in particular, that provides essential clues to the mysterious way in which the already established colonists became the chief beneficiaries of Ireland's mid-century disturbances. It also showed the remarkable extent to which the history of the pursuit of anglicization by the regime of the 1650s repeated in telescoped miniature the experience of the preceding one-hundred years: Marvell's 'foreshortened time' might almost have been part of the baggage of the Cromwellians. The history of the Irish remains obscure in this decade: some attempt to reach them is the virtue of Peter Berresford Ellis's unsure *Hell or Connaught*,[76] but the material for detailed study provided by R. C. Simington's compilation, *The transplantation to Connacht*,[77] has not yet been exploited.

The development of a lively interest in the sixteenth century has been perhaps the most exciting feature of the last decade, but the major advance was unquestionably the publication of *A New History of Ireland*, which set new standards of systematization and coherence, and from which an agenda for future research may be compiled without undue difficulty.

IRELAND, 1534 – 1660/AIDAN CLARKE/NOTES

[1] *A new history of Ireland.* Edited by T.W. Moody, F.X. Martin, and F.J. Byrne, Vol. iii: *Early modern Ireland, 1534 – 1691.* Oxford, 1976.

[2] G.E. Aylmer, in *E.H.R.*, xciii, (1978), pp 117–21.

[3] 'Early modern Ireland: an appraisal appraised', in *Irish economic and social history,* iv (1977), pp 56–65.

[4] 'Early modern Ireland', in *I.H.S.*, xx, no. 79 (1977), pp 272–285.

[5] 'Early modern Ireland: a speculative review', in *Retrospect: journal of the Irish history students' association* (1979), pp 53–6.

[6] Nicholas Canny, 'Hugh O'Neill, earl of Tyrone, and the changing face of Gaelic Ulster', in *Studia Hib,* no. 10 (1970), pp 7–35; 'Historical revision: xvii, The flight of the earls', in *I.H.S.,* xvii, no. 67 (1971), pp 380–399.

[7] R. Dudley Edwards, *Ireland in the age of the Tudors: the destruction of Hiberno-Norse civilization,* London, 1977.

[8] *N.H.I.,* iii, xl.

[9] Ibid., p. 40.

[10] 'Cromwellian reform and the origins of the Kildare rebellion', in *Trans R.H.S.,* 5th series, no. 27 (1977), pp 69–94.

[11] 'The Kildare rebellion and the early Henrician reformation' in *Historical Journal,* xix (1976), pp 807–30; 'Tudor policy and the Kildare ascendancy in the lordship of Ireland, 1496–1534', in *I.H.S.,* xx, no. 79 (1977), pp 235–71.

[12] 'The Silken Thomas Revolt', N.U.I., M.A. thesis, 1975.

[13] Brendan Bradshaw, *The dissolution of the religious orders in Ireland under Henry VIII,* Cambridge, 1974; 'The beginnings of modern Ireland', in Brian Farrell (ed.), *The Irish parliamentary tradition,* Dublin, 1973.

[14] K.W. Nicholls, *Land, law and society in sixteenth century Ireland,* O'Donnell Lecture, N.U.I., 1976.

[15] Hassocks, 1976

[16] See also, D. J. Kennedy, 'The presidency of Munster under Elizabeth I and James I', N.U.I., M.A. thesis, 1973.

[17] 'The Composition of Connacht, 1585 – 1630'; paper read at the annual conference of the Economic and Social History Society of Ireland, 1979.

[18] Nicholas Canny, 'Dominant minorities: English settlers in Ireland and Virginia, 1550–1650', in A.C. Hepburn (ed.), *Historical Studies; xii: minorities in history,* London, 1978.

[19] *The formation of the Old English elite in Ireland,* N.U.I., 1975.

[20] 'The Elizabethans and the Irish', in *Studies,* lxvi, no. 261 (1977), pp 38–50.

[21] 'The opposition to the ecclesiastical legislation in the first reformation parliament', in *I.H.S.,* xvi, no. 63 (1969), pp 285–303; 'The Edwardian reformation in Ireland', in *Archiv. Hib.,* xxxiv (1976), pp 83–99.

[22] *Historical Journal,* xxi (1978), pp 475–502.

[23] *Journal of Ecclesiastical History,* xxx, no. 4 (1979), pp 423–50.

[24] 'Recusancy and the Dublin Stanihursts', in *Archiv. Hib.,* xxxiii (1975); 'Richard Stanihurst (1547–1618) and Old English identity', in *I.H.S.,* xxi, no. 82 (1978), pp 121–143.

[25] 'Sermons and pamphlet literature in the Irish reformed church', in *Archiv. Hib.,* xxxiii, (1975), pp 110–121; 'Bishops and ministers in Ulster during the primacy of Ussher', in *Seanchas Ardmacha,* viii, no. 2 (1977), pp 24–8; 'Puritanism in Ireland in the seventeenth century', N.U.I., M.A. thesis, 1973.

[26] *I.H.S.,* xxi, no. 81 (1978), pp 106–11.

[27] 'The beginnings of modern Ireland', loc. cit., note 13 above.

[28] *The formation of the Old English elite.* See note 19 above. Compare Donal Cregan, 'Irish catholic admissions to the English Inns of Court, 1558–1625', in *The Irish Jurist,* v, new series, pt i (1970), pp 95–114.

[29] 'The counter-reformation and the people of catholic Ireland, 1596–1641', in T. D. Williams (ed.), *Historical studies, viii,* Dublin, 1971.

[30] 'Colonial identity in early seventeenth century Ireland', in T.W. Moody (ed.) *Historical studies, xi: nationality and the pursuit of national independence,* Belfast, 1978.

[31] 'Attitudes to the counter-reformation in Meath, 1600–1630'; 'Thomas Dease and ecclesiastical rights', in *Riocht na Midhe,* v (1972); vi (1975).

[32] 'Religion and state in seventeenth century Ireland', in *Archiv Hib.,* xxxiii (1975).

[33] T.J. Walsh, *The Irish continental college movement: the colleges at Bordeaux, Toulouse and Lille,* Dublin and Cork, 1973. Cathaldus Giblin, 'The Irish colleges on the continent', in Liam Swords (ed.), *The Irish-French connection, 1578–1978,* Paris, 1978.

[34] Helga Hammerstein, 'Aspects of the continental education of Irish students in the reign of Elizabeth I', in T. D. Williams (ed.), *Historical studies, viii,* Dublin, 1971.

[35] *James Archer of Kilkenny: an Elizabethan jesuit,* Dublin, 1979.

[36] *Studies,* lxiv (1975), pp 143–55.

[37] 'Violence and assimilation in Tudor Ireland', in Eoin O'Brien (ed.)

Essays in honour of J.D.H. Widdess, Dublin, 1978.

[38] 'Dominant minorities': see note 18 above.

[39] 'The permissive frontier: the problem of social control in English settlements in Ireland and Virginia, 1550–1650', in K.R. Andrews, P. Hair and N.P. Canny (ed.), *The westward enterprise: English activities in Ireland, the Atlantic and America, 1480–1650,* Liverpool, 1979.

[40] Donald Jackson, *Intermarriage in Ireland, 1550–1650,* Montreal, 1970.

[41] London, 1973.

[42] 'British settlement in County Tyrone, 1610–1666', in *Irish economic and social history,* v (1978), pp 5–26.

[43] 'Towns in the Ulster plantation', in *Studia Hib.,* no. 11 (1971), pp 40–78; 'Sir William Cole and plantation Enniskillen, 1607–41', in *Clogher Record* (1978), pp. 336–350

[44] 'The maps of the escheated counties of Ulster, 1609–10', in *Proc., R.I.A.,* 74, C, 4 (1974).

[45] 'The making of an Ulster great estate: the Chichesters, Barons of Belfast and Viscounts of Carrickfergus, 1599–1648', in *Proc., R.I.A.,* 79, C. 1 (1979).

[46] *Trans R.H.S.,* 5th series, no. 26 (1976), pp 77–94.

[47] 'The New English and Munster society in the early seventeenth century', Second conference of Irish historians in Britain, 1979.

[48] *N.H.I.,* iii, 174–7.

[49] *The trade of Elizabethan Chester,* Hull, 1970.

[50] 'The Irish customs administration in the sixteenth century', in *I.H.S.,* xx, no. 80 (1977), pp 384–417.

[51] 'The Anglo-Irish livestock trade in the seventeenth century', in *I.H.S.,* xviii, no. 72, (1973), pp 489–523.

[52] 'Christopher Lowther's Canary Adventure: a merchant venturer in Dublin, 1632–3', in *Irish economic and social history,* ii (1975), pp 22–34.

[53] D.R. Hainsworth (ed.), *Commercial papers of Sir Christopher Lowther,* The Surtees Society, vol 189, Gateshead, 1977

[54] *The Elizabethan conquest of Ireland,* Chap. I.

[55] *Cromwellian Ireland: English government and reform in Ireland, 1649–1660,* Oxford, 1975. Chap. IV.

[56] 'Irish towns in the sixteenth and seventeenth centuries', in R.A. Butlin (ed.), *The development of the Irish town,* London, 1977.

[57] 'The Irish parliament of 1569–70', in *Proc., R.I.A.,* 65, C, 4 (1966); 'The establishment of the farm of the Irish customs, 1603–13', in *E.H.R.,* xciii (1978), pp. 580–602.

[58] 'Population trends in seventeenth–century Ireland', in *The Economic and Social Review,* vol. 6, no. 2 (1975), pp 149–65.

[59] Dublin, 1972.

[60] 'Landownership and social structure in Co. Sligo', N.U.I., Studentship dissertation, 1978.

[61] 'Gaelic lordships in Ulster in the later middle ages', Dublin University, Ph.D. thesis, 1976.

[62] 'Warfare in the medieval Gaelic lordships', *The Irish Sword,* xii, no. 47 (1975), pp 98–109. 'The legal position of Irishwomen in the later middle ages', in *Irish Jurist,* x, new series (1975), pp 96–111.

[63] 'The relief of Athlone and the battle of Rathconnell'; 'Sir Richard Grenville, Governor of Trim; the career and character of an English soldier in Ireland', in *Riocht na Midhe,* v, no. 2, 3 (1972, 1973)

[64] *The Irish Sword,* xi, no. 45 (1974), pp 212–21.

[65] *Cromwell: our chief of men,* London, 1973.

[66] 'Owen Roe O'Neill's return to Ireland in 1642: the diplomatic background', in *Studia Hib.,* ix (1969), pp 48–64. 'Henry O'Neill and the formation of the Irish regiment in the Netherlands', in *I.H.S.,* xviii, no. 70 (1972), pp 481–8.

[67] 'Historical revision: xviii, The history of Poynings' law, 1615–41', in *I.H.S.,* xviii, no. 70 (1972), pp 207–22.

[68] 'Strafford, the Ulster Scots and the covenanters', in *I.H.S.,* xviii, no. 72 (1973), pp 524–51. See also David Stevenson, *The Scottish revolution, 1637–77. The triumph of the Covenanters,* Newton Abbott, 1973.

[69] 'Ireland and the general crisis', in *Past and Present,* 48 (1970), 79–99.

[70] 'The Ulster rising of 1641, and the depositions', in *I.H.S.,* xxi, no. 82 (1978), pp 144–67.

[71] K. Bottigheimer, 'Civil war in Ireland: the reality in Munster', in *Emory College Quarterly* (1966).

[72] 'The politics of the Munster protestants, 1641-9', in *Cork Hist. Soc. Jn.,* lxxvi (1971), pp 1–20.

[73] 'The Confederation of Kilkenny', in Brian Farrell (ed.), *The Irish parliamentary tradition,* Dublin, 1973.

[74] *English money and Irish land: the 'adventurers' in the Cromwellian settlement of Ireland,* Oxford, 1971.

[75] See note 55 above.

[76] *Hell or Connaught! The Cromwellian colonization of Ireland, 1652–1660,* London, 1975.

[77] I.M.C., 1970

Ireland, 1660 — 1800

J. I. Mc Guire

(a) Surveys and general works

(b) 1660–1691

(c) 1691–1750

(d) 1750–1800

(e) The workings of eighteenth century Irish politics

(f) Constitutional and administrative history

(g) Language, civilization and learning

Since 1970 Irish historical scholarship has lost the services of two eminent historians to whom it owes a considerable debt of gratitude, Maureen Wall in 1972 and J. G. Simms in 1979. Simms left behind him a considerable corpus of published work covering the period between the restoration and the early decades of the eighteenth century. Indeed this period was almost exclusively his own, and anyone seeking authoritative guidance through the Williamite land settlement, military developments (his particular joy), the politics of the penal laws, or simply the narrative of events may start and finish with Simms. Maureen Wall's published legacy was not so considerable in volume, but it is immensely important. Be it in her work on the emergence of a Catholic middle class or in her explanation for the decline of the Irish language she showed herself to be both a painstaking scholar and an intellectually imaginative historian. She could draw on her own personal acquaintance with rural Ireland in comprehending the past, or enter imaginatively into the political outlook of Anglo-Irish politicians.

My survey covers part of the period dealt with by Simms in the previous volume and all of the period covered so suggestively by Herbert Butterfield, a considerable friend and source of inspiration to historical studies in Ireland, who also died in 1979[1]. However my scope is more limited than Butterfield's or Simms's as religious, economic and social history have been dealt with elsewhere in this volume,[2] and works from these areas are only mentioned in so far as they have a bearing on the main developments.[3]

(a) Surveys and general works

Since most surveys or general works are syntheses of earlier scholarship it follows naturally that they lag behind the current frontiers of research or interpretation. Sometimes, of course, a general work can be the by-product of a major research project or represent a radical rethinking of ground well covered. But the first sort are more common than the second, and the recent historiography of the period 1660–1800 is no exception to the general rule.

Four major surveys cover the period more or less. T.W. Moody *et al* (eds.), *A new history of Ireland,* iii (Oxford, 1976), F.G. James, *Ireland and the empire, 1688–1770* (Cambridge, Mass., 1973), R.B. McDonnell, *Ireland in the age of imperialism and revolution, 1750–1801* (Oxford, 1979) and Edith Mary Johnston, *Ireland in the eighteenth century* (Dublin, 1974). The years 1660–1691 are covered in the final chapters of

A new history and here the major contributions are from J.G. Simms, with significant specialist pieces on the economy (L.M. Cullen), land and people (J.H. Andrews), and the Irish abroad (John J. Silke). Simms's narrative, a model of clarity and accuracy, is to a large extent a synthesis of his own earlier monographs and articles. It provides safe passage through the complexities of restoration and Jacobite politics, the land settlement and ecclesiastical policies. Its only possible weakness is an overemphasis on military developments

Between them F.G. James and R.B. McDowell cover the remainder of the period, i.e. between the 1688 revolution and the act of union. It has to be said that Professor Mc Dowell has done so more successfully for the second half of the century than Dr James has for the first half. There are good things in James, particularly where his own specialist knowledge emerges, but by and large it is rather old-fashioned in its conception and structure. Dr Mc Dowell's work, however, is quite remarkable, based as it is on a very wide range of primary sources and offering a lively political narrative of a period which he first adopted more than forty years ago. Its weakness may be Dr Mc Dowell's reluctance to take account of recent specialist work, a failure which detracts somewhat from the usefullness of his scene-setting introductory chapter, where not all his conclusions about the economy and society would find universal acceptance. Perhaps the most successful survey is Dr E.M. Johnston's contribution to the Gill History of Ireland series. It has admirably attempted to redress Lecky's concentration on the last decade of the century, so providing an authoritative account of the main political developments, though recent work would necessitate a revision of some of Dr Johnston's conclusions should a second edition be contemplated. There is due emphasis given to economic developments though like Professor McDowell, Dr Johnston is less sure-footed here than in her own areas of political and administrative history. If her survey suffers any serious defect, however, it is one of compression, a fault which could best be compensated for by the appearance of her long promised study of eighteenth century Ireland.

Finally, special note must be taken of J.C. Beckett's *The Anglo-Irish tradition* (London, 1976). Its time span is wider than the scope of this survey but it contains two stimulating chapters on the eighteenth century, one being entitled, revealingly, 'The eighteenth century achievement', where Professor Beckett comments that 'the Ireland of the protestant ascendancy was more prosperous and more liberal than has commonly been recognized' (p. 83).

(b) 1660–1691

In the months leading to the king's restoration in May 1660 developments in England, Scotland and Ireland were closely linked. Their course was charted a quarter of a century ago by Godfrey Davies in *The restoration of Charles II, 1658–1660,* Ireland being the subject of a useful, if not totally flawless, chapter. It has not yet been superseded. Recent work has been written around the topic, but not on it. Particularly useful in that respect is T.C. Barnard's *Cromwellian Ireland: English government and reform in Ireland, 1649–60 (London, 1975),* which provides an indispensable backdrop to the politics and government of protestant Ireland at and after the restoration. However, the key to understanding the politics of Ireland in the early months of 1660 may well lie in a study of the composition, policies and proceedings of the General Convention which started work in March 1660. Barnard himself has promised such a study.[4] Until it emerges his own assertion, that once Charles II's restoration in England became inevitable the Dublin convention 'was unable to take an independent line and it acquiesced meekly, but unenthusiastically, in Charles II's return', must remain open to question.

What is emerging is the conservative character of protestant politics at and after the restoration. Dr Karl S. Bottigheimer has argued convincingly that the dominant element in the political nation were the pre-Cromwellian settlers, the new English of the first half of the seventeenth century, who sometimes referred to themselves as the 'old English' or 'ancient protestants of Ireland' so as to distinguish themselves from more recent arrivals.[5] While the stranger to seventeenth century Ireland might find his reliance on contemporary terminology a trifle confusing, Dr Bottingheimer's views find independent support in the work of Dr Barnard, who has shown how the older settlers dominated Munster politics on the eve of the restoration and has pointed out that about half the Irish members returned to sit in each of the three protectorate parliaments were pre-1649 settlers.[6] A full scale analysis of the membership both of the Dublin convention and of the 1661–66 parliament would test the Bottigheimer-Barnard theses on the composition of protestant politics.[7] Meanwhile, Charles II's only Irish parliament still awaits the publication of a modern assessment or analysis of its work and politics, be it article or monograph.[8]

As in England the restoration of the monarchy in Ireland was followed soon after by the restoration of episcopalian protestantism as the state church. Indeed the composition of the Irish episcopal bench appears to have been common knowledge in London by the end of June 1660, although the consecration and installation of the bishops was delayed until the following January. This poses a number of problems: why were the Irish bishops appointed well in advance of the English? How much does this early decision to restore the bishops tell us anything about the government's religious policy after the restoration both in Ireland and in England? What was the character and composition of the restored episcopate? How does it compare with its English counterpart? So far there have been no specifically Irish answers to these essentially political questions, though some interesting points have emerged in recent historiography. Barnard believes that the Convention favoured an Erastian presbyterian system, but that since the protestant gentry's main concern was not with forms of church government but with the preservation and extension of the protestant interest in Ireland, the government's decision to restore episcopacy was accepted.[9] Green, in his important study of *The re-establishment of the Church of England 1660–1663* (Oxford, 1978), has underlined the necessity of bearing in mind developments in all three kingdoms, 'for every move that the king made in one country was bound to be regarded as a foretaste of their own settlement by his subjects in the other two kingdoms'. He attributes an episcopalian settlement to the predictable support of Ormond at court and the less predictable support of Broghill and Coote, and points out that the Irish episcopal bench included a far higher proportion of 'sufferers' than did the English.[10] Of course neither he nor Barnard has attempted to explain the Irish politics of the church settlement in any detail, since it was not central to their main concerns. Nor has Green fully integrated his illuminating analysis of the Irish appointments into the more central problem of the English settlement.

The problems which the Roman catholic church posed for the government were peculiarly Irish, largely because of the majority's allegiance to that church, and also because of the crucial role played by the clergy in the 1640s. But if the scale of the problem was peculiar to Ireland, the government's solution was essentially the same in both countries, to procure a group of loyal clergy prepared to renounce papal temporal power.[11] While a respectable corpus of articles and monographs exists on the clerical side of the Remonstrance controversy, nothing of note has been published on the government's aims and methods. This has led to a regrettable distortion of our knowledge of church-state relations, though a recent survey article makes the point that the most immediate effect of the remonstrance controversy seems to have been a more co-operative attitude to the government amont catholic clergy.[12] Certainly the government under Ormond was only deflected from its apparent divide and rule policies during the Popish plot crisis in England, and then for reasons that were essentially political.[13] The one significant victim of this period was Archbishop Plunkett of Armagh, whose canonization in 1975 occasioned a considerable body of historical and quasi-historical literature of varying degrees of scholarly interest.[14] Otherwise persecution was the exception to the rule in Charles II's reign.[15]

A constant theme in the history of English government in Ireland is the political pressure exerted at court or at Westminister to undermine a chief governor's position or policies. This was particularly true of the restoration period when Ormond, Berkeley and Essex, each in turn, were to find themselves embroiled in English domestic politics. The problems which such involvment posed have been skillfully analysed by J.C. Beckett, who has pointed out that 'every major political development in England had its echo in Ireland' and that a viceroy's 'authority in Ireland rose or fell with Irish opinion of his standing at court'. While Beckett has placed the emphasis on court intrigue, it has been argued elsewhere that court politics alone do not explain Ormond's dismissal in 1669 and that Charles II's diplomatic intrigues must also be taken into account.[17] The viceroy with the least enviable task was undoubtedly Henry Hyde, earl of Clarendon. As Dr John Miller has pointed out in his *James II: a study in kingship* (Hove, 1977), no sooner had Clarendon arrived in Ireland than Tyrconnel 'came to court to undermine his credit with the king'.[18] Clarendon found himself ordered to execute measures which he had not advised and did not like (p. 217). The making of policy for Ireland is only incidental to Dr Miller's wider task, but limited though his treatment may be, it has the very positive advantage of placing Irish developments in the wider setting of James's other, and more important, dominions. Not that Dr Miller has underestimated James II's Irish policies. For in 1977 he published 'The earl of Tyrconnel and James II's Irish policy, 1685–1688' *(Hist, Jn.,* xx (1977), pp 893–23). Adopting a thematic approach he has analysed James's relationship with Tyrconnel and the way in which Tyrconnel persuaded the king to adopt the sort of Irish policy he wanted, to abandon an 'English' policy in favour of an 'Irish' one. James alone must take the blame for the consequences of following Tyrconnel's advice, since he was not deprived of other advice but chose to follow Tyrconnel's for reasons which were emotional and religious rather than national and political, Dr Miller argues.[19]

It is generally accepted that James II's policies spelt disaster for protestant Ireland well before the legislation of the Jacobite parliament put paid to any hopes of reconciliation between the monarch and his protestant subjects. Yet normality was clearly maintained in some areas for longer than has been generally allowed.[20] The position of the Church of Ireland was particularly difficult, though more work needs to be done before a true picture can emerge. Recent published work has shown how the threats to the church's future forced William King to re-examine relations with protestant dissent and how the eventual extension of the 'glorious revolution' to Ireland did not create the same incidence of scruples or non-juring that the Church of England experienced.[21] The bulk of recent work on 1688–91 continues to centre on military matters.[22]

(c) 1691–1750

Viewing the piecemeal work that had been done on the penal laws up to 1970 Sir Herbert Butterfield commented that these laws called 'for a treatment both very detailed and highly synthetic – one in which the processes of change in various parts of the system will be treated chronologically'. This has not happened. Indeed, there has been a marked slowing down in published articles or monographs on the origins, enactment, and enforcement of the penal code, or on local case studies. The ultimate work of synthesis cannot yet be written. When it is, painstaking studies like J.G. Simms, 'The bishops banishment act of 1697' in *I.H.S.*, xvii (1970), pp 187–99, will prove invaluable, as will Tomás Ó Fiaich, 'The registration of the clergy in 1704', in *Seanchás Ardmhácha*, vi (1971), pp 46–96. The Public Record Office of Northern Ireland has issued an excellent set in its Education Facsimiles series under the general title *The penal laws*,[23] thereby making available, primarily to secondary school pupils, photocopies of documents illustrative of the laws and their impact.

The passage of the penal code, largely the work of William III's second Irish parliament (1695–99) and of Queen Anne's first Irish parliament (1703–11), represented a triumph for protestant public opinion, determined to preserve its land and security against any repetition of the events of the late 1680s. Initially the government underestimated the extent of the public grievances over religion, security, finance, land and allegations of official corruption. This emerged clearly from the failure of the 1692 parliament, when the lord lieutenant, Viscount Sydney, felt obliged to prorouge parliament after one month of political turbulence. I have argued in a recent publication that the issues raised in this parliament and the political acrimony which accompanied its prorogation led in time to a change in government policy, the adoption of a more sophisticated approach to political management and the emergence of a constitutional *modus vivendi* between executive and parliament. The lessons learned from the failure of 1692 enabled parliament to become a regular part of government over the succeeding century.[24]

Two important points have emerged from recent scholarship. In the first place it seems likely that the political management of the House of Commons was placed in the hands of 'undertakers' considerably earlier than historians like J.L. Mc Cracken and E.M. Johnston had allowed. Secondly, it is clear that Irish politics in Queen Anne's reign became caught up in whig-tory conflicts imported from England but which soon developed peculiarly Irish characteristics. The revisionist views are those of Dr D.W. Hayton who has revived interest in the neglected field of early eighteenth century Irish politics.[25] Dr Hayton is in effect doing for his chosen field what Geoffrey Holmes did for British political history in the late 1960s.[26] It is to be hoped that Dr Hayton's findings will be published in full in monograph form, thereby benefitting both British and Irish political studies.[27] His forthcoming article on the 1713 parliament substantially revises the views of Dr J.G. Simms.[28]

The development of sophisticated approaches to political management had the effect of defusing potentially explosive constitutional crises. The Woollen Act of 1699 and the Act of Resumption of 1700 underlined the subordinate status of the kingdom of Ireland and might well have led to a serious impasse in Anglo-Irish relations, preceded as they had been by the condemnation of William Molyneux's *Case of Ireland* by the English House of Commons. Molyneux's tract, oft cited but little read, was re-issued in 1977 in a limited edition, with an introduction by J.G. Simms and an 'afterword' by Denis Donoghue.[29] A year earlier, in connection with the American bi-centennial celebrations, Dr Simms published his *Colonial nationalism 1698–1776* (Cork, 1976) in which he showed the influences on Molyneux, examined the text, and traced its impact both in Ireland and colonial America. It is very much to be hoped that Dr Simms's fullscale biography, which he compledted shortly before his death, will soon be published, thereby enabling Molyneux the scientist and man of letters to appear alongside Molyneux the pamphleteer. While the neglected Molyneux receives overdue attention, Swift, the major personality of Irish politics and letters of the first half of the eighteenth century continues to excite scholarly attention, though not to the same extent as the ter-centenary celebrations occasioned in 1967 and immediately afterwards.[30]

Surveying the historiography of Ireland in the first half of the eighteenth century there seems hardly any need to qualify Butterfield's comment of a decade ago, that in this period ' "the march of history" still looks a very amorphous affair'.[31] It has not yet recovered from Lecky's imbalance, the devoting of only one of his five volumes to the period before 1760.[32] Admittedly some work has been or is being done but it has not yet found its way into print.[33] Were it not for Dr Hayton's publications, political historiography would indeed be in a sorry state. If historians or apprentice historians were less anxious to work on apparent 'turning-points' or periods of activity they might find an ample supply of topics in the politics and administration of Ireland before 1750, and in the process add considerably to the political history of both islands.

(d) 1750–1800

If the political history of pre-1750 Ireland still has the appearance of a *tabula rasa,* Irish politics after 1750 continue to attract the research worker and historian, and a revisionist school is hard at work. In a sense it is a tribute to the pioneering work of Professor J.L. Mc Cracken that it is his findings which have provided the impetus for the revisionists, so that a genuine historiographical debate is now possible. But even the revisionists themselves are not always of one mind. This emerges in the findings of Dr Declan O'Donovan and Dr J.C.D. Clark on the nature of the relationship between Irish and English politics.[34] Both have studied the political crises of the 1750s and both have drawn different conclusions. To Dr O'Donovan 'England was coming more and more to see Ireland in a colonial light', while Dr Clarke writes, not of 'England', but of English and Irish politics, his aim being to show 'that the detailed course of events in the two capitals must be explained together and in parallel if it is to be understood in either, and that many of the longterm developments in English politics can be found echoed in Dublin in such a way as to suggest that it was very often the Irish example which served as the unacknowledged precedent for English innovations'.[35] Dr Clarke's work has involved him in both Irish and English politics of the 1750s and from that vantage point he seems entitled to criticise both British and Irish historians for not having recognized 'the close texture of the reciprocal influence of English and Irish politics in the mid-eighteenth century'.[36] At the same time Dr O'Donovan's thesis, that the 1753 money bill dispute 'provided a focus and accelerator for gathering patriotic sentiments, which were to culminate in the establishment of legislative independence in 1782',[37] reminds us that Irish political history is multidimensional and that the British domestic dimension is not the only one, however regrettable its neglect.

Looking at Irish political history after the accession of George III Butterfield suggested that 'we need a fuller reconstruction – a complete account of Townshend's lord lieutenancy for example – and every scrap of evidence on the English side ought to be assembled.'[38] In the case of Townshend's lieutenancy Dr Thomas Bartlett has supplied the need.[39] While regarding the Townshend government as 'the key administration of the period 1690–1798', he has argued against the traditional view which saw Townshend being sent to Ireland with instructions to reside constantly and to break the power of the undertakers by 'bringing administration back to the castle'.[40] Instead, he suggests that Townshend was the decision maker and that the role of the British cabinet was merely one of granting formal approval to Townshend's policies, in particular the decisions to reside in Ireland, to curb the power of the great undertakers and to create a 'castle' party. It was his control of patronage, particularly the Revenue Board's patronage, which enabled him to maintain this 'castle' party.[41] And here lies Townshend's enduring significance, for the party survived the constitution of 1782, the regency crisis, the Fitzwilliam episode and in fact was 'instrumental in undertaking the greatest project of all – the union'.[42] It was appropriate that Townshend's party should have had a role to play in carrying the union, Dr Bartlett argues, since the seeds of union were sown during his viceroyalty with the exacerbation by his new system of the central weakness of the Anglo-Irish governmental structure, the separation of executive from legislature.[43] In the light of Dr Bartlett's findings what are required now are detailed analytical narratives of the immediately succeeding administrations.

That the American colonial rebellion had a profound impact on Anglo-Irish relations and Irish domestic politics hardly needs remarking, yet there is a danger in drawing too easy parallels between Ireland and the colonies. Undoubtedly there were constitutional similarities between the two areas and valuable work continues to be produced demonstrating the comparative possibilities.[44] But there are pitfalls which recent research seems to underline. A case in point is Thomas F. Moriarty's study of the controversy surrounding the Irish absentee tax of 1773.[45] In itself a valuable account of the problem, Dr Moriarty has placed it firmly in the context of 'imperial reorganization', believing as he does that 'the new imperial policy for Ireland began to unfold' during Townshend's viceroyalty when 'the crown intended to govern Ireland more directly' (p.370). But attractive as this imperial framework may be, it must now be seriously questioned in the light of Dr Bartlett's findings, at least so far as Ireland is concerned.[46] And after the outbreak of war there were few in Ireland prepared to endorse the rebels' aims or methods. Professor Maurice R. O'Connell's conclusion, 'that the American revolution did not have any major ideological effect on Ireland in its own day', seems reasonable particularly when he shows that Volunteer reformers looked to British, not American, radicals for their inspiration,[47] though it must be mentioned that British radicalism was an important element in American revolutionary ideology and *vice versa*[48]

The real impact on Ireland of American developments was the result of war not ideology.[49] The threats from external enemies and internal disorders led to the formation of the Volunteers, who started as an unofficial militia and rapidly developed into a formidable extra-parliamentary political pressure group.[50] Dr Peter Smyth has examined the relationship between the Volunteers and parliament and in so doing has shown the reasons for their ultimate failure as a political force, divided as they were by conflicting loyalties, political equality *versus* social deference, legislative freedom *versus* the British connection, 'and above all, their immediate experience of successful political intervention conflicted with basic and long-held beliefs that armed interference in politics was wrong'.[51] Their's was 'the first successful example of the bringing of the gun into Irish politics' (p.126)! Were they, as Dr Senior maintained, 'the progenitor of both the United Irishmen and the Orange movement'?[52] Analysis of the Volunteers at local level has led Oliver Snoddy to suggest 'that they can be more firmly placed in the pattern and tradition of loyal, local, military service evinced at other times in the eighteenth century in the militia and yeomanry units'[53] Two studies of the Volunteering bishop of Derry have recently appeared, one long and popular, the other short and valuable.[54] Lecky's narrative of the period has received a welcome overhaul, called for by Butterfield (art.cit., p.64), in Professor Mc Dowell's recent survey.[55]

The granting of legislative independence in 1782 was followed both by government attempts to define Anglo-Irish constitutional and commercial relations and by 'patriot' attempts to secure reform and to consolidate what had been gained. Dr Peter Jupp has clarified the renunciation question as an issue in English politics,[56] thereby complementing Theresa M. O'Connor's study of the renunciation problem as an issue in the Irish patriot movement ('The conflict between Flood and Grattan, 1782–3', in H.A. Cronne, *et al*, eds, *Essays on British and Irish history in honour of James Eadie Todd,* London, 1949). The politics of Pitt's attempts to gain trading concessions in return for a modification in the constitutional relationship between the two countries has been studied by Dr Paul Kelly who argues that 'at the end of the day the government lost little and the whigs gained nothing'.[57] Dr Edith M. Johnston provides a brief but useful account of the Rutland administration in an introduction to her edition of an invaluable contemporary analysis of the members of Irish parliament of 1784–7.[58] In a lively essay Professor J.J. Lee has undermined many of the more pious illusions about the effect of legislative independence, particularly with regard to its allegedly benign impact on the economy.[59] A more sympathetic view is to be found in Dr A.P.W. Malcomson's, *John Foster. The politics of the Anglo-Irish ascendancy* (Oxford, 1978), ch. 8.

The increasing pace of political movement at the centre from the 1760s onwards was matched by a growth in social unrest in the rural areas. By the 1790s the political implications of this unrest would underline the structural weaknesses in the Irish constitution. While rural disturbance had long been a feature of the Irish countryside, the emergence of the Whiteboys in 1761 marked a new departure in the character and aims of agrarian violence. The emergence of this phenomenon has been analysed by Dr James S. Donnelly Jr.[60] In numbers, geographical spread, organization and coordination the Whiteboys represented a new and formidable means for rectifying grievances. Though initially short lived their example would be taken up again by a new generation, and here too Dr Donnelly provides the analysis.[61] In this very important article Dr Donnelly discerns certain distinctive features of the movement which mark it off from both its predecessors and successors: its peculiar techniques of mobilisation, its low level of serious violence, its high degree of effectiveness, and the active leadership of some members of the protestant gentry, with the encouragement or neutrality of many more (p.201). This latter point is particularly important as it challenges the more simplisitic interpretations of social and sectarian division in rural Ireland, at least before the 1790s.

What was the initial motivation of the agrarian secret societies? Maureen Wall argued that Whiteboys and Rightboys 'had their origin, as had the Oakboys and Hearts of Steel, in stated grievances largely economic'.[62] Similarly Professor Lee has suggested that the issues at stake were 'predominantly economic',[63] a view challenged by Dr M.R. Beames.[64] It was not, he argues, merely economic grievances that lay at the heart of Whiteboy complaints, rather it was 'the awareness that the relationship between landlord and tenant is being disrupted and abused'. Socially conservative, the Whiteboys (and Dr Beames uses the term comprehensively) wished to restore the landlord-tenant relationship to a position where it was recognised that there were 'certain obligations on each side' (p.503). This view of the secret societies' aims as essentially conservative is supported, in the case of the Rightboys, by Dr Donnelly, who argues that 'direct challenges to the fundamentals of the tenurial system were uncommon'.

In the 1790s sectarianism and political radicalism became inextricably entangled with agrarian unrest. Maureen Wall attributed the rise of sectarianism to 'the ruling class', who were 'determined to maintain protestant ascendancy' and so represented the agrarian disturbances in the south as 'popish conspiracies'. Hence the upsurge of sectarianism leading to the formation of the Peep O'Day Boys, the Defenders and the Orange Order.[65] More recent work by Dr Donnelly and W.H. Crawford must cast doubt on this interpretation, founded as it is on the notion of a gentry conspiracy. Dr Donnelly has demonstrated actual gentry involvements in Rightboy activities in the 1780s,[66] and Mr Crawford's recent study of late eighteenth century Ulster shows the development of sectarian in-fighting to have had more complex causes.[67] He argues that 'the Orange troubles were a single response to two contrasting kinds of change in society: social change in the case of the rise of the Roman catholics, and economic change in the decline in the standard of living of the hand loom weavers' (p.203). The rise of the Orange Order is described by Dr Hereward Senior in an essay which draws on his own earlier monograph, *Orangeism in Ireland*.[68] While Aiken Mc Clelland provided useful information as to Orange strength in Co. Monaghan,[69] Dr Simms showed how the cult of William III was developed in the eighteenth century, becoming by the end largely the preserve of the Orange Order.[70] There are no comparable studies of the Defenders and it is unlikely that there ever will be owing to a lack of documentation of what was, in the words of Dr C. J. Woods, 'a number of localized secret societies with a largely illiterate membership'.[71]

Political radicalism in the 1790s was inspired by French revolutionary principles and was the preserve of the United Irishmen. But the middle class United Irishmen failed to understand the sectarian and social tensions of their day. In an important reflective article Dr Marianne Elliott argues that the protestant exponents of theoretical republicanism 'had become so accustomed to political and social dominance that they failed to anticipate the different interpretation which the Catholic rank and file might impose on the new republicanism and were shocked to discover that Catholic republicanism was as much a weapon to oust the protestant planter as to destroy English rule'.[72] Her thesis is best incapsulated by her comment that 'the catholics had been invited to join the republican movement, but finished by taking it over' (p.428). While some of Dr Elliott's arguement is based on a rather facile view of pre-eighteenth century Ireland, the fundamental thesis is important and finds some support in an article published some years earlier by W. Benjamin Kennedy.[73] As Dr Kennedy put it, 'The Irish pesants backed up their dimly-conveived notions of Jacobinism with a nativist and agrarian revolt and laid the foundations for an Irish catholic nationalism that looked bact to '98 as the origin of a tragic and proud tradition' (p.121). Elsewhere Dr Elliott has demonstrated the links between Irish republicanism and English revolutionary activity, placing the United Irish Society very much in the context of 'one of the many British reform associations inspired by the idealism of the French revolution'.[74] This Irish dimension of a wider British problem is discussed more generally by Albert Goodwin in *The friends of liberty* (London, 1979), chapter xi.

What of the actual rebellions of 1798? No substantial account has appeared since the publication of Thomas Pakenham's *The year of liberty* in 1969, so it remains the most authoritative account to date.[75] Work published, however, has continued to add to our knowledge, in some cases to suggest a need for further revision. Some contributions have been concerned with preparations, military and diplomatic,[76] while others have analysed local situations.[77] Sr Maura Duggan has argued that there was a weakening of clerical influence in Co. Carlow in 1798, pointing to 'the absence of clerical support at any level for the rebellion in the county'.[78] Particularly interesting is Thomas Powell's conclusion that what most likely made the Wexford rebellion what it was 'is the unequivocal depression in its unique malt and barley trade'.[79] The most suggestive comment comes from W.H. Crawford, who has argued that 1798 in Ulster 'was not for the rank-and-file a crusade against the British government', but 'a "turn-out" of the restless elements in the countryside, who followed local leaders because their pride would not let them turn back from encounters which turned out to be more bloody than affrays at fairs and markets'. Mr Crawford must now develop this fully.[80]

In November 1800, Friedrich von Gentz, later to be Metternich's secretary at the Congress of Vienna, greeted the enactment of the union enthusiastically, 'Irland kann nicht ohne England, England kann schwer ohne Irland bestehen'. His views, published originally in the *Historisches Journal,* have been usefully summarised and quoted by Dr M.A. Bond.[81] Another useful collection of documents, designed for use in the school, illustrates the politics and contemporary views of the union.[82] Although the publication of G.C. Bolton's *The passing of the Irish act of union: a study in parliamentary politics* in 1966 removed the likelihood of any further substantial work in that area for some time, Dr A.P.W. Malcomson has thrown more light on the passing of the union in his immensely important *John Foster. The politics of the Anglo-Irish ascendancy*,[83] while Gearóid Ó Tuathaigh has written a lively narrative of the events leading to the union in the first chapter of his *Ireland before the famine 1798–1848* (Dublin, 1972).

(e) **The workings of eighteenth century Irish politics**
Work on the structure and character of eighteenth century Irish politics, so essential for an understanding of political issues and divisions, is now at a promising stage, though the last years of the century continue to be the focus of attention. The Public Record Office of Northern Ireland have done an invaluable service by their publication of calendars of primary source material.[84] In addition, the recent publication of a register of Irish parliamentary lists, twenty-two for the commons and nine for the lords, opens up considerable possibilities for students of the earlier period, enabling the testing of theories about the structure of Irish politics, be it whig-tory divisions in Queen Anne's reign, or the compositon of the 'Irish' and 'English' interests in the lords in George I's reign, to give but two examples.[85]

For the last two decades of the eighteenth century Dr Malcomson's *John Foster: the politics of Anglo-Irish ascendancy* is a work of unusual significance. Not only does it provide a penetrating analysis of one of the key figures in ascendancy politics, more importantly it amounts to a full scale description of both the nature and the workings of the Irish political system. In so doing it overturns many of the previously held commonplaces concerning eighteenth century politics. Dr Malcomson has examined the role of parliamentary influence through the 'command of seats' (ability counted for more than electoral interest), the significance of patronage (too much stress has been laid on the role of patronage and jobbery was not a peculiarly Irish vice), and the operation of election politics ('interest' is synonymous with influence, property *per se* did not determine who was elected for a county, issues could be an important element).

Indeed election politics have received considerable attention over the past decade. Here Dr Peter Jupp also requires us to revise our assumptions.[86] In his study of 'County Down elections, 1783–1831' *(Irish Historical studies,* xviii, 1972, pp 177–206) he plays down the traditional stress on fraud, bribery, nepotism and oppressive tactics, arguing that elections were dominated in Co. Down by two powerful landed families through 'the establishing and maintenance of organisational resources involving a broad spectrum of the proprietorial class and depending upon an acquiescing rather than an oppressed tenantry'.[87] Similarly, Dr Malcomson has argued, from his analysis of Strabane borough, that 'patron control was not something which was imposed forcibly and artificially from the top downwards, in negation of the political aspirations of the electorate, and of the much more numerous unenfranchised inhabitants'.[88] And what of the representatives of the close boroughs when they got to parliament? Inevitably it is to Dr Malcomson that we must turn again for guidance: the Irish government 'depreciated the currency of its patronage, and was the main victim of the ensuing inflation'. Does any other argument explain the fact that patrons and close borough representatives 'did not prevent, as numerically they could have done, the winning of free trade in 1779 and the constitution of 1782, did not prevent the passing of many popular measures, above all, did not prevent successful opposition being given to the union in 1799'.[89] The extent and significance of this revisionism will soon necessitate a work of synthesis which will bring its fruits to a wider audience. Perhaps the Dublin Historical Association might consider commissioning a new pamphlet in its Irish History series. Not that the work has yet been completed, for both Dr Edith M. Johnston and Dr Malcomson are currently presiding over the launching of a 'History of the Irish parliament' on the lines of the Westminister project sponsored by the History of Parliament Trust. This will extend the area of inquiry outside the environs of Ulster county and borough politics to the rest of the country, thus ensuring a more even geographical spread. In addition, it is planned to include an analysis of the membership of Commons' committees.

(f) Constitutional and administrative history

Like its English exemplar the projected 'History of the Irish parliament, 1690–1800' will be largely concerned with membership. While this is immensely important, there is another perspective which has hardly been touched upon, parliament as an institution. Here two recent works by British historians could provide models for similar work on the Irish parliament, Sheila Lambert, *Bills and acts. Legislative procedures in eighteenth-century England* (Cambridge, 1971), and P.D.G. Thomas, *the House of Commons in the eighteenth century* (Oxford, 1971). There will be source problems, admittedly, and it is unlikely that anything as extensive as Miss Lambert's or Dr Thomas's works could be produced for Ireland. Nevertheless, Dermot Englefield has published an invaluable account of the Irish parliament's printed papers, indicating what is still extant[91], and here there is centainly scope for original work. A useful introductory survey of the composition and powers of the Irish parliament has been provided by Professor J.L. Mc Cracken in *The Irish parliament in the eighteenth century* (Dundalk, 1971).[92]

Long before parliament became part of the regular machinery of government in the 1690s, the presidency system of provincial administration had been abolished. Yet in the case of Munster, at least, the restored presidency between 1660 and 1672 appeared to be flourishing, thanks entirely to the efforts of its ambitious and efficient president, the earl of Orrery. Liam Irwin has shown how Orrery used the presidency to further economic development in Munster and to secure it from internal and external military threats, real or imaginary.[93] He has also studied the operation of the presidency courts, arguing that 'the popularity and efficiency of the Munster court' during the 1660s is well attested, and that in 1672 'the valuable judicial role which the Irish presidencies had played was ignored in the interests of short-term and opportunist English political ends'.[94] Mr Irwin's articles underline the need for a full-scale study of Orrery's role as politician and administrator.

There has been no authoritative account of the army's function and organization for the period as a whole. Professor Beckett has written of the army in Ireland in an uncharacteristic period, the restoration, uncharacteristic because it was the only time when the army was raised and organised primarily for service in Ireland.[95] He stops short in 1685, pointing out that while James II's army was administratively the same, it had radically changed in its composition and purposes (p.41). It would be appropriate if Professor Beckett's stimulating essay were to be followed up by detailed studies of the army before and after the Williamite revolution.

The workings of central government continue to be neglected. While political, economic and social historians are reasonably active, there are few administrative historians in the field, particularly for the period before 1760. Any new contribution is therefore welcome. In that respect J.C. Sainty has provided a useful introduction to his lists of officials of the secretariat of the chief governors between 1690 and 1800,[96] describing in particular the organization of the secretariat (pp 3–12). Dr David Dickson has contributed a number of useful local studies of the revenue service, pointing out that it was 'the most pervasive agency of central government in eighteenth century Ireland throughout the country'.[97] Thomas Bartlett has assessed the significance of Townshend's revenue reforms between 1767 and 1773[98] But anyone requiring a comprehensive treatment of government financial administration must rely on T.J. Kiernan's *History of the financial administration of Ireland to 1817*, published in 1930.

Two areas of administrative innovation in eighteenth century Ireland were the establishment of a registry of deeds in 1708 and of a Dublin metropolitan police force in 1786. Both were essentially Irish innovations. In the case of the former Dr Peter Roebuck has argued that the Irish registry, if not entirely unique, a Scottish registry having been in existence since the mid-sixteenth century and a registry in the west riding of Yorkshire since 1704, nevertheless developed far wider functions that its counterparts in Scotland or England.[99] Dr Kevin Boyle has traced the origins of police organization in Ireland before the union, taking as his point of departure the passage by the Irish parliament of the Dublin Police Act of 1786, a measure almost identical to that rejected by the Westminister parliament for the establishment of a city of London police not long before.[100] Dr Boyle has useful things to say about the problems of law enforcement in pre-union Ireland.

(g) Language, civilization and learning

One of the more significant achievements of *A new history of Ireland*, volume iii, has been the inclusion of chapters specifically devoted to culture and civilization, Brian Ó Cúiv's 'The Irish language in the early modern period' (ch. xx), Alan Bliss's 'The development of the English language in early modern Ireland' (ch. xxi), and Benignus Millett's 'Irish literature in Latin 1550–1700' (ch. xxii). It is significant because up to recently cultural history was neglected by those mainstream historians who seemed unaware of the potential importance to historical explanation of work by scholars in other disciplines.

Experts in language have a particularly important role to play. Alan Bliss has selected and analysed twenty-seven 'representative texts' in his *Spoken English in Ireland 1600–1740* (Dublin, 1979), and as part of his introduction to Jonathan Swift's *A dialogue* he has written on 'The

English language in Ireland in the eighteenth century' (pp 25–41).[101] In Irish the figure of Daniel Corkery remains dominant, although his interpretative uses of eighteenth century Gaelic poetry were skillfully challenged by Louis Cullen in ' "The hidden Ireland" reassessment of a concept', in *Studia Hibernica,* ix (1969), pp 2–47.[102] Another look has been taken at Corkery's contribution in Seán Ó Mórdha (ed.), *Scríobh* 4,[103] and Emmet Larkin has offered a brief reconsideration of Corkery's ideas on cultural nationalism in *Éire–Ireland,* viii (1973), pp 42–51. Padraig Ó Snodaigh's discovery of a *Hidden Ulster* (Dublin, 1973) brought him into the field of contemporary political controversy.[104] Less controversial, but more important, are M.H. Risk's 'Seán Ó Neachtain: an eighteenth century Irish writer', in *Studia. Hib.,* xv (1975), pp 47–60, and Pilip Ó Mórdha, 'Peter Urson, hedge schoolmaster', in *Clogher Rec.,* viii (1975).

The intellectual climate of Anglo-Ireland has received some attention and has even been the source of some controversy. T.C. Barnard's arguments about an earlier beginning for intellectual and scientific inquiry than K.T. Hoppen allowed for in *The common scientist in the seventeenth century* (London, 1970), has been vigorously answered by Dr Hoppen.[105] Dr David Berman has prepared a scholarly introduction (pp 7–27) to his edition of William King's *Sermon on predestination,*[106] and has written two articles in the field of Berkeley studies.[107] Edward Mc Parland has made two important contributions to the history of visual arts, 'James Gandon and the Royal Exchange competition, 1968–69', in *R.S.A.I. Jn.,* cii (1972), pp 58–71, and 'The Wide Streets Commissioners: their importance for Dublin architecture in the late eighteenth and early nineteenth century', in *Ir. Georgian Soc. Jn.,* xv (1972), pp 1–32.[108] Dr Mc Parland's work on the Wide Streets Commissioners, some of it as yet unpublished, also makes an important contribution to the political history of the period.

[1] See J.G. Simms, 'Seventeenth-century Ireland 1603–1702', and Herbert Butterfield, 'Eighteenth-century Ireland, 1702–1800, in T.W. Moody (ed.), *Irish historiography 1936–70* (Dublin, 1971), pp 43–54 and pp 55–70.

[2] See the contributions by P.J. Corish and J.J. Lee.

[3] I wish to record my gratitude to Mrs Clara Cullen, Dr David Doyle, Mr Gerard Lyne and Miss Maeve Bradley for their assistance in the preparation of this article.

[4] Barnard, op.cit., p.24.

[5] Karl S. Bottigheimer, 'The restoration land settlement in Ireland: a structural view', in *I.H.S.*, xviii (1972), pp 1–21.

[6] T.C. Barnard, 'Lord Broghill, Vincent Gookin and the Cork elections of 1659', *E.H.R.*, lxxxviii (1973), pp 352–65. Dr Barnard has reproduced here a number of letters relating to this contest.

[7] There is a useful list of members with some biographical details in Fergus M. O'Donoghue, 'Parliament in Ireland under Charles II' (National University of Ireland, U.C.D., M.A. thesis, 1970).

[8] It was not dealt with at all in Brian Farrell (ed.), *The Irish parliamentary tradition* (Dublin, 1973).

[9] Barnard, op.cit., pp 130–4.

[10] Green, op.cit., pp 16–18, p.32.

[11] For English parallels see John Miller, *Popery and politics in England 1660–1688* (Cambridge, 1973), pp 42–4, pp 95–6.

[12] Conor Ryan, 'Religion and state in seventeenth-century Ireland', in *Archiv.Hib.*, xxxiii (1975), pp 122–132.

[13] See John Kenyon, *The popish plot* (London, 1974, paperback ed.), pp 224–5, pp 233–4, for references to Ireland.

[14] See in particular John Hanly (ed.), *The letters of Saint Oliver Plunkett 1625–1681* (Dublin, 1979), and Tomas Ó Fiaich, *Oilibhear Pluincéid* (Baile Átha Cliath, 1976); see also P.G. Murray, 'A previously unnoticed letter of Oliver Plunkett's, and J. Hanly, 'An unpublished letter of Saint Oliver Plunkett', in *Seanchas Ardmhacha,* viii (1976), pp 23–33 and pp 3–6 respectively.

[15] Leonard Howard, 'The penal laws in north Kerry, 1677–1685', in *N. Munster Antiq. Jn.,* xiv (1971), pp 49–52.

[16] J.C. Beckett, 'The Irish viceroyalty in the restoration period', in *R. Hist. Soc. Trans.,* 5th series, xx (1970), pp 53–72, and reprinted in J.C. Beckett, *Confrontations* (London, 1972), pp 67–86.

[17] J.I. Mc Guire, 'Why was Ormond dismissed in 1669', in *I.H.S.,* xviii (1973), pp 295–312. There is a sizeable collection of material of Irish

interest for the 1660s in F.J. Routledge (ed.), *Calendar of the Clarendon state papers,* (Oxford, 1970), vol. v.

[18] Clarendon's worries and frustration are echoed in his secretary's correspondence and notes, which have been published in *Anal.Hib.,* xxvii (1972), pp 125–182, with a brief introduction by Patrick Melvin. Tyrconnel's erstwhile secretary, Thomas Sheridan, dismissed early in 1688, wrote a 'Narrative', which historians in recent years have regarded as dubious. However, Dr Miller has concluded that, if it should still be used with caution, 'it deserves a certain respect and sheds valuable light on James II's Irish policy', 'Thomas Sheridan (1646–1712) and his "Narrative" ', in *I.H.S.,* xx (1976), pp 105–28. The period between June 1687 and February 1689 is covered in *Calander of state papers, domestic series, James II* (London, 1972) vol. iii.

[19] See also Sir Charles Petrie, *The great Tyrconnel* (Cork, 1972), a popular biography which adds little to our knowledge or understanding of its subject.

[20] Dr David Dickson has shown how a protestant collector of revenue in Co. Kerry survived in office up to 1689 despite the wholesale catholicisation of public office, 'The account-book of a Kerry revenue official, 1687–9', in *Kerry Arch. Soc. Jn.,* vi (1973), pp 76–82.

[21] Andrew Carpenter, 'William King and the threats to the Church of Ireland during the reign of James II', in *I.H.S.,* xviii (1972), 22–8; J.I. Mc Guire, 'The Church of Ireland and the "glorious revolution" of 1688', in A. Cosgrove and D. Mc Cartney (eds.), *Studies in Irish history* (Dublin, 1979). See also C.C. Ellison, 'Bishop Dopping's visitation book', in *Riocht na Midhe,* v (1974), nos 2, 3 and 4.

[22] Dr J.G. Simms wrote a new introduction for the 1971 reissue of John T. Gilbert (ed.), *A Jacobite narrative of the war in Ireland, 1688–1691.* Patrick Melvin has made two interesting contributions, 'Irish troop movements and James II's army in 1688', and 'Irish soldiers and plotters in Williamite England', in *Ir. Sword,* x (1971), pp 87–105 and xiii (1978), pp 256–67 respectively. See also Michael Hewson, 'Robert Stearne's diary of the Williamite Campaign', in *An Cosantóir,* xxxvii (1977), pp 49–53.

[23] Public Record Office of Northern Ireland, *The penal laws,* (Education facsimiles 101–120, Belfast, 1971 and 1975). For a gradual change in protestant churchmen's attitudes towards catholics and dissenters see 'The church of Ireland in the early 18th century', in *Historical Magazine of the Protestant Episcopal Church* (Austin, Texas), xlviii (1979), pp 433–451. See also Peadar McCann, 'Cork city's eighteenth-century char-

ity schools. Origins and early history' in *Cork Hist. Soc. Jn.,* lxxxiv (1979), pp 102–111.

[24] James I. Mc Guire, 'The Irish parliament of 1692', in Thomas Bartlett and D.W. Hayton (eds.), *Penal era and golden age. Essays in Irish history, 1690–1800* (Belfast, 1979), pp 1–31.

[25] See D.W. Hayton, 'The beginnings of the "undertaker system" ', in Bartlett and Hayton, *Penal era,* pp 32–54; D.W. Hayton, 'Tories and whigs in Co. Cork, 1714', in *Cork Hist. Soc. Jn.,* lxxx (1975), pp 84–88. Dr Hayton's views are summarised in his introduction to *Ireland after the glorious revolution* (Education facsimiles 221–240, Belfast, 1976).

[26] Geoffrey Holmes, *British politics in the age of Anne* (London, 1969).

[27] See Dr Hayton's Oxford D. Phil. dissertation, submitted in 1975, 'Ireland and the English ministers 1707–16'. See also F.G. James, 'The active Irish peers in the early eighteenth century', in *Jn. Brit. Studies,* xviii (1979), 52–69.

[28] 'The crisis in Ireland and the disintegration of Queen Anne's last ministry', accepted for publication in a forthcoming issue of *Irish Historical Studies.*

[29] William Molyneux, *The case of Ireland stated* (Dublin, 1977). This is the fifth volume in a series published by the Cadenus Press under the general title, 'Irish writings from the age of Swift'.

[30] Two articles in particular should be noted: J.C. Beckett, 'Swift: the priest in politics', in J.C. Beckett, *Confrontations,* pp 111–122 and Andrew Carpenter, 'Archbishop King and Swift's appointment as dean of St. Patrick's', in *Long Room,* xi (1975), pp 11–13. See also J.G. Simms, 'Dean Swift and County Armagh', in *Seanchas Árdmhacha,* vi (1971), pp 131–140, A Norman Jeffares, 'Swift and the Ireland of his day', in *Ir. Univ. Rev.,* ii (1972), pp 115–132, and Matthew N. Coughlan, ' "This deluge of brass": rhetoric in the first and fourth Drapier letters', in *Éire–Ireland, xi (1976), pp 77–91.*

[31] Butterfield, 'Eighteenth-century Ireland, 1702–1800', in T.W. Moody (ed.), *Irish historiography 1936–70,* p. 63.

[32] Ibid., p.61.

[33] See Joseph Griffin, 'Parliamentary politics in Ireland during the reign of George I' (N.U.I., U.C.D., M.A. thesis, 1977).

[34] Declan O'Donovan, 'The money bill dispute of 1753', in Bartlett and Hayton, *Penal era,* pp 55–87, and J.C.D. Clark, 'Whig tactics and parliamentary precedent: the English management of Irish politics, 1754–1756', in *Hist.Jn.,* xxi (1978), pp 275–301.

[35] O'Donovan, art.cit., p.87; Clarke, art. cit., p.276.

[36] Clarke, art.cit., p.275. Dr Clarke makes the point that the 'lieutenancy was not a backwater, but was held by peers of the first political rank' (p.276). See also his article, 'The decline of party, 1740–1760', *E.H.R.*, xciii (1978).

[37] O'Donovan, art.cit., p.87.

[38] Butterfield, art.cit., p.63.

[39] Thomas Bartlett, 'The Townshend viceroyalty 1767–72' (The Queen's University of Belfast, Ph.D. thesis, 1977). Dr Bartlett has been publishing his findings in articles, which will be referred to in subsequent footnotes. In addition his article, 'Opposition in late eighteenth century Ireland: the case of the Townshend viceroyalty', will be published in a forthcoming issue of *Irish Historical Studies.*

[40] See his edition of the papers of Townshend's chief secretary, published as *Macartney in Ireland 1768–72. A calendar of the chief secretaryship papers of Sir George Macartney* (Belfast, n.d., 1979?). Dr Bartlett's introduction is particularly valuable.

[41] In 'Viscount Townshend and the Irish Revenue Board, 1767–73', *R.I.A. Proc.*, lxxxix (1979), sect. C, pp 153–175.

[42] Thomas Bartlett, 'The Townshend viceroyalty, 1767–72', in Bartlett and Hayton (eds), *Penal era,* pp 88–112.

[43] Ibid., p. 112.

[44] See John P. Reid, *In a defiant stand: the conditions of law in Massachusetts Bay, the Irish comparison and the coming of the American revolution* (Pennsylvania, 1978). See also David N. Doyle, *Ireland, Irishmen and revolutionary America 1760–1820* (Cork, 1980) and David N. Doyle and Owen Dudley Edwards (eds), *America and Ireland, 1776–1976. The American identity and the Irish connection* (London and Westport, Conn., 1980), both of which are due for publication in spring, 1980.

[45] Thomas F. Moriarty, 'The Irish absentee tax controversy of 1773: a study in Anglo-Irish politics on the eve of the American revolution', in *Amer. Phil. soc. Trans.*, cxviii (1974), pp 370–408.

[46] Bartlett, *Penal era,* pp 88–112 *passim.* A very different approach to Anglo–Ireland's relationship with the empire is R.B. Mc Dowell's 'Ireland in the eighteenth century British empire', in J.G. Barry (ed.), *Historical Studies,* ix (1974), pp 49–63.

[47] Maurice R. O'Connell, 'The American revolution and Ireland', in *Éire–Ireland,* xi (1976), no. 3, 3–12. For an Irishman who contributed to the American revolution see Cyril M. White, 'Charles Thomson: the Irish-born secretary of the Continental Congress 1774–1789, in *Studies,*

lxviii (1979), pp 33–45.

⁴⁸ Colin C. Bonwick, *English radicals and the American revolution* Chapel Hill, North Carolina, 1977).

⁴⁹ See Marcus de la Poer Beresford, 'Ireland in French strategy during the American war of independence', in *Ir. Sword*, xii (1976), pp 285–297 and xiii (1977), pp 20–28 for details of intelligence work and invasion plans.

⁵⁰ Dr. Peter Smyth has written a useful introduction (18pp) to *The Volunteers, 1778–84* (Education facsimiles 141–160, Belfast, 1974); see also his 'The Volunteers of 1782', in *An Cosantóir*, xxxvi (1976), pp 110–116; ' "Our cloud-cap't grenadiers": the Volunteers as a military force', in *Ir. Sword*, xiii (1978), pp 185–207. In addition see K.P. Ferguson, 'The Volunteer movement and the government, 1778–1793' in *Ir. Sword*, xiii (1978), pp 208–216.

⁵¹ P.D.H. Smyth, 'The Volunteers and parliament, 1779–84', in Bartlett and Hayton (eds), *Penal era*, pp 114–136.

⁵² Senior, *Orangeism in Ireland and Britain* (London, 1966), p.6.

⁵³ Pádraig Ó Snodaigh, 'Notes on the Volunteers, militia, yeomanry and Orangemen of County Monaghan', in *Clogher Rec.*, ix (1977), pp 142–166. See also his studies of the Volunteers in other counties: *Louth Arch. Soc. Jn.*, xviii (1976), pp 279–93 (Co. Louth), *Ir. Sword*, x (1971), pp 125–40 (Co. Limerick), *Galvia*, xi (1977), pp 1–31 (Co. Galway), *Ir. Sword*, xii (1975), pp 15–35 (Co. Roscommon). The article in *Galvia* is in the Irish language.

⁵⁴ Brian Fothergill, *The mitred earl: an eighteenth century eccentric* (London, 1974), John R. Walsh, *Frederick Augustus Harvey, 1730–1803* (Maynooth, 1972). The latter is an interesting biographical essay, concentrating on Harvey's work for religious toleration.

⁵⁵ R.B. Mc Dowell, *Ireland in the age of imperialism and revolution, 1760–1800* (Oxford, 1979).

⁵⁶ Peter Jupp, 'Historical revision xvii. Earl Temple's viceroyalty and the renunciation question, 1782–3', in *I.H.S.*, xvii (1971), pp 499–520.

⁵⁷ Paul Kelly, 'British and Irish politics in 1785', in *E.H.R.*, lxxx (1975), pp 536–63. See also his 'British parliamentary politics, 1784–1786', in *Hist. Jn.*, xvii (1974) pp 733–753. See also Sheila Lambert, ed., *House of commons sessional papers of the eighteenth century* (Wilmington, Delaware, 1975), vols 51 and 52, George III 1785. This series, which covers the period 1715–1800 in 130 volumes, contains many other papers of Irish interest as well.

⁵⁸ Edith M. Johnston, 'Members of the Irish parliament, 1784–7', in

R.I.A. Proc., 71 (1971), C, pp 139–246.

[59] J.J. Lee, 'Grattan's Parliament', in B. Farrell (ed.), *The Irish parliamentary tradition* (Dublin, 1973). A recent account of Fitzwilliam's short-lived government can be found in E.A. Smith, *Whig principles and party politics. Earl Fitzwilliam and the whig party 1748–1833* (Manchester, 1975), pp 175–218 in particular, but material of Irish interest occurs elsewhere. Fitzwilliam's political overtures are shown to have had prior knowledge in London.

[60] James S. Donnelly, Jr, 'The Whiteboy movement, 1761–5', in *I.H.S.,* xxi (1978), pp 20–54.

[61] 'The Rightboy movement 1785–8', in *Stud. Hib.,* xvii–xviii (1978), pp 120–202. For a different interpretation see Maurice J. Bric, 'The disturbances of 1785–86 in Cork and Kerry' (N.U.I., U.C.C., M.A. thesis, 1977).

[62] M. Wall, 'The Whiteboys', in T.D. Williams (ed.), *Secret societies in Ireland* (Dublin, 1973), pp 13–25. In this essay she made the point that agrarian societies 'may have prevented the type of wholesale eviction which took place in Scotland in the last half of the eighteenth century' (p. 24).

[63] J. J. Lee, 'The Ribbonmen', in Williams, *Secret societies,* p. 26.

[64] M. R. Beames, 'Peasant movements: Ireland, 1785–1795', *Jn. Peasant Studies,* ii (1975), pp 502–6. The argument in this article is attractive but it is not sufficiently supported by primary sources. However, it should be noted that Dr Beames is author of a doctoral dissertation, 'Peasant disturbances, popular conspiracies and their control: Ireland 1798–1852', (Manchester University Ph. D. thesis, 1976). See also G. E. Christianson, 'Secret societies and agrarian violence in Ireland, 1790–1840', in *Agricultural History,* xlxi (1972), pp 369–84.

[65] Wall, 'Whiteboys', in Williams, *Secret societies,* p. 25.

[66] Donnelly, 'Rightboys', p. 201.

[67] W. H. Crawford, 'Change in Ulster in the late eighteenth century', in Bartlett and Hayton, *Penal era,* pp 186–203.

[68] H. Senior, 'The early Orange Order, 1795–1870', in Williams, *Secret societies,* pp 36–45'.

[69] A. Mc Clelland, 'Orangeism in County Monaghan', in *Clogher Record,* ix (1978), pp 384–404. He mentions that Lodge 434 constituted the Monaghan militia (p. 385).

[70] J. G. Simms, 'Remembering 1690', in *Studies,* lxiii (1974), pp 231–42. See also Peter Gibbon, 'The origins of the Orange order and the United Irishmen', in *Economy and Society,* i (1972), pp 135–63, and by

the same author, *The origins of Ulster unionism* (Manchester, 1975).

71 C. J. Woods, 'Ireland and the French revolution', in *Éire–Ireland*, vii (1973), no. 2, pp 34–41.

72 Marianne Elliott, 'The origins and transformation of early Irish republicanism', in *International Review of Social History*, xxiii (1978), pp 405–28.

73 W. B. Kennedy, 'The Irish Jacobins', in *Studia Hib.*, xvi (1976), pp 109–121. With reference to the United Irishmen see also the following: A. T. Q. Stewart, ' "A stable unseen power": Dr William Drennan and the origins of the United Irishmen', in J. Bossy *et al* (eds.), *Essays presented to Michael Roberts*, pp 80–92; J. L. Mc Cracken, 'The United Irishmen', in Williams, *Secret societies*, pp 58–67; Public Record Office of Northern Ireland, *The United Irishmen* (Education facsimilies 61–80, Belfast, 1971 and 1974). Two historiographical pieces are worth mentioning, both of them by Dr Leon Ó Broin: 'R. R. Madden, historian of the United Irishmen', in *Ir. Univ. Rev.*, ii (1972), pp 20–33, and *An Maidineach, staraí na hÉireannach aontaithe* (Dublin, 1971).

74 M. Elliott, 'Irish republicanism in England: the first phase, 1797–9', in Bartlett and Hayton, *Penal era,* pp 204–21. See also Dr Elliott's 'The "Despard conspiracy" reconsidered', in *Past and Present,* lxxv (1977), pp 46–61.

75 See also Public Record of Northern Ireland, *The '98 rebellion* (education Facsimiles 81–100, Belfast, 1970).

76 See C. J. Woods, 'The secret mission to Ireland of Captain Bernard Mac Sheehy, an Irishman in French service, 1796', in *Cork Hist. Soc. Jr.,* lxxviii (1973), pp 93–108; Paul M. Kerrigan, 'The defences of Ireland 1793–1815', in *An Cosantoir,* xxxvii (1977), pp 150–3 and pp 245–7; Russell Mc Kay, 'The fortifications of Lough Swilly and Lough Foyle: temporary expedients, 1798–1800', in *Donegal Annual,* xii (1977), pp 40–48. J. J. St. Mark has an uncritical introduction to some useful documents in his 'Wolfe Tone's diplomacy in America: August –December, 1795', in *Éire–Ireland,* vii (1972), no. 4, pp 3–11..

77 See Peadar Mac Suibhne, *'98 in Carlow* (Carlow, 1974), and by the same author, *Kildare in 1798* (Naas, 1978). See also Pádraig Ó Snodaigh *'98 and Carlow: a look at the historians,* (Ceatharlacha, 1979), 28 pp.

78 M. Duggan, 'The "Popish plot" in county Carlow', in *Carloviana,* ii (1977), no. 26, pp 7–10. Sr. Duggan completed a dissertation in 1970 entitled 'Carlow in the 1790s' (N.U.I., U.C.D., M.A. thesis).

79 T. Powell, 'An economic factor in the Wexford rebellion of 1978', in *Studia Hib.,* xvi (1976), pp 140–57. See also his thesis abstract, 'The

background to the Wexford rebellion, 1790–1798', in *Ir. Econ. Soc. Hist.,* ii (1975), pp 61–3.

[80] W. H. Crawford, 'Change in Ulster in the late eighteenth century', in Bartlett and Hayton, *Penal era,* pp 186–203. This article has already been cited in n.67.

[81] M. A. Bond, 'A German view of Anglo-Irish relations in 1800: Friedrich von Gentz on the act of union', in *Éire–Ireland,* viii (1973), no. 1, pp 13–20. See also H. L. Calkin, 'For and against an union', in *Éire–Ireland,* xiii (1978), no. 4, pp 22–33.

[82] Public Record Office of Northern Ireland, *The Act of Union* (Education Facsimiles 41–60, Belfast, 1970 and 1973).

[83] See in particular pp 76–85. See also John Patrick Ehrman, *The younger Pitt. The years of acclaim* (London, 1969), passim.

[84] *Eighteenth century Irish official papers in Great Britain. Private collections* (Belfast, 1973), vol. i; T. Bartlett (ed.), *Macartney in Ireland 1768–72. A calendar of the chief secretaryship papers of Sir George Macartney* (Belfast, no date); A. P. W. Malcomson (ed.), *The extraordinary career of the 2nd earl of Massereene, 1743–1805: a volume of select documents with explanatory notes and introduction* (Belfast, 1972); *An Anglo-Irish dialogue: a calendar of the correspondence between John Foster and Lord Sheffield, 1774–1821* (Belfast, 1976). See also A. P. W. Malcomson, 'A catalogue of the bibliographical material in the Foster-Massereene papers, Public Record Office of Northern Ireland', in *Ir. Booklore,* ii (1972), pp 89–102.

[85] David Hayton and Clyve Jones (eds), *A register of parliamentary lists 1660–1761* (Leicester, 1979). This register covers England, Ireland and Scotland separately. The first Irish list dates from 1695.

[86] See P. Jupp, *British and Irish elections, 1784–1831* (Newton Abbot, 1973); Public Record Office of Northern Ireland, *Irish elections, 1750–1832* (Education Facsimiles 21–40, Belfast, 1970).

[87] Jupp, 'County Down elections', p 199. Dr Jupp also makes the point that radical politics 'make hardly any impact upon the electoral system'.

[88] A. Malcomson, 'The politics of "natural right": the Abercorn family and Strabane borough, 1692–1800', in G. A. Hayes–Mc Coy (ed.), *Historical Studies* x (1976), pp 43–90. See also A. Malcomson, 'Election politics in the borough of Antrim 1750–1800', in *I.H.S.,* xvii (1970), pp 32–57; A. Malcomson, 'The Newtown Act of 1748: revision and reconstruction', in *I.H.S.,* xviii (1973), pp 313–344.

[89] A. Malcomson, 'The parliamentary traffic of this country', in Bartlett and Hayton, *Penal era,* pp 137–161.

⁹⁰ See also the following by A. Malcomson: 'The struggle for control of Dundalk borough, 1782–92', in *Louth Arch. Soc. Jn.*, xvii (1970), 'The Foster family and the parliamentary borough of Dunleer, 1683–1800', ibid., xvii (1971), 'The earl of Clermont: a forgotten Co. Monaghan magnate of the late eighteenth century', in *Clogher Rec.*, vii (1973), pp 19–72, and 'The earl of Clermont: revisions and corrections', ibid., pp 384–6; in addition see M. Duggan, 'The structure of politics and power: county Carlow in the last quarter of the eighteenth century', in *Carloviana,* new series, i (1971), no. 20, pp 35–40; Desmond Murphy, 'Parliamentary politics in Co. Donegal 1790–1832', in *Donegal Annual,* xii (1978), pp 266–75. Desmond Fitzgerald, knight of glin, 'A "sovereign" row in Naas', in *Kildare Arch. Soc. Jn.,* xv (1971), pp 22–8 deals with disturbances at an election for mayor of Naas in 1730.

⁹¹ Dermot Englefield, *The printed records of the parliament of Ireland 1613–1800. A survey and biographical guide* (London, 1978).

⁹² See also A. P. W. Malcomson, 'John Foster and the speakership of the Irish House of Commons', in *R.I.A. Proc.,* lxxii (1972), c, pp 271–303, and A.P.W. Malcomson, 'Speaker Pery and the Pery papers', in *N. Munster Antiq. Jn.,* xvi (1973–4), pp 33–60.

⁹³ L. Irwin, 'The role of the presidency in the economic development of Munster, 1660–72', in *Jn. Cork Hist. Soc.,* lxxxii (1977), pp 102–14; L. Irwin, 'The earl of Orrery and the military problems of restoration Munster', in *Ir. Sword,* xiii (1977), pp 10–19.

⁹⁴ L. Irwin, 'The Irish presidency courts, 1569–1672', in *Ir. Jurist,* new series, xii (1977), pp 106–114.

⁹⁵ J. C. Beckett, 'The Irish armed forces, 1660–1685', in Bossy and Jupp (eds.), *Essays presented to Michael Roberts,* pp 41–53.

⁹⁶ J. C. Sainty, 'The secretariat of the chief governors of Ireland, 1690–1800', in *R.I.A. Proc.,* lxxvii (1977), c, pp 1–33.

⁹⁷ D. Dickson, 'Edward Thompson's report on the management of customs and excise in County Kerry in 1733', in *Kerry Arch. Soc. Jn.,* vii (1974), pp 12–20. See also two other pieces by Dr Dickson, 'The account-book of a Kerry revenue official, 1687–9', ibid., vi (1973), pp 76–82, and 'A Donegal revenue inspection of 1775', in *Donegal Annual,* x (1972), pp 172–82. In addition see Diarmuid Ó Doibhlin, 'Hearth money and subsidy rolls of the barony of Dungannon, 1666', in *Seanchas Árdmhacha,* vi (1971), pp 24–45, and Brian De Breffny, 'Employees of the Irish revenue in 1709', in *Ir. Ancestor,* vi (1974), pp 6–16.

⁹⁸ T. Bartlett, 'Viscount Townshend and the Irish Revenue Board, 1767–73', in *R.I.A. Proc.,* lxxix (1979), c, pp 153–75.

[99] P. Roebuck, 'The Irish registry of deeds: a comparative study', in *I.H.S.*, xviii (1972), pp 61–73.

[100] K. Boyle, 'Police in Ireland before the union', in *Ir. Jurist*, new series, vii (1972), pp 115–37, and viii (1973), pp 90–116, pp 323–48. See also Stanley H. Palmer, 'The Irish police experiment: the beginnings of modern police in the British isles, 1785–1795', in *Social Science Quarterly*, 56 (1975), pp 410–424.

[101] A Bliss (ed.), *A dialogue in Hybernian stile* (Dublin, 1977). This is the sixth volume in the Cadenus Press's 'Irish writings from the age of Swift'.

[102] See Butterfield, *art. cit.*, p. 57.

[103] In particular see Seán Ó Tuama, 'Donall Ó Corcora' (pp 94–108) and Breandán Ó Buachalla, 'Ó Corcora agus an Hidden Ireland' (pp 109–137).

[104] British and Irish Communist Organisation, *"Hidden Ulster" explored. A reply to Pádraig Ó Snódaigh's "Hidden Ulster"* (Belfast, 1973).

[105] T. C. Barnard, 'The Hartlib circle and the origins of the Dublin Philosophical Society', in *I.H.S.*, xix (1974), pp 56–71, K. T. Hoppen, 'The Hartlib circle and the origins of the Dublin Philosophical Society', in *I.H.S.*, xx (1976), pp 40–48. See also T. C. Barnard, 'Myles Symner and the new learning in seventeenth-century Ireland', in *R.S.A.I. Jn.*, cii (1972), pp 129–142.

[106] This edition was published in Dublin in 1976 as the fourth volume in the Cadenus Press's 'Irish writings from the age of Swift'.

[107] B. Berman, 'Francis Hutcheson on Berkeley and the Molyneux problem', in *R.I.A. Proc.*, lxxiv (1974), c, pp 259–265, and 'A note on Berkeley and his catholic countrymen', in *Long Room*, xvi–xvii (1978), pp 26–8.

[108] See also Anne Crookshank and the knight of Glin, *The painters of Ireland, c. 1660–1920* (London, 1978); Esther K. Sheldon, 'The Hibernian Academy: an eighteenth-century group experiment in modern education', in *Long Room*, xi (1975), pp 23–34; T. J. Walsh, *Opera in Dublin 1705–1797: the social scene* (Dublin, 1973). In addition three articles by Richard C. Cole are worth mentioning, 'Smollett and the eighteenth century Irish book trade', in *Bibliographical Society of America, papers*, lxix (1975), pp 345–56, 'Community lending libraries in eighteenth-century Ireland' and 'Private libraries in eighteenth-century Ireland' in *Library Quart.*, xliv (1974), pp 111–123 and pp 231–247 respectively. Recently published is J. C. Beckett, 'Literary life in 18th century Ireland', in S. Dyrvik, *The satellite state in the 17th and 18th centuries* (Bergen, Norway, 1979), pp 157–68.

Ireland, 1800 – 1921

M. A. G. Ó Tuathaigh

The nineteen-seventies has, on the whole, been a prosperous decade for historical writing on Ireland under the Union. The sheer volume of published work is intimidating, and the increasing number of professional historians working on this period has meant that a high proportion of this work has been of good quality. The local history societies, for their part, have maintained a high level of activity, not least in their publications; and, while some of this work is of mixed quality, the best of it is such that professional historians cannot afford to neglect it.[1]

The fruits of the decade's historical writing have not, of course, been evenly distributed. The most significant area of growth, perhaps, has been in social and economic history, and the supply of original work has, on balance, been more plentiful for the post-famine decades than for the earlier period. Several factors have contributed to this situation. For one thing, historians have become progressively less inhibited in adopting and adapting concepts from the social sciences in formulating new questions and in offering new interpretations of familiar historical problems. Methodologically, the application of techniques of quantification has become more common and more sophisticated during the past decade, as historians search for greater precision in measuring that which is measurable in Irish historical data. This development has not been without risk, particularly where non-historians have sought to quantify and interpret historical data. But, on balance, the results of this increasing awareness among historians, of the possibilities of sensible quantification, have been beneficial.

Perhaps the most eloquent testimony to the growing specialisation in Irish historical writing (and to the growth in output) has been the appearance during the past decade of several new specialist societies and journals. The two most notable of these have been the *Economic and Social History Society of Ireland*,[2] and the *Irish Labour History Society*.[3] There have also been indications of a quickening of interest in business history,[4] while archival studies have also made considerable progress during the past decade.[5]

Turning from types of history to major themes, it would seem to us that three main areas in Irish historical writing have been particularly well served during the seventies. These are: the land question, the study of popular movements (social and political), and the Ulster question. So far as the land question of the 19th and early 20th centuries is concerned, the aspects which have attracted most scholarly attention are: landlord-tenant relations (actual as well as legal), the determinants of changes in land ownership and use, and the impact of market forces and of changing social structures. Changes in social structure have also been very much in evidence in the investigation of popular movements, while the role of leadership, the relationship between economic distress and social protest and the dynamics of popular politics have also received a good deal of attention. As regards Ulster, it is sad but true that the troubles of the past decade have been an important factor in provoking several new analyses of the origins and nature of the Ulster problem. This in no sense exhausts the list of themes where, during the decade, Irish historical scholarship[6] has shed light into corners hitherto darkened by ignorance or by prejudice and polemics.

The supply of bibliographical aids has improved continuously. While the annual consolidated listing in the September issue of *Irish Historical Studies* remains an essential reference for a comprehensive bibliography of writings in Irish history, it may be supplemented by annual lists of relevant publications in the specialist journals. For example, *Irish Economic and Social history* has included such a list since its inception, while *Saothar 5* (pp. 97–108) included a bibliography of *Irish Labour History (1973–77)*, compiled by Deirdre O'Connell.[7] Since 1976 the Royal Historical Society has published an *Annual bibliography of British and Irish history*, Ed. G. R. Elton; it includes (beginning with the publication of 1975) a select list of Irish publications under various headings. Two large volumes published under the direction of the *Royal Historical Society* and the *American Historical Association* contain substantial Irish sections: L. Brown and J. Christie (ed.), *Bibliography of British History 1789–1851* (Oxford, 1977), and H. J. Hanham (ed.), *Bibliography of British history, 1851–1914*.[8] More specialised works are G. H. Martin and S. MacIntyre (ed.), *A Bibliography of British and Irish municipal history, Vol. i.* (Leicester, 1972), and J. J. Silke's useful survey, 'The Roman Catholic Church in Ireland, 1800–1922: a survey of recent historiography' in *Studia Hibernica*, VX, pp. 61–104 (1975).[9] Two concise historiographical essays by Helen Mulvey appeared in the predecessor of this volume,: 'Nineteenth Century Ireland, 1801–1914' and 'Twentieth Century Ireland, 1914–70', in T. W. Moody (ed.), *Irish historiography 1936–70*,

(Dublin, 1971), pp. 71–102 and pp. 103–36 respectively. Henry Boylan's *Dictionary of Irish Biography* (Dublin, 1978) is aimed at the general reader,[10] while Irish M.P.s of the union period are covered in Michael Stenton's (ed.), *Who's Who of British members of parliament, vol. I., 1832–85* (Hassocks, 1976) and *vol. II* (with S. Lees), *1885–1918,* (Hassocks, 1978).

Turning from bibliographical aids to general surveys of the period, one is immediately struck by the volume and variety of work of the past decade. While no single volume coincides exactly with the union period, the relevant volumes of the Gill history of Ireland are: Gearóid Ó Tuathaigh, *Ireland before the Famine 1798–1848* (Dublin, 1792), Joseph Lee, *The modernisation of Irish Society 1848–1918* (Dublin, 1973), and John A. Murphy, *Ireland in the Twentieth Century* (Dublin, 1975). The most detailed survey of the post-famine era is F.S.L. Lyons's *Ireland since the Famine* (London, 1971), while M. E. Collins's, *An outline of modern Irish history, 1850–1951* (Dublin, 1974) is a useful introduction. The period of the union features prominently in a number of very different interpretations of Irish history. Patrick O'Farrell's provocative *Ireland's English Question* (London, 1971) argued for the centrality of religion in an explanation of Anglo-Irish conflict since the reformation, and in a later work, *England and Ireland since 1800* (London, 1975), the same author stressed the importance of images and perceptions in interpreting the tensions of Anglo-Irish relations under the Union. While Farrell's works consistently subordinate economic and social factors to broadly ideological forces, other interpretations have taken a very different line. Thus, for example, Michael Hechter, a sociologist, discusses the persistence of ethnicity in the Celtic fringe of Britain and Ireland in, *Internal Colonialism: The Celtic fringe in British national development, 1536–1966* (London, 1975). Hechter uses the model of a core-periphery relationship (with England as the industrial 'core') in arguing his case, and while his emphasis on the cultural division of labour and regional economic inequalities as the main causes for the persistence of ethnicity may seem too narrow an explanation to many historians, his discussion of Wales and Scotland in this context adds a welcome comparative dimension to his analysis for Ireland. Irish nationalism is discussed in a detailed but conventional manner by Robert Kee in *The Green Flag* (London, 1972), while E. R. Norman's *A history of modern Ireland* provides a strong counter-blast to Gladstonian liberal sympathy with the Irish sense of grievance.[11] Finally, in addition to several highly individual general histories,[12] we may note a first attempt at providing an *Atlas of Irish history,* by Ruth Dudley Edwards (London, 1973).

In Irish political history the most encouraging development of the past decade has been the shift in emphasis from, in Theo Hoppen's phrase, 'national politics to local realities'. This is in no way meant to belittle the substantial body of quality work along traditional lines – high politics, political biography, platform and parliament – which we discuss below. However, it is in the study of regional variations in the support of political movements, of the social composition of these movements, of the local relationships of power and patronage through which 'national' issues were filtered; it is here, in the micro-politics of nineteenth century Ireland, that the most significant advances have been made. While the Dutch social geographer, Hendrik H. Van der Wusten, has analysed the regional variations in the support for different political movements throughout the union period,[13] most of the other serious contributions to political history have concentrated on shorter periods. The politics of the immediate post-union decades remain strangely neglected. Peter Jupp has added further to his valuable work on post-union elections.[14] But the fate or fortunes of the survivors of the old Irish parliament under the new union disposition, their integration into Westminister politics, the factors which determined who would prosper and who would fail under the new order, the Irish dimension in the politics of revolution and counter-revolution in the early nineteenth century;[15] these and other no less important questions require detailed investigation. It is one of the many virtues of Anthony Malcomson's fine study of Speaker Foster that it provides an illuminating case-history of one of the pillars of the old ascendancy who did not succeed at Westminister.[16]

Writings on O'Connellite politics have built steadily on Angus MacIntyre's work,[17] and have also struck out in new directions. Here, too, local realities have come to the fore. Both Jacqueline Hill and Feargus D'Arcy have looked at the impact of religious and class factors in determining the strength and the limits of O'Connell's repeal campaign in Dublin.[18] The 'educative' role of the emancipation campaign of the twenties in the initiation of Catholic laymen (largely drawn from the middle class of the towns) into national politis has been examined by Fergus O'Ferrall, with particular reference to Waterford, Cork and Longford,[19] and Cork politics in the repeal period have also been analysed by Maura Murphy.[20] An illustrated interpretative essay,[21] an assessment of O'Connell as parliamentarian,[22] contributions on his finances, his views on religious freedom, violence and slavery;[23] suggestions on the Gaelic dimension to his popular support and on his place in

Irish folklore;[24] further studies on the British dimension of his political activities;[25] – this by no means exhaustive litany gives some idea of the attention given to O'Connellite politics during the seventies.[26]

Finally, and most importantly, the decade has seen the publication of Maurice O'Connell's massive six volume edition of the collected letters of O'Connell.[27] While this has been a labour of love, it has also been an enterprise of sustained excellence in scholarship and presentation, and it makes a new full-length study of O'Connell a more feasible and a more desirable undertaking. However, a few brief comments may serve here as an interim report on the 'state of play' in the historiography of O'Connellite politics. On balance, it is hard to disallow O'Connell's claims for consideration as a belated 'enlightenment' presence in Ireland, a genuine, if unusual, utilitarian. With certain reservations (e.g. his complicity in the contraction of the franchise in 1829) O'Connell's title to being 'the founding father of Irish democracy' may also be allowed, if we understand it to mean the mobilisation and organisation of the masses of the population to achieve definite political objectives through non-violent political exertions. But the nature of his support – the views, perceptions and expectations of the masses who made his movements the formidable political forces that they were – is more problematic. The extent to which forces making for 'the modernisation of Irish society' were present in O'Connellite politics remains open to debate. On the one hand, the crucial role of an 'improving' middle class leadership (in town and country), the 'rational' pursuit of political objectives, the emphasis on discipline and on improved communications, the shift from local to 'national' issues – all of these modernising elements undoubtedly feature in O'Connellite politics. But they are not the whole story. Some of the more backward aspects of the peasant mentalité, superstition, prophecy, fatalism, millenialism, and messianism[28] are also present in O'Connellite 'popular' politics and, indeed, in all popular movements of the pre-famine period. Hugh Kearney, in a recent piece,[29] has argued the case of Fr. Matthew's temperance movement as a modernising gospel, not only because of its temperance element, but also because of its emphasis on literacy, thrift, moral and social welfare and a general Smilesean programme of improvement. But Kearney also acknowledges the charismatic and miraculous aspects of the Mathewite crusade. Regional and local variations (reflecting differences in economic conditions, literacy and communications) are obviously important in explaining the geographical and social bases of political movements. But, whatever about the recruitment of a local leadership cadre, it is now becoming clear that a simple urban – cosmopolitan – modernistic/rural – localist – backward dichotomy will simply not fit the data for the O'Connellite movement. Theo Hoppen has ably demonstrated that, in terms of electoral support, to say nothing of the non-enfranchised majority, O'Connell's repeal movement (i.e. a 'national' question) enjoyed more consistent support in the counties than in the boroughs (where local issues could easily come to dominate). Furthermore, Hoppen has shown that the constantly shrinking electorate of the O'Connell era was not as uniformly 'respectable', in borough or county, as historians have hitherto supposed it to be.[30] Clearly, then, there are many pertinent questions still to be asked of O'Connellite politics.

In moving to the mid-victorian decades, our first obligation must be to salute the work of Theo Hoppen on Irish electoral politics during the past decade.[31] Indeed, in view of their range and implications, it would probably be more accurate to describe Hoppen's essays as contributions towards a study of 'Irish politics and society' between O'Connell and Parnell. If we say that Hoppen is 'doing a Hanham' for Ireland in these decades, the intention is not to diminish the originality of his work, but rather to emphasise its worth. Ranging over a territory where John Whyte has long been a lone pioneer, Hoppen has carefully unravelled the intricacies of nineteenth century electoral law, but more than that, he has painted a convincing picture of the turbulent but highly localist nature of borough electoral politics during the fifties and early sixties, in contrast to the relative quiescence of county constituencies under a temporary revival of landlord influence during the same period. According to Hoppen, it was the renewed interest in the county constituencies which signalled the beginning of a new phase in 'national' politics in the 1870's. Above all, however, in demonstrating the extreme localism of Irish electoral politics in the mid-nineteenth century, Hoppen would have us consider this as the normal form of Irish politics, which only gave way to coherent national politics, on national issues, under the exceptional circumstances of an O'Connell or a Parnell-inspired national movement. This is no place to discuss the implications of this interpretation, only the bare bones of which have geen given here. But clearly Hoppen's historical psephology provides not only a crucial insight into mid-nineteenth century Ireland but also a good platform from which to look forward to the styles of politics in the Irish state after 1922, and also backwards to the politics of the late eighteenth century. When we add to this the invaluable volume on Irish election results during the union period prepared by Brian Walker and the same author's study of the Irish electorate from 1868 to

1914,[32] then we may indeed take satisfaction in the progress of Irish electoral history during the past decade.[33] The traditional emphasis on parliamentary politics and policy-formation is now being balanced by the investigation of, as it were, 'grass-roots' politics in the Irish constituencies.[34]

Whether or not national politics and ideology gave way to unbridled localism in the post-repeal years, it is certainly the case that, historiographically, the Young Irelanders and their impact have received comparatively little attention during the past decade.[35] Happily the same cannot be said of the Fenians. Leon Ó Broin's *Fenian Fever: an Anglo-American dilemma* (London, 1971) has established itself as the most complete account of the climax of the Fenian conspiracy and its aftermath in the middle and late sixties, though the sources available to the historian of clandestine movements (preponderantly intelligence reports of various kinds) inevitably affect the structure of the account. Two books and a number of articles have examined aspects of the Fenian presence in North America,[36] while Seán Ó Lúing's second volume of Rossa's biography has been joined by a full-length study of Kickham by R. V. Comerford.[37] The publication of original documents and the listing of Fenian papers in the Catholic University of America have thrown further light on the movement,[38] as indeed has K. B. Nowlan's essay on the Fenians in Ireland, and A. J. Sample's essay on Fenian infiltration of the British army.[39] With the exception of Seán Ó Lúing's admirable work on Kerry,[40] no local studies on Fenianism have been produced. This is regrettable as there is a particular need for such studies if we are to 'place' Fenianism in the history of 19th century popular politics. For example, we need to know more about its antecedents in different localities – Young Irelanders or Ribbonmen or others; was its largely town constituency (artisans, clerks, shop boys and the like) unable anywhere to link with forces of agrarian discontent?[41] Still more important than its antecedents we need to know more of its 'after-life' after 1867 in different localities. In this regard we should note Leon Ó Broin's *Revolutionary underground: the story of the Irish Republican Brotherhood, 1858–1924* (Dublin 1976). While it lacks the cohesion of *Fenian Fever,* one important achievement of Ó Broin's study of the I.R.B. is his disclosure of the complex network of clandestine societies operating in Ireland in the later nineteenth and early twentieth centuries. This twilight zone of the secret societies is also examined in several worthwhile essays in T.D. Williams (ed.), *Secret Societies in Ireland* (Dublin 1973).[42] But some of the general statements need to be tested by local studies. For example, the hardening consensus among historians that Fenian influences played a crucial role in 'preparing the way' for the mobilisation of the tenantry in the land war,[43] and particularly its role in politicising hitherto political backward areas in the west; this and other contentions need to be tested by local studies, with special attention, perhaps, to the activities of the Amnesty Association.

The Fenian movement represented the most extreme version of Irish nationalist demands during the union period, the demand for total separation. But, of course, the problems encountered by the imperial parliament in dealing with the demands of Irish nationalism, in its manifold forms, did not begin in the eighteen-sixties. The old firm of 'coercion and conciliation' had been in businesss as long as the union itself – indeed longer – and in the first half of the nineteenth century both the Whigs and Peel resorted to this strategy in seeking to secure the safe government of Ireland. But the Fenian threat did serve to bring the Irish nationalist demand into sharp focus; it certainly forced the issue on the attention of Gladstone, traditionally acknowledged in Irish historiography as the one British statesman of the union era who fully comprehended Irish nationalism, and who sought to reach a just and generous accommodation with it. This view of Gladstone's Irish policy has been undergoing sustained re-examination during the past decade. David Steele, in particular, has offered a number of re-valuations for the mid-Victorian years in Anglo-Irish relations.[44] For Steele, the question of 'Irish nationality' and the reconciling of its claim with the demands of Empire, constituted the central issue of the sixties, affecting all major policy matters, from Church-State relations to the Irish land question. The different modes of Irish nationalism (for Steele, Paul Cullen is as ardent a nationalist as the most die-hard Fenian) called for different government strategies. But by the 1880s, as Irish nationalism settled into its cohesive, electorally significant, Home Rule mould, its claims for substantial appeasement, if not total satisfaction, were stronger than at any time since the union. Steele sees Gladstone's developing views on Ireland as having been rooted in a deep personal sense of religious and moral responsibility and a "nobility of purpose" in striving for a 'just' solution. But these elements were wedded to an acute appreciation of the importance of timing and the realities of power in the launching of political initiatives, and, above all, 'generosity' towards Ireland was, for Gladstone, at all times bounded by the instincts and the priorities of 'the patriot and the imperial statesman'.[45]

The Parnellite years have continued to attract a steady stream of historians during the last decade, and the result has been a considerable refinement in our understanding of Parnell himself, of his relationship with 'the movement' during the 1880's, and of the 'context' – in Wicklow and Westminister, in private houses and on the hustings – in which Parnell operated. F. S. L. Lyons's *Charles Stewart Parnell* (London 1977), the result of almost thirty years research and reflection on its subject, is meticulous in its scholarship and balanced in its judgments. On balance, Lyons is critical of the Parnell of 1886–91, and highly critical of his failure to address himself in any serious way to the problem posed by Ulster unionists to any Home Rule scheme proposed for the whole island. Roy Foster's contextual biography of Parnell in his domestic and local setting admirably complements Lyons's work.[46] Apart from a study of William O'Brien which, while quite useful, in no way exhausts the subject, and a number of local studies of election contests,[47] the major discussion of the significance of the Parnell era in Irish domestic politics has centred on the role of the Catholic Church in relation to Parnell and to the Home Rule movement in general, and on the significance for Irish politics of the strength and geographical concentration of Ulster unionism.[48] The one significant exception to this generalisation is Peter Alter's *Die irische National-bewengung zwischen Parlament und Revolution: der Konstitutionelle Nationalismus in Ireland, 1880–1918.* (Munich and Vienna 1971). Alter's work is less remarkable for its straight-forward summary of Irish parliamentary history in the Home Rule era than for its imaginative discussion of the importance of 'symbols' – flags, songs, colours – in the formation of popular political consciousness.[49] He also provides, in his analysis of the activities of the National League in Cork city and county from 1881–85, the only detailed local study we have of the 'inner' workings of nationalist politics in a particular area.

The English context of Home Rule politics has undergone major revision during the past decade. Alan O'Day's *The English face of Irish Nationalism: Parnellite involvement in British politics 1880–86* (Dublin 1977) has some interesting things to say on the 'profile' of the Irish party at Westminister, while other studies have looked again at government policy towards Ireland in the aftermath of 1886,[50] or have examined the Home Rule issue as a test case for assessing the scope and limits of British radicalism.[51] But the most radical revision of the policies of the eighties has been the work of A. B. Cooke and J. R. Vincent. In addition to publishing a considerable body of new and important source material,[52] Cooke and Vincent have placed the Home Rule crisis of 1885–6 in a context of high intrigue and ruthless calculation, of pronounced fluidity in party politics and in a struggle for power *within* the main parties no less than *between* them. The governing passion consumes all the main serious political figures in this game, and the intrinsic merits (moral or other) of the Irish case are very incidental indeed. The Gladstone of Cooke and Vincent in 1885–6 seems a very different animal indeed to Steele's moral man of noble purpose.[53]

The historiographical significance of the work of the 'high politics' school lies in its insistence on the need for scholarly discrimination in the use of sources by historians seeking to understand and to explain the motives and actions of politicians. One of the major criticisms made of this kind of history is that it seriously underestimates the role of ideas and ideology in the conduct of politics, to say nothing of the more intangible (and mostly unwritten) attitudes and prejudices of those politicians and of the wider public, and their implications for party politics. Recent contributions on those aspects of the Home Rule crisis have largely confirmed and amplified the existing body of work.[54] This can certainly not be said of the recent histiography of 'the Ulster question', and of Irish unionism in general. Indeed, the re-examination of the historical development of Irish unionism has been one of the few unequivocally healthy consequences of the troubles in northern Ireland during the seventies. What has emerged is an extremely rich and varied range of interpretations of Irish unionism under the union. On one point only is there something like a consensus, namely, on the historical, cultural and economic differences which distinguished the Ulster unionists (a geographically compact, multi-class community) from southern unionists, and the very different political strategies which these differences dictated to the different elements of Irish unionism in their dealings with Irish nationalism and with British imperial policy throughout the union era.

The most comprehensive treatment of the subject is Patrick Buckland's two volume history of Irish unionism (together with a collection of documents which is particularly useful for a discussion of Ulster unionism).[55] Studies of southern unionism have, for the most part, concentrated on biographical studies or on particular constituents of the patrician mentalité of southern unionism. The aggregate impact has been highly evocative, even if at times over–nostalgic.[56] Ian d'Alton's valuable essays on Cork unionism, however, are valuable precisely because they analyse a southern unionist community as it actually functioned.[57] Turning to Ulster unionism, it is hardly an exaggeration to say that the past decade has seen a dramatic increase, in bulk and sophistication, in historical writings on this topic. The long-term context of community conflict in Ulster has been analysed, from many different perspectives, by T. W. Moody, Liam de Paor, Owen Dudley Edwards and A.T.Q. Stewart, whose work stresses the continuities of place and perception which community conflict in Ulster has evidenced through the centuries.[58] David Miller has offered a particularly interesting interpretation of Ulster loyalism, seeing it as involving 'conditional loyalty', something going back to planter days and very different from the almost 'automatic loyalty' associated with modern nationalism.[59] John F. Harbinson's somewhat institutional history of the unionist party supplements Buckland's story at a number of points.[60] But the most radically revisionist writing on Ulster unionism during the past decade has come from a group of young Marxist historians. A common Marxist background, however, does not mean that their interpretations run along the same track; far from it. Michael Farrell's work is closest to the orthodox Marxist position on Ulster, by stressing the essential imperialist nature of the problem and the necessity for the completion of national sovereignty as a precondition to a solution of conflict in Ulster.[61] A very different interpretation of the historic development of Ulster unionism was offered by Peter Gibbon in 1975 in his book, *The origins of Ulster Unionism: the formation of popular Protestant politics and ideology in nineteenth century Ireland* (Manchester 1975). Since then, Gibbon's thesis has been refined and, in certain aspects, amplified by Gibbon himself and by Paul Bew and Henry Patterson.[62] Seeing the essence of the Ulster problem in the uneven development of Irish captialism, this group (to summarise rathern brutally) concentrate on, as it were, the *independent* forces and forms of Ulster unionism — the specific conditions of economic and social geography, and the ideological sources, of the unionist alliance, as it developed particularly from the sixties to its climax in the creation of the Ulster Unionist Council in 1905. These Marxist contributions, while leaving many questions still unanswered, and while often couched in language which some historians will find difficult if not impenetrable, have made an important contribution to the historiography of Irish unionism. Finally, there have been important studies of community politics and conflict in Belfast by Budge and O'Leary, Sybil Baker, and A.C. Hepburn.[63] The latter's work puts the Belfast experience in a comparative context in northern Ireland and underlines the need for more local studies of areas other than Belfast.

The final phase of the union era, from 1900 to the crisis of 1912–22, culminating in the establishment of the 'two states' in Ireland in 1920–22, has been the subject of a rather vast amount of important historical writing during the past decade. In the first place, there has been a virtual bonanza in biographies, a small number of which have been of exceptional quality.[64] In the face of such riches it may seem greedy to ask for more, but Craig, Carson, Redmond and Joe Devlin are due a serious revaluation. Whatever the case about the major figures, however, the political context in which they operated (and which they participated in shaping) has been the subject of an extraordinarily large body of historical writing during the past decade. Much of this writing has been revisionist in intention, drawing on newly accessible source materials or reflecting on familiar material from fresh perspectives. It would be impossible to attempt here a summary account of writings of such mass and variety. However, the bulk of the new writing has been concerned with defining, as precisely as possible, the context in which policy towards Ireland was formulated – the inter-relationship between imperial interests, party politics at Westminister, the personal ambitions and rivalries of politicians, the advice, authority and energy of bureaucrats, and political developments within Ireland itself. The main issues covered have included the development of Liberal strategy towards Home Rule up to 1914, and particularly their tardy appreciation of the gravity of the Ulster problem;[65] the Conservative strategies to defeat Home Rule and, in particular, the primacy of British imperial interests in all their calculations and the effect of the Liberal-Irish alliance of 1910 on the weapons which they felt admissible in the battle against Home Rule;[66] the impact of the great war and of the rebellion of 1916 and its aftermath on the prospects for an Irish settlement;[67] the realignment of political forces in Ireland during 1916–1919, culminating in the establishment of Dáil Eireann in 1919;[68] the American dimension;[69] the final stage of negotiation, leading to partition, truce and treaty. The refinement of analysis which this impressive body of work represents has been helped, of course, by the availability of new sources, among which Thomas Jones's *Whitehall Diary*, vol. iii, ed. Keith Middlemas (London 1971) deserves special mention.

In conclusion, let us turn to a very different kind of political history in the revolutionary era. 1977 saw the belated publication of an English version of Erhard Rumpf's pioneering work on the social geography of twentieth century nationalist politics in Ireland,[71] a work which included an interesting backward glance to nineteenth and early twentieth century politics. David Fitzpatrick has recently returned to 'the geography of Irish nationalism' for the period 1910–21.[72] Revising Rumpf's figures on 'violence' and 'voting', Fitzpatrick examines closely the numbers and activities of local nationalist organisations as an index of nationalism in different localities. He holds that post–1918 Sinn Fein integrated both the violent and the constitutional strands in Irish nationalism. Moreover, he suports the view that it was during the period 1870–1910 that the centre of gravity of Irish nationalist activity moved from the towns to the countryside, although, as we have noted in discussing Theo Hoppen's work, the politics of the mid-Victorian decades may allow another point of view on the issue. Fitzpartick draws much of his local data from County Clare, which is the locus of his *Politics and Irish Life, 1913–21* (Dublin 1977), perhaps the most exciting work published on the revolutionary era for some time. In demonstrating the impact of the revolutionary years on various groups in county Clare, Fitzpatrick has not only produced a case-history, integrated with great assurance into the 'national' picture, but he has also given a clear demonstration of how an historian should seek out, and, having found, make intelligent use of a great variety of source material. Fitzpatrick's desire to measure as accurately as possible that which lends itself to measurement (from inch columns in the press to flying columns in the countryside) never becomes a fetish. What emerges is a fascinating study of the essential resilience of the dominant groups in Irish politics, and the manner in which the accommodation of 'new men' to political prominence was accomplished without serious social dislocation. The socially conservative nature of the Irish national revolution of 1913–21 is here confirmed. It remains for others to test the validity of Fitzpatrick's thesis (and, hopefully, to show his resourcefulness in seeking out sources) for other areas in Ireland. But it is a pleasure to be able to close this survey of a decade's writing on constitutional and political history on a note of unreserved praise.

Turning to the general area of administrative and military history, it has to be admitted that work in this area has not been particularly prolific or exciting during the past decade. Oliver Mac Donagh's chapter on Ireland in *Early Victorian Government* (London 1977) is perceptive, but brief; while Edward Brynn's *Crown and Castle: British rule in Ireland 1800–1830* (Dublin 1978) can only be described, with much charity, as a missed opportunity. With very few exceptions, the impact of changes in local government structures during the nineteenth century – in town and country, corporations and grand juries – has been largely ignored, particularly the impact of the new county councils after 1899.[73] It is, perhaps, appropriate that it is at the interface between politics and administration, so rich in controversy during the nineteenth century, that some of these few exceptions are to be found. An example here is William

Feingold's work on the politicisation of the Boards of Guardians elections during the 1870s[74]

Writings on the development of the centralised elementary education have also been as much concerned with politics as with administration. On both counts, D. H. Akenson's admirable work, *The Irish Education Experiment* (London and Toronto 1970) fits the bill, though a recent essay by Mark Daly looks at the state system as it actually affected the schools.[75] A large body of work has concerned itself with the relationship between the state elementary school system and the various churches in Ireland, with local histories of individual educational institutions featuring prominently in the literature.[76] Significantly, most of the writing on education – at all levels – has had to do with its political or its institutional aspect.[77] The actual content of education has been sorely neglected, if one except J. M. Goldstrom's *The Social content of Education 1808–1870: a study of the working class school reader in England and Ireland* (Shannon 1972), and a number of minor pieces.[78] Too often, however, the content of Irish education – in state and private institutions – is still being inferred from the impressionistic evidence of biographical studies. This is no substitute for the systematic analysis that is needed of the content of nineteenth century Irish education, with its implications for literacy, ideology and social conformity (or the lack of it).

The administration of poor relief, under various forms, has received some attention, most notably from Timothy P. O'Neill,[79] and there have also been a few items of interest on prisons, places of detention, and on aspects of public health.[80] While there have been a few institutional biographies of various hospitals,[81] we are still awaiting work on the unexplored world of the doctor and of medicine in the countryside, and on the social history of medicine in 19th century Ireland. An outstanding work which goes beyond the limits of administrative history is J. H. Andrews's *A Paper Landscape: the Ordnance Survey in nineteenth century Ireland* (Oxford 1975), A solid piece on the board of works during the famine virtually completes the recital.[82]

On the military and the police, Galen Broeker's *Rural disorder and police reform in Ireland 1812–36* (London and Toronto 1970) is useful in elucidating aspects of the official response to Irish crime. Two general histories of the Irish police contain historical background,[83] while M. A. G. Ó Tuathaigh's *Thomas Drummond and the government of Ireland 1835–41* (Dublin 1978) places the police reforms of the thirties in the general context of administrative reform. The use of the army in aid of the police and civil power has been discussed by Richard Hawkins,[84] while various aspects of intelligence work emerge in some interesting studies by Leon Ó Broin and K. R. M. Short.[85] Finally, J. Anthony Gaughan's edition of the memoirs of an especially interesting police constable from the end of the union period is a rare example of the kind of insight into the 'policeman in society' which needs to be investigated much more than heretofore.[86] The same applies to the army, where the impact of 'the garrison' on Irish towns of the nineteenth century, and on Irish life in general, has yet to be studied. Developments in military techniques, the story of individual regiments, campaigns and officers continue to receive attention in the journal of the military history society, *The Irish Sword*[87] while H. J. Hanham's study of 'Religion and Nationality in the mid-Victorian army,'[87a] has a good deal on the Irish element. The literature on the revolutionary period 1913–22 is more plentiful, and, ironically, here we have nearly as much on the unofficial or guerilla army as on the official army. On the latter, Charles Townshend's *The British Campaign in Ireland 1919–21* (Oxford 1975) is excellent, while there have been a number of valuable studies on the I.R.A. during this period.[87b] Finally, the crucial changes in the administration of justice – through various kinds of courts – which accompanied the war of independence, the establishment of the Sinn Fein apparatuses of state post–1918, and the gradual eclipse of the British system, have received some attention, but demand a whole lot more.[88]

If politics have deeply penetrated Irish administrative history, the same is true with even greater force of Irish ecclesiastical and religious history. Indeed, church-state relations – irrespective of whichever church or state might be involved – has long dominated the literature on this topic. During the past decade, however, there have been some signs of a greater interest in the internal life of the churches, their social role and the devotional life of their communities.

The Church of Ireland faced many problems in the immediate post-union years. Not the least of these was coming to terms with the new political and constitutional arrangements. Even the Church's most indulgent friends acknowledged that major reforms were necessary in its organisation – in revenues, discipline and appointments. The question was, whether these changes would be agreed or imposed.[89] The political circumstances in Westminister and in Ireland decreed that, in large measure, they would be imposed, and during the thirties there was radical reform of the Church organisation and a solution of sorts to the vexatious problem of church tithes. However, even after the reforms of the thirties the established status of the Church remained vulnerable to the attacks of the majority community of Irish Catholics and of Dissenters in Ireland and in Britain. Eventually, under the 'right' conditions at Westminister, these attacks prevailed, and the Church of Ireland was disestablished in 1869. D. H. Akenson's *The Church of Ireland: ecclesiastical reform and revolution, 1800–85. (New Haven, 1971)*, is careful study of the institutional church during these decades, and there have been a number of contributions on the disestablishment crisis itself.[90] A concise and affectionate portrait of the post-disestablishment church is R. B. McDowell's *The Church of Ireland 1869–1969* (London 1975), while the resilience of the Church of Ireland and its rich contribution to Irish life in the century after disestablishment is the subject of a collection of essays edited by Michael Hurley, *Irish Anglicanism 1869–1969* (Dublin 1970). In addition to surveying the contribution of the Anglican community to economic, political and cultural life in Ireland, this volume also includes an account of the background to disestablishment by K. B. Nowlan. A different aspect of 'renewal' is discussed by Desmond Bowen in two books which discuss the work of the evangelical Protestants of the mid-nineteenth century and the controversies which attended their efforts to convert Irish Catholics to Protestantism.[91] Bowen's basic sympathy with the evangelists results in a very warm and detailed treatment of their motives and methods, but he does not always show sufficient appreciation of the historic cultural circumstances which rendered their activities so productive of controversy. Finally, interesting biographies of Church of Ireland figures have been disappointingly few.[92]

Few also have been the studies of Irish Presbyterianism, though what has been written during the decade is of considerable interest. Apart from a number of biographies of different congregations,[93] the most arresting contribution has undoubtedly been David Miller's analysis of the impact on Ulster Presbyterianism of the 'modernisation' of the north-east under the spur of industrialisation during the 19th century.[94] Miller sees the essential change as being from prophetic to conversionist evangelicalism, with the rebellion of the 1790s serving as 'the last flicker of a dying flame' (i.e. the 'prophetic' element, emphasising miraculous and apocalyptic versions of divine intervention, which many Catholics as well a Presbyterians subscribed to), and the 1830s seeing the mature emergence of 'conversionist' evangelicalism more suited to the empirical world of early industrial Ulster. Miller's interpretation should be read in conjunction with the discussion of Ulster Presbyterianism which is to be found in several of the works on Ulster unionism, including Miller's, discussed earlier in this essay. Finally, there is also an interesting essay on the attitued of the Presbyterian Church to the Government of Ireland act, 1920.[95]

Turning to the other Protestant churches, we may notice a few 'church' histories for Methodist churches,[96] and an impressive body of work on the Irish Baptists. This work, published in the *Irish Baptist History Society Journal* since 1968, includes not only the story of the Baptist mission in different parts of the country, but also discusses source material and education.[97] All in all, it is a considerable achievement. On the Irish Jews, see Louis Hyman's *The Jews of Ireland: from earliest times to 1910* (Shannon 1972) for a good account.

In the writings of the past decade on the history of Irish Catholicsm under the union there is cause for satisfaction, tinged with a little regret. The regret concerns the demise of the *Irish Ecclesiastical Record* and the abandonment (after the appearance in fascicle form of about half the projected volumes) of the ambitious *A history of Irish Catholicism* under the editorship of P. J. Corish. However, the publication of sources and documents – from diocesan and other archives – has continued steadily throughout the decade, with the completion of Peadar Mac Suibhne's collection of Paul Cullen's letters and Fr. Corish's calendar of the Kirby papers being but two of the important contributions.[98] However, the work which has probably caused most excitement during the seventies has been the work of Emmet Larkin and David Miller. Three volumes of Emmet Larkin's long-awaited history of Irish Catholicism in the 19th century have now appeared.[99] Larkin has been criticised for the manner in which he presents his findings – in the form of a 'mosaic' where the narrative is structured on extensive quotations from his sources (chiefly episcopal correspondence) with occasional interventions by Larkin himself. Whatever its defects, the technique does allow us an unusual intimacy with the way in which the bishops saw Irish politics, and their role in those politics, during the years 1878–91, the period covered by these three volumes. Larkin's thesis, however, goes beyond episcopal strategy; he argues that during these years there came into existence a *de facto* Irish state, in which the bishops came to terms with and gave benediction to the dominant Irish nationalist 'machine' in return for an acknowledgment of their special authority in certain key areas of social policy, most notably education. This 'concordat' of the eighties paved the way for the creation of the *de jure* Irish confessional (but not clericalist) state after 1922. The problem with this bold interpretative line is that it is based very much on the way the bishops saw the situation in Ireland (this is inevitable given Larkin's sources), and takes too little account of the wider – non-episcopal, extra-ecclesiastical – dimensions of popular nationalist politics. David Miller's *Church, State and Nation in Ireland 1898–1921* (Dublin 1973), is a chronological sequel to Larkin's work and shares many of the same questions. But paradoxically, because episcopal archives for the later period were not available to him, he paints a wider canvas (and in a less complicated framework) of church involvement in politics than does Larkin for the earlier period. But, essentially, Miller too is concerned with explaining how the Catholic Church maintained her interests and her influence in the crucial period during which the British state was gradually giving way to the reality of Irish nationalist political power over four-fifths of the country, until eventually in 1922 the Church was able, without any great anxiety, to confer her blessing on new 'Catholic' state.

While the work of Larkin and Miller, and other scholars who have contributed to the discussion of Church-State relations in Ireland in the late-Victorian and early 20th century,[100] has been of major value for its richness of material and, in certain areas, its conceptual originality, it must be borne in mind that the problems of the Church in coming to grips with the dynamics of popular politics (indeed popular 'nationalist' politics of a decidedly secular character) had already been faced in the O'Connell era, as the work of Oliver MacDonagh and Kevin B. Nowlan has shown clearly.[101] MacDonagh's claim, that the Catholic Church had, to a very great extent, to 'follow' O'Connell's initiatives when they were clearly in accord with popular Catholic instincts and objectives, suggests that the question of whether the bishops were more a passive than a drastic element in the politics of 19th century Irish Catholicism may be more complicated than Larkin has been prepared to admit. As we have noted, not all the writing on Irish Catholicism has been concerned with church-state relations.[102] A full-length biography of Croke,[103] a perceptive profile of Moriarty,[104] the systematic collection of data on priests from several dioceses[105] and a flourishing industry in parish, diocesan and 'institutional' histories (even if the quality is uneven), are all signs of vitality[106] Most significant of all, perhaps, have been the few articles which have examined the 'internal' life and social role of the 19th century Catholic Church. Emmet Larkin's article on the 'devotional revolution' is a major landmark[107] and, taken in conjunction with David Miller's 'Irish Catholicism and the great famine', (in *Journal of Social History*, ix, no. 1, 84–98, it gives us an outline interpretation of collective devotional practice in 19th century Catholic Ireland. Summarising rather drastically, the new orthodoxy (for such it has become) goes like this: the impact of the great famine and the influence of Paul Cullen and his episcopal supporters created between 1850–1875 the form of Irish Catholicism – with its emphasis on regular attendance at the sacraments, novenas, missions and a generally church-centred religion – which we now accept as 'traditional'. In the pre-famine decades a shortage of manpower (despite a gradual improvement in supply) relative to the massive population increase with its attendant social problems, together with the inadequacies in discipline prevalent in a church still recovering from severe dislocation, combined to restrict the influence of the church as an instrument of social control or of canonical devotional orthodoxy. Miller estimates attendance rates as being as low as 30 per cent to 40 per cent in the eighteen thirties. The famine and post-famine population losses (heavily concentrated in the 'problem' categories of Irish society) solved the problem of manpower and prepared the way for the devotional revolution of the Cullenite era. Both Larkin and Miller offer explanations for the receptivity of the post-famine Irish Catholic to the new devotional orthodoxy. For Larkin the loss of the Irish language led to an identity crisis, with Catholicism, ripe for emphasis, becoming the 'proxy' for national identity consequent on the loss of the language. Miller seeks a wider context, arguing for the collapse of a whole peasant belief system (based on wakes, superstitions, patterns and like) under the traumatic impact of the famine, and its replacement (at an uneven rate throughout the country) by the Cullenite devotional revolution. We may note in passing the areas of comparison between changing patterns of belief and devotion in Catholic and Presbyterian communities in the 19th century which underlie Miller's analysis.

There is much else in these essays on Irish Catholic devotion which the lack of space prevents us from discussing here. One major obstacle to a balanced judgement on the new orthodoxy is the relative dearth of studies on the social role of the Church in the pre-famine decades. We know that there were indeed problems of discipline in various dioceses, causing distress to local bishops and to Rome. But there is need for much more work on all aspects of the pre-famine Catholic Church, as well as a closer study of the agencies which were used in implementing the devotional revolution.[109] Clearly, the role of Maynooth and its priests is very important here. But, apart from a recent piece from Fr. Corish,[110] Maynooth is most often discussed in the context of relations between the Catholic church and the British State.[111] However, there are grounds for optimism here. A recent thesis by Seán Connolly on *Catholicism and Social Dscipline in pre-famine Ireland* (soon to be published) gives us hope that we may be on the threshold of important work in this neglected area.[112]

As Irish economic history is the subject of a separate essay in this volume, the survey of it here will be extremely summary. L. M. Cullen's *An Economic History of Ireland since 1660* (London 1972) was an ambitious attempt to provide an up-to-date scholarly text-book on the subject. And, while it has been faulted for its overemphasis on trade and market forces, it remains the essential survey on the subject, as well as suggesting where further work is required. For a welcome comparative dimension to Irish economic history there is L. M. Cullen and T. C. Smout (ed), *Comparative aspects of Scottish and Irish Economic and Social history* (Edinburgh 1977). It may be perverse to begin on a negative note, but let us turn first to those areas where the seventies have not been particularly fruitful. With a few significant exceptions, there has been little work on investment patterns in industry and manufactures, or case-studies of individual industries or firms,[113] or of key market institutions,[114] or of that most intractable problem – the supply and quality of entrepreneurs.[115] On banking and credit, G. L. Barrow's *The emergence of the Irish banking system, 1820–45* (Dublin 1975) is a careful institutional history of Irish banking from the crisis of 1820 to the famine, and while it leave untouched many of the more thorny problems of money supply and credit and their impact on the pre-famine economy, it does confirm the view that what was lacking in pre-famine Ireland (and, it may be said, for some time after) was not capital as such, but rather a demand which would put it to use in risk investment.[116] A useful introduction to one aspect of infrastructure is K. B. Nowlan (ed), *Travel and Transport in Ireland* (1973), while there is an extensive literature on Irish railways, though much of it is directed towards the aficionados.[117] However, we need a more precise chronology for the penetration of the Irish market (or, more precisely, local markets) by large, centralised producers, as a consequence of changes in transport and communications during the 19th century.

There is still much that is unclear about the pre-famine agricutltural economy, a situation for which deficiencies in the statistical data are only partly responsible.[118] However, it does seem at the moment that the 'dual economy' model has, as it were, served its time, and that a more refined version of the relationship between cash and subsistence sectors in the Irish economy is gradually taking its place.[119] The absorption into the market economy of those areas which remained isolated longest has been discussed in a series of articles by Liam Kennedy.[120] The range of topics covered in Kennedy's work is wide, and includes the expansion of the retail network, rural credit facilities (to which controversy a lively article by Peter Gibbon and Michael D. Higgins provided the initial spark),[121] the role of the Catholic Church and of the co-operative movement in the economic and social development of rural Ireland in the later nineteenth century.[122] Kennedy's work is of methodological interest, in as much as it combines the analysis of historical data with constructs from economic theory.

In historical demography, the last decade has seen further modifications of the orthodoxy that has emerged from post-Connell revisionism.[123] The two most significant developments have been: i) F. J. Carney's claim, based on data from the Trinity College estates, that it wasn't only the rate of population increase but also the actual level of population that was declining during the 1830s;[124] and ii) Cormac Ó Gráda's revision of post-famine regional variations in population, suggesting that Connacht's post-famine emigration rate was not lower than the national average, as had been supposed, but that its rate of population increase may have been significantly higher.[125] In the analysis of social structure, Samuel Clark's *Social Origins of the Irish Land War* (Princeton 1979) is the most sustained and comprehensive treatment of changes in Irish social structure (and its implications for politics and social conflict) to appear to date. Michael Beames has sought to clairfy the terminology used in discussing pre-famine rural society, and has also sought greater precision in identifying the social contours of agrarian violence,[126] while the structure of the 'peasant' family is the subject of an interesting essay by Peter Gibbon and Chris Curtin.[127]

Above all else, however, it is the land question which has been the subject of the most intense investigation and which has produced the most exciting work of the past decade in Irish economic and social history. There has been a thorough reassessment of the economic and social role of the landlord, and of the full range of landlord-tenant relations.[128] One of the most important reasons for this reassessment has been the use made by Maguire, Donnelly, Ó Grada, Vaughan and others of a mass of estate papers which had not been used before. This plus the intelligent use of local newspapers as well as the more conventional offical data, and an awareness of certain concepts in social theory, have utterly transformed the historiography of the land question.

Irish urban history (in the sense in which urban history is now understood among professional historians) is as yet in its infancy in Ireland,[129] but labour history has been making considerable progress in the past few years. Apart from biographical work and several studies of Labour's place in the 'national question', the decade has seen the publication of one major study of Labour in Irish politics,[130] an impressive (if somewhat institutionalised) study of Irish trade unions after 1894,[131] and, most welcome of all, a growing body of the work on the actual working and living conditions of the labouring classes in Ireland.[132] To date, the progress has been uneven; but all the signs indicate that a healthy growth is in store for Irish labour history during the eighties.[133]

A 'healthy growth' would also describe the enormous increase in output during the past decade in the literature of Irish emigration and on the expatriate Irish. Not surprisingly, perhaps, the American-Irish experience has produced the heaviest crop, and here the old assumptions of 'the uprooted', which underpinned the bulk of emigrant studies of the Irish to-date, have been replaced (at least in the best of the new work) by a more sophisticated analysis of the ways in which emigrants from peasant communities translate to an urban industrial environment; the kind of analysis exemplified in the works of Stephen Thernstrom.[134] While the Irish-American literature is the most voluminous on emigration,[135] there has also been a growth in the study of Irish emigrants in Australia,[136] New Zealand,[137] Canada,[138] and Britain,[139] of which Lynn Lee's *Exiles of Erin* (Manchester 1979) is an outstanding example. It has also been shown that emigrant behaviour, in addition to its intrinsic interest, can tell us much about the society from which the emigrants have emigrated.[140]

On Irish intellectual history, or the social history of language and literature (as distinct from literary history),[141] the works of the last decade have been relatively few, but full of interest. Irish historians have reflected on their subject and on some of its practitioners in times past,[142] and there have been a number of forays into the history of ideas and their dissemination.[143] In this context, also, we should note that throughout the seventies Irish social and cultural geographers have continued to insist, very properly, on the importance of 'habitat' and of the physical environment in any explanation of history, and their writings have helped irish historians move a little closer to the most fruitful aspects of *annaliste* historical writing.[144] Physical evidence of the past, though of a very different kind, can be found in the growing number of photograph collections which have been published during the decade.[145] Finally, the social history of leisure has had a few extra items added to its shelf; but here, as in so many other areas of social history, there is an abundant harvest awaiting the resourceful student.[146]

In conclusion we may say that it has long been acknowledged that the nineteen thirties was the crucial decade in the establishment of professional historical scholarship in modern Ireland. The conceptual and methodological innovations of the past decade, and the widening horizons on the scope and significance of economic and social history, suggest that, at least so far as the period of the Union is concerned, the nineteen seventies may come in time to be recognised as another, equally significant, watershed in Irish historical scholarship.

IRISH HISTORIOGRAPHY, 1800–1921

1 The end of the decade saw the establishment of the federation of local history societies in Ulster; this ought to give a lead to the rest of the country, and, hopefully, to raise general standards.

2 Its journal, *Irish Economic and Social History* (1974–) is published annually.

3 Its journal, *Saothar: The journal of the Irish Labour History Society* (1975–) is published annually.

4 See, for example, Trevor Parkhill, 'Business records in Co. Kildare' in *Kildare Arch. Soc. Jn.*, xv, 262-7. Ibid., 'Business records survey in Co. Longford', in *Teathbha*, i, 226-7. John O'Brien, 'Business history' in *Ir. Archives Bull.*, ii. no. 1., pp. 50–7

5 The *Irish Archives Bulletin* (the journal of the *Irish Society for Archives)* began publication in 1971. Among the new publications of more limited interest one should note the *Irish Baptist History Society Journal* (1968–).

6 This, of course, means writings on Irish history, and not by Irish historians only. In fact, some of the most innovative work (conceptually and methodologically) of the seventies has come from non-Irish historians – from North American, continental European, British and Australian scholars.

7 Also, the annual lists of relevant publications in such journals as the *Economic History Review* or the *Agricultural History Review* contain Irish entries.

8 See also the more limited bibliographical handbooks: Joseph L. Altholz, *Victorian England, 1837–1901* (Cambridge 1970), and Alfred F. Havighurst, *Modern England, 1901–1970* (Cambridge, 1976); D. J. Munroe (ed.), *Writings in British History, 1949–51* (London, 1975), all of which contain Irish entries.

9 See also 'A bibliography of works on Irish history published in the U.S.S.R.' in *Saothar 2.*, pp. 62–3.

10 See also a brief survey on *Libraries and Archives: no. 10 — Ireland* by C. J. Woods and R. J. Hunter in *History,* lviii, pp. 392–6 (1973).

11 For a very different perspective, see Thomas E. Hachey, *Britain and Irish separatism from the Fenians to the Free State, 1867–1922* (Chicago, 1977). See also Maurice Goldring, *Irlande: ideologie d'une revolution nationale* (Paris, 1975); Francis Shaw's assault on the militant separatist tradition in 'The Canon or Irish history – a challenge', in *Studies,* lxi, 117–53 (1972). In Brian de Breffry (ed.), *The Irish World* (London,

1977), there are two chapters on the period of the Union, Gearóid ó Tuathaigh, 'The Distressed Society 1800–1918', and Kevin B. Nowlan, 'Modern Ireland: the birth and growth of the new state', pp. 172–98 and 256–80 respectively.

[12] R. Dudley Edwards, *A new history of Ireland* (Dublin, 1972); Pierre Joannon, *Histoire de l'Irlande* (Paris, 1973); René Fréchet, *Histoire d'Irlande; Tome I. Milieu et Histoire* (Paris 1970), Lawrence J. McCaffrey, *Ireland from colony to nation-state* (Englewood Cliffs, N. Jersey, 1979); Oliver MacDonagh, *Ireland: the union and its aftermath*. (Revised edn. London, 1977)

[13] H. H. Van der Wusten, *Iers verzet tegen de staatkurdige eenheit den Britise Eilanden 1800–1921: een politick geographische studie van integratie – en disintegratieprocessen*. (Amsterdam, 1977)

[14] Peter Jupp, *British and Irish elections, 1784–1831*, (Newton Abbot, 1973); and 'County Down elections 1783–1831', in *I(rish) H(istorical) S(tudies)*, xviii, pp. 177–206 (1972).

[15] For an interesting glimpse of clandestine politics see Marianne Elliott, 'The Despard Conspiracy reconsidered' in *Past and Present*, no. 75 (1977), pp 46–61.

[16] A.P.W. Malcomson, *John Foster: The politics of the Anglo-Irish ascendancy* (Oxford, 1978). Also, Public Record Office of Northern Ireland, *An Anglo-Irish dialogue: a calendar of the correspondence between John Foster and Lord Sheffield, 1774–1821* (Belfast, 1976).

[17] Angus MacIntyre, *The Liberator: Daniel O'Connell and the Irish Party, 1830–47* (London and New York, 1965).

[18] Jacqueline Hill, 'Nationalism and the Catholic Church in the 1840's: views of Dublin repealers', in *I.H.S.*, xix, 371–95.

F. A. D'Arcy, 'The artisans of Dublin and Daniel O'Connell, 1830–47: an unquiet liaison', in *I.H.S.*, xvii, 221–43.

Also, P. Holohan, 'Daniel O'Connell and the Dublin trades: a collision, 1837–8', in *Saothar, I.*, 1–17 (1975)

[19] See, Fergus O'Ferrall, 'The growth of political consciousness in Ireland 1824–1848' (Thesis abstract) in *Ir. Econ. and Soc. Hist.*, vi (1979), pp. 70–71; 'The struggle for Catholic emancipation in county Longford 1824–29', in *Teathbha: Journal of the Longford Hist. Soc.*, I 4 (1978), pp. 259–69.

[20] Maura Murphy, 'Municipal reform and the Repeal movement in Cork, 1833–44' in *Cork Hist. Soc. Jn.*, lxxxi, 1–18; 'Repeal, popular politics and the Catholic clergy of Cork, 1840–50', in *ibid*, lxxxii, 39–48.

[21] R. Dudley Edwards, *Daniel O'Connell and his world* (London, 1975).

²² Essay by Oliver MacDonagh in Brian Farrell (ed.), *The Irish Parliamentary Tradition* (Dublin, 1973).

²³ Maurice R. O'Connell, 'Daniel O'Connell: income, expenditure and despair' in *I.H.S.*, xvii, 200–20; 'Daniel O'Connell and religious freedom' in *Thought,* 1, no. 197, 176–87; 'O'Connell, Young Ireland and violence' in *Thought* liii, no. 207, 318–46; Raymond Moley, *Daniel O'Connell : nationalism without violence* (New York, 1974); Douglas C. Riach, 'Daniel O'Connell and American anti slavery' in *I.H.S.*, xx, 3–25.

²⁴ Gearóid Ó Tuathaigh, 'Gaelic Ireland, popular politics and Daniel O'Connell' in *Galway Arch. and Hist. Soc. Jn.*, xxxiv, 20–34; Caoimhín Ó Danachair, 'O'Connell i mbéalaibh na ndaoine' in *Studia Hibernica,* xiv, 40–66.

²⁵ A. D. Kriegel, 'The Irish policy of Lord Grey's government', in *E.H.R.*, lxxxvi, 22–45. Also A. D. Kriegel (ed.), *The Holland House Diaries, 1831–1840* (London, 1977); G. I. T. Machin, 'Resistance to Repeal of the Test and Corporation Acts, 1828' in *Hist. Jn.*, xxii, no 1, 115–139. Norman Gash, *Sir Robert Peel* (London, 1972).

²⁶ See also: Gerald J. Lyne, 'Daniel O'Connell, intimidation and the Kerry elections of 1835', in *Kerry Arch. Soc. Jn.*, iv, 74–97; Leon Ó Broin, 'The trial and imprisonment of O'Connell in 1843' in *Eire–Ireland,* viii, no. 4, 39–54; Francis Griffith, 'Daniel O'Connell's most famous case: the trial of John Magee, 26 July, 1813' in *Eire–Ireland,* ix, no. 2., 90–106; Maurice O'Connell, 'O'Connell reconsidered' in *Studies,* lxiv, 107–19; Elizabeth Petuchowski, 'Mr. Punch and Daniel O'Connell', *Eire–Ireland,* vii, no. 4, 12–31.

²⁷ Maurice O'Connell (ed.), *The Correspondence of Daniel O'Connell,* 6 vols. (vols, 1–2 Shannon, vols. 3–6 Dublin, 1972–79).

²⁸ For a stimulating discussion of these elements in Irish history, see: Patrick O'Farrell, 'Millenialism, messianism and utopianism in Irish history', in *Anglo-Irish Studies,* ii, 45–68; also, K. Danaher, *The Year in Ireland* (Cork, 1972); 'The Death of a tradition' in *Topic 24.*, pp. 5–18 (1972).

²⁹ H. F. Kearney, 'Fr. Matthew: Apostle of modernisation' in Art Cosgrove and Donal McCartney (ed.) *Studies in Irish History* (Naas, 1979) pp. 164–175.

³⁰ K. Theodore Hoppen, 'Politics, the law, and the nature of the Irish electorate 183–1850', in *E.H.R.*, xcii, no. CCXV, pp. 746–76

³¹ K. Theodore Hoppen,: Landlords, society and electoral politics in mid-nineteenth century Ireland', in *Past and Present,* no. 75 (1977), 62–93; 'Tories, Catholics and the general election of 1859' in *Hist. Jn.,* xii

(1970), 48–67; 'National politics and local realities in mid-nineteenth century Ireland', in Art Cosgrove and Donal McCartney (ed.), *Studies in Irish History* (Naas, 1979), pp. 190–227.

[32] B. M. Walker (ed.), *Parliamentary Election Results in Ireland, 1801–1922*. (Dublin, for the Royal Irish Academy, 1978); 'The Irish Electorate, 1868–1914' in *I.H.S.*, xviii, 359–406; 'Irish election poll-books, 1832–72: part I' in *Irish Booklore*, iii, no. 1., pp. 8–27.

[33] On a minor chord, see also : W. V. Hadden, 'The election of 1841 or the reign of terror in Carlow' in *Carloviana*, new series, i, no. 19, pp. 21–4; P. J. Kavanagh, 'Thomas Kavanagh, M.P. 1767–1837 and his political contemporaries' in *Carloviana*, ii, no. 26, pp. 4–6; Liam McNiffe, 'The 1852 Leitrim election', *Breifne*, v, no. 18, 185–205.

[34] Two valuable essays on the conduct of politics under the impact of the famine are: F. Darrell Munsell, 'Charles Edward Trevelyan and Peelite Irish famine policy 1845–6' in *Societas,* i (1971), pp. 299–315; and K. B. Nowlan's essay on parliament's response to the famine in Brian Farrell (ed.) *The Irish Parliamentary Tradition* (Dublin, 1973)

[35] But, for exceptions, see Mary Buckley, 'John Mitchel, Ulster and Irish nationality, 1842–8.' in *Studies,* lxv, 30–44; Sean Cronin, 'John Mitchel's call to protestant Ulster' in *Capuchin Annual,* 1976, pp. 81–92, and 'The country did not turn out: the Young Ireland rising of 1848' in *Eire–Ireland,* xi, no. 2, 3–17. Also, Brendán Ó Cathaoir, *John Mitchel* (Dublin, 1979).

[36] W. S. Neidhardt, *Fenianism in north America* (Pennsylvania 1975); Hereward Senior, *The Fenians and Canada* (Toronto 1978); D. C. Lyne and Peter M. Toner, 'Fenianism in Canada, 1874–84', in *Studia Hibernica,* xii, 27–76; Peter Toner, 'The military organisation of the Canadian Fenians, 1866–70' in *Irish Sword,* x, 26–37; also, E.E.R. Green, 'The Fenians Abroad' in T. D. Williams (ed.), *Secret Societies in Ireland* (Dublin 1973), 79–89.

[37] Seán Ó Lúing, *Ó Donnabháin Rossa II* (Baile Átha Cliath 1979); R. V. Comerford, *Charles Kickham: Fenian Leader and Popular Novelist* (Dublin, 1979). Also, Breandan Ó Cathaoir, 'John O'Mahony, 1815–77' in *Capuchin Annual,* xliv, pp. 180–93.

[38] T. W. Moody and Leon Ó Broin (ed.), 'The I.R.B. supreme council 1868–78', in *I.H.S.,* xix, 286–332; Leon Ó Broin, 'A Charles Kickham correspondence' in *Studies,* lxiii, 251–8; Denis Clarke, 'Letters from the underground: the Fenian correspondence of James Gibbons' in *American Catholic Hist. Soc. of Philadelphia Records,* lxxxi, 83–95; Séamas Pender, 'Fenian papers in the Catholic University of America: a prelimi-

nary survey', 8 parts, in *Cork Hist. Soc. Jn.,* lxxv, 36–53; lxxvi, 25–47, 137–149; lxxviii, 14–26, lxxix, 1–13, lxxx, 61–73; lxxxi, 120–133.

[39] K. B. Nowlan, 'The Fenians at home' in T. D. Williams (ed.), *Secret Societies in Ireland* (Dublin 1973), pp. 90-99; A. J. Sample, 'The Fenian infiltration of the British Army' in *Journal of the Society for Army Historical Research* (London, Autumn 1974), LIII, no. 211, pp. 133-60.

[40] Seán Ó Lúing, 'Aspects of the Fenian rising in Kerry', 5 parts: in *Kerry Arch. Soc. Jn.,* iii, 131-53; iv, 139-64; v, 103-32; vi, 172-94; vii, 107-33.

[41] For Fenian links with international socialism, see Cormac Ó Gráda, 'Fenianism and socialism: the career of Joseph Patrick McDonnell' in *Saothar,* I (1975), 31-41; John W. Boyle, 'Ireland and the First International', in *Jn. of British Studies,* xi, no. 2 (1972), pp. 44-62. See also, Paul Rose, *The Manchester Martyrs: a Fenian Tragedy* (London 1970).

[42] J. Lee, 'The Ribbonmen', pp. 26-35; H. Senior, 'The Early Orange Order 1795-1840', 36-45; T. de Vere White, 'The freemasons', 46-57; R Hawkins, 'Government versus secret societies: the Parnell era', 100-112; Leon Ó Broin, 'The Invincibles', 113-25; T. D. Williams, 'The Irish Republican Brotherhood', 138-149.

See also: W. F. Mandle, 'The I.R.B. and the beginnings of the Gaelic Athletic Association', in *I.H.S.,* xx, no. 80, 418-38; Leon Ó Broin, 'Revolutionary nationalism in Ireland: The I.R.B. 1858-1924' in T. W. Moody (ed.), *Nationality and the pursuit of national independence* (Belfast 1978), pp 97-119.

[43] See: Joseph Lee, *The Modernisation of Irish Society 1848-1918* (1973) for a strong presentation of this case. A recent study which addresses itself to some of these issues is Paul Bew, *Land and the National Question in Ireland 1852-82* (Dublin 1978).

[44] E. D. Steele, 'Gladstone and Ireland' in *I.H.S.,* xvii (1970), pp 58-88; 'Cardinal Cullen and Irish nationality' in *I.H.S.,* xix, (1975), pp. 239-60; 'Tenant-right and Nationality in 19th century Ireland' in *Proc. Leeds Phil. and Lit Soc.,* xv, pt. 4 (1974); *Irish Land and British Politics: Tenant-Right and Nationality 1865-70* (Cambridge 1974); 'Gladstone, Irish violence, and Conciliation' in Cosgrove and McCartney (ed.), *Studies in Irish history* (Naas 1979), pp. 257-78.

[45] Steele has also argued that Mill's radicalism on Ireland was more limited than has been supposed, and was limited by Mill's being a patriot and an imperialist. See: E. D. Steele, 'J. S. Mill and the Irish Question' Parts I and II, *Historical Journal,* xiii (1970), no. 2, 216-236 and no. 3, 419-450.

[46] R. F. Foster, *Charles Stewart Parnell: the man and his family* (Sussex 1976). See also: F. S. L. Lyons, 'The political ideas of Parnell' in *Historical Journal*, xvi (1973), 749-75; 'Parnellism and crime' in *Royal Hist. Soc. Trans.*, xxiv (1974), 123-40; Ged Martin, 'Parnell at Cambridge: the education of an Irish nationalist', in *I.H.S.*, xix, 72-82; Michael V. Hazel, 'The Young Charles Stewart Parnell' in *Eire-Ireland*, viii, no. 2, 42–61; T. W. Moody, 'Anne Parnell and the Land League' in *Hermathena*, cxvii, 5–17; Frederick C. Stern, 'The other Parnell' in *Eire-Ireland*, vii, no. 3, 3–11; Joyce Marlow, *The uncrowned queen of Ireland: the life of Kitty O'Shea* (London, 1975); J. Enoch Powell, 'Kilmainham – The Treaty that never was', *Hist. Jn.* xxi (1978), 949–959.

[47] Joseph V. O'Brien, *William O'Brien and the course of Irish politics, 1881-1918* (Berkeley 1976); P. M. Bottomley, 'The north Fermanagh elections of 1885 and 1886: some documentary illustrations' in *Clogher Record*, vii (1974), 167–93; John Magee, 'The Monaghan election of 1883 and the "invasion of Ulster",' in *Clogher Record*. vii, (1974), 147–66; Frank Thompson, 'The Armagh elections of 1885–6' in *Seanchus Ardmhacha*, vii, 360–85

[48] Both of these areas are discussed below.

[49] See also: P. Alter, 'Symbols of Irish Nationalism', *Studia Hibernica*, no. 14 (1974), 104–23.

[50] Peter Davis, 'The Liberal Unionist Party and the Irish policy of Lord Salisbury's government, 1886–92' in *Historical Journal*, xviii (1975), 85–104. Also: Paul Felix Thiede, *Chamberlain, Irland und das Weltreich 1880-95*. (Frankfurt um Main 1977).

[51] T. W. Heyck, *The dimensions of British radicalism: the case of Ireland 1874-95*. (Urbana 1974); Feargus D'Arcy, 'Charles Bradlaugh and the Irish question: a study in the nature and limits of British radicalism 1853–91', in Cosgrove and McCartney (ed.) *Studies in Irish History* (Naas 1980), 190-227. See also: Joseph M. Hernon, 'The historian as politician: G. O. Trevelyan as Irish chief secretary' in *Eire-Ireland*, viii, no. 3, 3–15.

[52] A. B. Cooke and J. R. Vincent, 'Herbert Gladstone, Forster and Ireland, 1881–2', 2 parts, in *I.H.S.*, xvii, 521–48 and xviii, 74–89; 'Lord Spencer on the Phoenix Park murders', in *I.H.S.*, xviii, 583–91; *Lord Carlingford's Journal: reflections of a Cabinet Minister, 1885*. (Oxford, 1971); A. B. Cooke, 'A Conservative party leader in Ulster: Sir Stafford Northcote's diary of a visit to the province, October, 1883' in *R.I.A. Proc.*, lxxv, C, pp. 61–84.

[53] A. B. Cooke and J. R. Vincent, *The Governing Passion: Cabinet*

Government and Party Politics in Britain 1885–6. (Brighton 1974); J. R. Vincent, *Gladstone and Ireland* (1979); Also, *Andrew Jones, The Politics of Reform,* 1884 (Cambridge 1972). For those who would like the 'real' Gladstone to speak up, see: M. R. D. Foot and H. C. G. Matthew (ed.), *The Gladstone Diaries,* 6 volumes to date, 1825–68 (Oxford 1968).

[54] For ideology, see: C. Harvie, *The Lights of Liberalism: University intellectuals and the challenge of Demorcracy 1860-86* (London 1976); 'Ideology and home rule: James Bryce, A. V. Dicey and Ireland, 1880–87' in *E.H.R.,* xci, 298–314; T. H. Ford, 'Dicey's conversion to unionism' in *I.H.S.,* xviii, 552–82; 'Dicey's polemic against Parnell', in *Studies,* 1xv, 210–24; T. R. Green, 'The English Catholic Press and the home rule bill, 1885-6' in *Eire-Ireland,* x, no. 3, pp. 18–37. For prejudices see, L. P. Curtis, *Apes and Angels: the Irishman in Victorian caricature* (Newton Abbot 1971); R. N. Lebow, *White Britain and Black Ireland: the influence of stereotypes on Colonial Policy* (Philadelphia 1976); Danie T. Dorrity, 'Monkeys in a menagerie: the imagery of unionist oppostion to Home Rule, 1886–93', in *Eire-Ireland,* xii, no. 3, 5–22.

[55] Patrick Buckland, *Irish Unionism: vol. 1. The Anglo-Irish and the new Ireland 1885-1922* (Dublin 1972); *Irish Unionism: vol. II. Ulster Unionism and the origin of northern Ireland, 1886-1922* (Dublin and New York 1973); *Irish Unionism,.1885-1923: a documentary history* (Belfast 1973); 'The unity of Ulster Unionism, 1886–1939' in *History,* 1x, 211–23.

[56] J. C. Beckett, *The Anglo-Irish Tradition* (London 1976); Terence de Vere White, *The Anglo-Irish* (London 1972); W. B. Stanford and R. B. McDowell, *Mahaffy: a biography of an Anglo-Irishman* (London 1971); L. P. Curtis, 'The Anglo-Irish predicament', *Twentieth Century Studies;* (November 1970); See also, F. S. L. Lyons, *Culture and Anarchy in Ireland, 1890-1939* (Oxford 1979), especially pp. 57–83. For a personal perspective see, Jack White, *Minority Report: the Protestant community in the Irish Republic* (Dublin 1975).

[57] Ian d'Alton, 'Southern Irish unionism: a study of Cork unionists' in *Roy. Hist. Soc. Trans.,* 5th series, xxiii, 71–88; 'Cork unionism: its role in parliamentary and local elections 1885–1914' in *Studia Hibernica,* xv (1975), 143–61; 'A contrast in crises: Southern Irish Protestantism, 1820–43 and 1885–1910', in A. C. Hepburn (ed), *Minorities in History* (London 1978), 70–83.

[58] T. W. Moody, *The Ulster Question, 1603-1973* (Dublin and Cork 1974); Liam de Paor, *Divided Ulster* (London 1970); Owen Dudley Edwards, *The sins of our fathers: roots of conflict in Northern Ireland.* (Dublin 1970); A. T. Q. Stewart, *The narrow ground: aspects of Ulster*

1609-1969. See also Gilbert A. Cahill, 'Some nineteenth century roots of the Ulster problem, 1829-1848' in *Irish University Review*, i, 215–37.

⁵⁹ D. W. Miller, *Queen's rebels: Ulster loyalists in historical perspective* (Dublin 1978).

⁶⁰ John F. Harbinson, *The Ulster Unionist Party, 1882-1973: its development and organisation* (Belfast 1973)

⁶¹ Michael Farrell, *Northern Ireland: The Orange State* (London 1976).

⁶² Paul Bew, 'The problem of Irish Unionism' in *Economy and Society*, vi, no. 1, 89-109; Henry Patterson, 'Conservative politics and class conflict in Belfast', *Saothar*, 2, 22–32; 'The new unionism and Belfast' in *Soc. for the Study of Labour Hist. Bull.*, no. 35, pp. 7-9. For an excellent review of the Gibbon thesis, see Sybil Gribbon, 'The social origins of Ulster Unionism' in *Jr. Econ, and Soc. Hist.*, iv (1977), pp 66–72; See also, Paul Bew, Peter Gibbon and Henry Patterson, *The State in Northern Ireland 1921–72* (Manchester 1979), Ch. 2., 44–50; F. Wright, 'Protestant politics and ideology in Ulster', in *European Jn. of Sociology*, xiv (1973), 213–80.

⁶³ I. Budge & C. O'Leary, *Belfast: Approach to crisis* (London 1973); S. E. Baker, 'Orange and Green: Belfast 1832–1912', in H. J. Dyos and M. Wolff (ed.), *The Victorian City: Images and Realities* (London 1973), II, pp 789–814; A. C. Hepburn, 'Catholics in the North of Ireland 1850–1921' in A. C. Hepburn (ed.), *Minorities in History.* (London 1978), 84–101. Also, Aiken McClelland, 'Orangism in county Monaghan' in *Clogher Rec.*, ix, 3, pp 384–404.

⁶⁴ F. X. Martin and F. J. Byrne (Ed.), *The Scholar Revolutionary: Eoin Mac Neill: 1867-1945;* (Dublin 1973); N. P. Mansergh, 'Eoin Mac Neill: a reappraisal' in *Studies*, 1xiii (1974), 133–40; Richard P. Davies, *Arthur Griffith and non-violent Sinn Fein* (Dublin 1974); Donal McCartney, 'Arthur Griffith' in *Jn. Contemp. Hist.*, viii, no. 1, 3–19; Seán Ó Lúing, 'Arthur Griffith, 1871–1922: thoughts on a centenary' in *Studies*, 1x, 127–38; Carlton Younger, *A State of Disunion: Arthur Griffith, Michael Collins, James Craig and Eamonn de Valera* (London 1972); Seán Ó Lúing, *I die in a good cause: a study of Thomas Ashe, idealist and revolutionary* (Tralee 1970); J. Anthony Gaughan, *Austin Stack: Portrait of a separatist* (Dublin 1977); Diarmuid Ó Murchadha, *Liam de Róiste* (Dublin 1976); Ruth Dudley Edwards, *Patrick Pearse: the triumph of failure* (London 1977); David Thornley, 'Patrick Pearse and the Pearse family', in *Studies* 1x, 322–46; Frank Pakenham and Thomas P. O'Neill, *Eamonn de Valera* (London 1970); Tomás P. Ó'Neill agus P. Ó Fiannachta, *Eamonn de Valera* (Baile Atha Cliath 1970), iml. ii; Andrew

Boyle, *The riddle of Erskine Childers* (London 1977); B. Wilkinson, *The Zeal of the convert: the life of Erskine Childers* (Washington 1976); Tom Cox, *Dammed Englishman: a study of Erskine Childers* (New York 1975); Michael McInerney, *The riddle of Erskine Childers* (Dublin 1971); C. Desmond Greaves, *Liam Mellows and the Irish Revolution* (London 1971); Margery Forester, *Michael Collins - the lost leader* (London 1971); Brian Inglis, *Casement* (London 1973); B. L. Reid, *The lives of Roger Casement* (New Haven and London 1976); Karin Wolf, *Sir Roger Casement und die deutsch-irischen Beziehungen* (Berlin 1972); Samuel Levenson, *Maud Gonne* (London 1976); Sean Cronin, *Young Connolly* (Dublin 1978); Roger Faligot, *James Connolly et le mouvement revolutionaire irlandais* (Paris 1978); Owen Dudley Edwards and Bernard Ransom (ed.), *James Connolly: selected political writings* (London 1973); Seán Cronin, 'Connolly's leap in the dark' in *Capuchin Annual*, xliv, 309–24; Carol and Ann Barton Reeve, *James Connolly and the United States: the road to the 1916 Irish rebellion.* (Atlantic Highlands, N. J. 1978); Tomás Ó Dochartaigh, *Cathal Brugha* (Dublin 1971); Labhrás Breathnach, *An Pluincéadach* (Dublin 1971); Earnán de Blaghad, *Slán le h– Ultaibh* (Dublin 1970) and *Gaeil á Múscailt* (Dublin 1973)

[65] Patricia Jalland, 'A Liberal Chief Secretary and the Irish question: Augustine Birrell 1907–14' in *Hist. Jn.*, xix (1976), 421–51; 'United Kingdom Devolution, 1910–14: political panacea or tactical diversion' in *E.H.R.*, xciv, (1979), 757–85; A. C. Hepburn, 'The Irish Council Bill and the fall of Sir Anthony MacDonnell, 1906–7', in *I.H.S.*, xvii, no. 65, 89–112; George Dangerfield, *The Damnable Question* (London 1977); D. G. Boyce, 'Dicey, Kilbrandon and devolution' in *Political Quarterly*, xlvi, 280–92; John D. Fair, 'The King, the constitution and Ulster: inter-party negotiations of 1913 and 1914' in *Eire-Ireland*, vi, no. 1. 35–52; D. W. Savage, 'The Parnell of Wales has become the Chamberlain of England: Lloyd George and the Irish question' in *Jn. British Studies*, xii, 86–108; Ronan Fanning, 'The Irish policy of Asquith's government and the cabinet crisis of 1910' in Cosgrove and McCartney (ed.), *Studies in Irish history* (Naas 1979), pp 279–303; J. O. Baylen, 'What Mr. Redmond thought: an unpublished interview with John Redmond, December 1906' in *I.H.S.*, xix, 169–189.

[66] Catherine B. Shannon, 'The Ulster Liberal Unionists and local government reform, 1885–98' in *I.H.S.*, xviii, 407–23; D. G. Boyce, 'British Conservative opinion, the Irish question and the partition of Ireland', in *I.H.S.*, xvii, 89–112; Ronan Fanning, op. cit., no. 65; see also: Wolfgang Hunseler, *Das Deutsche Kaiserreich und die Irische Frage*

1900-1914. (Frankfurt am Main 1978).

[67] D. G. Boyce and Cameron Hazlehurst, 'The Unknown Chief Secretary: H. E. Duke and Ireland, 1916–18' in *I.H.S.,* xx. 286–311; J. M. McEwen, 'The Liberal Party and the Irish question during the first world war' in *Jn. Brit. Studies,* xii, 109–31; John Kendle, 'Federalism and the Irish problem in 1918' in *History,* lvi, 207–30; R. B. McDowell, *The Irish convention 1917–18* (London Toronto 1970); D. G. Boyce, 'British opinion, Ireland and the war, 1916–18' in *Hist Jn.,* xvii (1974), 575–93; Alan J. Ward, 'Lloyd George and the 1918 Irish conscription crisis', in *Hist. Jn.,* xvii (1974), 107–129; A. P. Haydon, 'Sir Matthew Nathan: Ireland and before' in *Studia Hibernica,* xv, 162–76; Leon Ó Broin, *Dublin Castle and the 1916 Rising* (Revised edn. London 1970).

[68] Brian Farrell, *The Founding of Dáil Eireann: parliament and nation building.* (Dublin 1971); Michael Laffan, 'The Sinn Fein party 1916–21' in *Capuchin Annual,* xxxvii, 227–35; 'The unification of Sinn Fein in 1971' in *I.H.S.,* xvii (1971), 353-79.

[69] M. H. Hopkinson, 'Irish Americans and the Anglo-Irish treaty of 1921', in Peter Jupp and John Bossy (ed), *Essays presented to Michael Roberts* (Belfast 1976); see also, Sean Cronin (ed.), *The McGarrity papers: revelations of the Irish revolutionary movement in Ireland and America, 1900-40* (Tralee 1972); Thomas E. Hachey, 'The British foreign office and new perspectives on the Irish issue in Anglo-American relations, 1919-21' in *Eire-Ireland,* vii, no. 2. 3–13; Donal McCartney, 'De Valera's mission to the United States, 1919–20' in Cosgrove and McCartney (ed.), *Studies in Irish history* (Naas 1979), 304–323.

[70] John D. Fair, 'The Anglo-Irish treaty of 1921: unionist aspects of the peace', *Jn. Brit. Studies,* xii, 132-49; Thomas E. Hachey, 'The partition of Ireland and the Ulster dilemma' in T. E. Hachey (ed.), *The problem of partition: peril to world peace* (Chicago 1972); Joseph M. Curran, 'Lloyd George and the Irish settlement, 1921–22' in *Eire-Ireland,* vii, no. 2, 14-46; D. G. Boyce, *Englishmen and Irish Troubles* (London 1972); 'British Conservative opinion, the Ulster question, and the partition of Ireland 1919-21' in *I.H.S.,* xvii, 98–112; Oliver Snoddy, 'From the bridge to the abyss' in *Capuchin Annual,* xxxix, 315-50; Alec Wilson, *PR elections in Ulster, 1920* (London 1972); Virginia E. Glandon, 'John Dillon's reflections on Irish and general politics, 1919-21' in *Eire-Ireland,* ix, no. 3, 21-43; David W. Harkness, 'England's Irish question' in G. Peele and C. Cooke (ed.), *The politics of re-appraisal* (London 1975). For a particularly perceptive treatment of the partition question, see N. P. Mansergh, 'The Government of Ireland Act, 1920, its origins and purposes: the

working of the official mind' in *Historical Studies,* ix, 19–48; and, *The prelude to partition: concepts and aims in Ireland and India* (Cambridge 1978). The Irish debate on the Treaty is discussed in two chapters by F.S.L. Lyons in Brian Farrell (ed.), *The Irish Parliamentary Tradition* (Dublin 1973).

[71] E. Rumpf and A. C. Hepburn. *Nationalism and Socialism in twentieth century Ireland* (Liverpool 1977) is, in fact, a revised and re-written edition of Rumpf's original work.

[72] David Fitzpatrick, 'The geography of Irish nationalism, 1910–21' in *Past and Present,* no. 78 (1978), 112-144.

[73] See, A. Alexander, 'Local government in Ireland' in *Administration,* xvii, no. 1, 3–30; Ann Barry, 'Youghal corporation records' in *Ir. Arch. Bull.,* iv, 30–33; B. M. H. Patterson, 'The Chapter closes', in *Nth. Ir. Leg. Quart.* xxi, 33–46

[74] William L. Feingold, 'The tenants movement to capture the Irish poor law boards, 1877–86' in *Albion,* vii, no. 3 (1975). *The Irish boards of poor law guardians, 1872–86: a revolution in local government.* (Unpublished Ph.D. thesis, Univ. of Chicago, 1974).

[75] Mary Daly, 'The development of the national school system, 1831–40' in Cosgrove and McCartney (ed.), *Studies in Irish history* (Naas 1979), 150–163; see also Patrick J. Dowling, *A History of Irish education* (Dublin 1971); T. J. Duncan, *History of Irish Education since 1800* (Merioneth 1972).

[76] P. J. McCusker, 'Nineteenth century National Schools in the parish of Donacavey', in *Clogher Rec.,* x, 52–109; M. Tóibín, 'The school beside the chapel', *The Past,* 8 (1970), 18–23; Sr. Mary de Lourdes Fahy, *Education in the diocese of Kilmacduagh in the 19th century* (Gort 1972); Harold O'Sullivan, 'The emergence of the national system of education in north county Louth (diocese of Armagh)', in *Louth Arch. Soc. Jn.,* xviii, 7–38; Harry Gott, 'Education in Enniscorthy, 1800–1900', 2 parts, *The Past,* x, xi, pp. 3–18, 37–57; Dorothy Rudd, *Rochelle, The history of a school in Cork, 1829-1979;* Mary Malone, 'Education in Drogheda through the ages' in *Old Drogheda Soc. Jn.,* 1976, 29–36; Kenneth Milne, 'Irish Chapter Schools', in *Ir. Jn. Education,* viii, 1974, 3–29; John Logan, 'Education and proselytesing in Ireland' in *Capuchin Annual,* 1976, 241–50; 'Oughteragh in 1826: a case study of rural sectarianism' in *Breifne,* v, 74–120; Aiken McClelland, 'The early history of Brown street primary school' in *Ulster Folklife,* xvii, 52–60; Michael Quane, 'Primary education in Kerry one hundred years ago' in *Kerry Arch. Soc. Jn.,* v, 133–59; Tadhg Ó Ceallaigh, 'Disestablishment and Church education' in

Studia Hibernica, x, 36–69; *St. Patrick's College, Drumcondra, Centenary booklet 1875–1975 (Dublin 1975);* T. B. Cunningham and D. Gallogly, *St. Patrick's College and the earlier Kilmore Academy a centenary history* (Cavan 1974); Nollaig Ó Gadhra, *Eamonn Iognáid Rís* (Dublin 1977); Seamas Ó Buachalla, 'Education as an issue in the first and second Dáil' in *Administration*, xxv, i, 57–75; Mary McNeill, *Vere Foster 1819–1900: an Irish benefactor* (Newton Abbot 1971); F.O.C. Meenan, 'The Catholic University School of Medicine 1860–80' in *Studies,* lxvi, no. 262, pp. 135–44.

[77] See also, the discussion of nineteenth century education at all three levels in P. J. Corish (ed.), *A History of Irish Catholicism,* vol 5, fasc. 6 (Dublin 1971).

[78] e.g. Justin Wallace, 'Science teaching in Irish schools 1860–1970', in *Irish Jn. of Educ.,* vi, 50–64; R. Grenfell Morton, 'Mechanics Institutes and the attempted diffusion of useful knowledge in Ireland 1825–79' in *Irish Booklore,* ii, 59–74; P. P. Ó Conchubhair, 'The early National Teachers' in *Oideas,* xviii, 5–16; see also: G. O'Flynn, 'Some aspects of the education of Irish women through the ages', *Capuchin Annual,* 1977, 114–79.

[79] Timothy P. O'Neill, 'The Catholic Church & the relief of the poor, 1815–45', in *Archivium Hibernicum,* xxxi, 13–45; 'Clare and Irish poverty, 1815–51' in *Stud. Hib.,* xiv, 7–27; Also, Thomas G. Conway, 'The approach to an Irish poor law, 1828–33' in *Eire-Ireland,* vi, no. 1, 65–81; John J. Meagher, 'South Dublin Union, 1847–52' in *Repertorium Novum,* iv, 135–58; Margaret Quinn, 'Enniskillen poor law union' in *Clogher Record,* vii, 498–513; J. A. Robins, 'Carlow workhouse during the famine years' in *Administration,* xx, 63–70; Frank Corrigan, 'Dublin workhouses during the great famine' in *Dublin Hist. Rec.,* xxix, 59–65; Michael Farrell, *The Poor Law and the workhouse in Belfast 1838-1948.* (Belfast 1978)

[80] e.g. Arthur P. Williamson, 'Armagh district lunatic asylum: the first phase', in *Seanchas Ardmhacha,* viii, 111–20; Timothy P. O'Neill, 'Fever and public health in pre-famine Ireland' in *R.S.A.J. Jn.,* cii (1973), 1–34. Also, P. Froggatt, 'Sir William Wilde, 1817–76' in *R.I.A. Proc.,* lxxxvii, section C, 261–78.

[81] e.g. J. B. Lyons, *St. Michael's hospital, Dun Laoghaire 1876-1976* (Dublin 1976); Lesley Whiteside, *A history of the King's Hospital* (Dublin 1975); J. D. H. Widdes, *The Richmond, Whitworth and Hardwicke hospitals, 1772-1972* (Dublin 1972); R. Allison, *The Seeds of Time: being a short history of the Belfast General and Royal Hospital, 1850-1903.*

(Belfast 1972).

[82] A. R. G. Griffiths, 'The Irish Board of Works in the Famine years' in *Hist. Jn.*, xiii, 634–52. Also of interest are: R. M. Wilcocks *The postal history of Great Britain and Ireland: a summarised catalogue to 1840* (London 1972), and D. Feldman and W. Kane *Handbook of Irish postal history* (Dublin 1975). Greagóir Ó Dúill, 'Founding the office: archival reform in the nineteenth century' in *Administration,* xxv, no. 4, 561–80; John McColgan, 'British Cabinet office records and the partition of the Irish administration' in *Irish Archives Bull.,* iv, 14–30.

[83] Conor Brady, *Guardians of the Peace* (Dublin 1975); Seamas Breathnach, *The Irish police force from earliest times to the present day* (Tralee 1974).

[84] Richard Hawkins, 'An army on police work, 1881–2: Ross of Bladensburg's memorandum' in *Irish Sword,* xi, 75–117; 'Government versus secret societies: the Parnell era' in T. D. Williams (ed), *Secret Societies in Ireland* (Dublin 1973) pp 100–112. See also: Peter Young, 'Military archives in the defence forces' in *An Cosantóir,* xxxvii, 274–5.

[85] Leon Ó Broin, *The Prime Informer: a suppressed scandal* (London 1971); K. R. H. Short, *The Dynamite War: Irish-American Bombers in Victorian Britain* (Dublin 1979).

[86] Jeremiah Mee, *Memoires of Constable Jeremiah Mee.* Ed. J. Anthony Gaughan. (Dublin 1975).

[87] e.g. Henry Harris, *The Royal Irish Fusiliers: the 87th and 89th regiment of foot.* (London 1972); Peter Verney, *The Micks: the story of the Irish Guards* (London 1970). See also occasional pieces in *An Cosantóir,* the journal of An Gárda Síochána.

[87a] H. J. Hanham, 'Religion and Nationality in the mid-Victorian army' in M. R. D. Foot (ed), *War and Society: Essays in honour and memory of J. M. Western 1928-71* (London 1973), 159–181.

[87b] J. Bowyer Bell, *The Secret Army* (London 1970); Tim Pat Coogan, *The I.R.A.* (London 1971); Tim Bowden, 'The Irish underground and the war of independence 1919–21' in *Jn. Contemp. Hist.,* viii, no. 3, 3–23; 'Bloody Sunday – a reappraisal' in *European Studies Rev.,* ii, 25–42; Phil Conran, 'Military and naval aviation in Ireland, 1913–22' in *An Cosantóir,* xxxii, 158–62; Ewan Butler, *Barry's Flying Column* (London 1971); M. R. D. Foot, 'The IRA and the origins of SOE' in M. R. D. Foot (ed), *War and Society,* pp. 57–69; Pierre Joannon, *Michael Collins, la naissance de l'IRA* (Paris 1978); See also a series on the war of independence in different localities in the *Capuchin Annual,* 1970. For a salutary reminder of the hazards awaiting an historian of guerilla warfare, see

Liam Deasy, *Towards Ireland Free*, Ed. John E. Chisholm (Dublin 1973), and Tom Barry, *The reality of the Anglo-Irish war 1920-21 in West Cork: refutations, corrections, and comments on Liam Deasy's 'Towards Ireland Free'* (Dublin 1974).

[88] James Casey, 'Republican courts in Ireland, 1916–22' in *Irish Jurist*, n.s. V (1970), 321–42; 'The genesis of the Dail courts' in *Irish Jurist*, ix (1974), 326–38; W. N. Osborough, 'Law in Ireland, 1916–26' in *North. Ireland Legal Quart.*, xxiii (1972), 48–81.

[89] See, for example, Edward Brynn, 'Some repercussions of the act of union on the Church of Ireland, 1801–1820', in *Church Hist.*, xl, 284–96; 'Robert Peel and the Church of Ireland', in *Jn. Relig. Hist.*, vii, 191–207.

[90] John D. Fair, 'The Irish disestablishment conference of 1869', in *Jn. Eccl. Hist.*, xxvi, 379–94; Hugh Shearman, *How the Church of Ireland was disestablished* (Dublin 1970).

[91] Desmond Bowen, *Souperism - Myth or Reality?* (Cork 1970); *The Protestant Crusade in Ireland 1800-70*. (Dublin 1978). For excellent background to the proslytising activities see, P. de Brún (ed), *Filíocht Sheáin Uí Bhraonáin* (Dublin 1972), and 'Forógra do Ghaelaibh 1824', in *Studia Hibernica*, 12, 142–166.

[92] R. P. C. Hanson, 'William Connor Magee', *Hermathena*, cxxiv, 42–55; E. W. Lavell, *A green hill far away: a life of Mrs. C. F. Alexander* (Dublin 1970).

[93] John M. Barkley, *St. Enoch's Congregation 1872-1972.* (Belfast 1972); George Carson, *The first one hundred years: a short history of Kells Presbyterian Church, Co. Antrim.* (Kells 1974); C. W. P. MacArthur, *Dunfanaghy's Presbyterian Congregation and its times* (Dunfanaghy 1978).

[94] David W. Miller, 'Presbyterianism and "modernization" in Ulster' in *Past and Present*, no. 80, 66–90. See, also, R. F. G. Holmes, 'Dr. Henry Cooke: the Athanasius of Irish Presbyterianism' in D. Baker (ed), *Religious motivation* (Oxford 1978).

[95] J. N. Barkley, 'The Presbyterian Church in Ireland and the Government of Ireland act (1920)', in D. Baker (ed), *Studies in Church History* (Oxford, 1975).

[96] David M. Weir, *Rathgar Methodist Church: Brighton Road, Dublin* (Dublin 1974); Raymond Gillespie, *Wild as Colts Untamed: Methodism and Society in Lurgan 1750-1950* (Lurgan 1977).

[97] e.g. H. D. Gribbon, 'Sources of Irish Baptist history'; 'Some lesser known sources of Irish Baptist history'; R. McMullan, 'Baptist education in Ireland'; in, respectively, *Irish Baptist History Society Journal*, viii,

14–26; vi, 61–72; iii, 21–54.

⁹⁸ Peadar Mac Suibhne (ed), *Paul cullen and his contemporaries, with their letters from 1820-1902.* iv, v (Naas 1974, 1977); P. J. Corish (ed), 'Irish College. Rome: Kirby Papers. Guide to material of public and private Interest, 1852-94' in *Archiv. Hib.*, xxx, 29–115, xxxi, 1–94, xxxii, 1–62; Also, Mark Tierney, 'A short-title calendar of the papers of archbishop William Croke in Archbishop's House, Thurles', in *Collect. Hib.*, xiii, 100–138 xvi, 97–124, xvii, 110–144; Evelyn Bolster, 'The Moylan correspondence in Bishop's House, Killarney', in *Collect. Hib.*, xiv, 82–142, xv, 56–109; P. J. Murphy, 'The papers of Nicholas Archdeacon 1800–23', in *Archiv. Hib.*, xxxi, 124–31; Raymond Murray, 'The Armagh diocesan archives', *Archiv. Hib.*, xxxii, 93–7; Katherine Walsh, 'Two letters of Cardinal Cullen, 1841 and 1873', in *Collect. Hib.*, xix, 184–212; Bartholemew Egan, 'An annotated calendar of the O'Meara papers', in *Archiv. Franciscanum Historicum,* lxviii, 78–110, 366–420; Patrick O'Donoghue, 'The Holy See and Ireland, 1780–1803', *Archiv. Hib.*, xxxiv, 99–108.

⁹⁹ Emmet Larkin, *The Roman Catholic Church and the Creation of the Modern Irish State 1878-86.* (Philadelphia 1975); *The Roman Catholic Church and the Plan of Campaign in Ireland 1886-8.* (Cork 1978); *The Roman Catholic Church in Ireland and the Fall of Parnell 1888-91.* (Liverpool 1979). Also, 'Church, state and nation in modern Ireland', in *A.H.R.*, 80, no. 5, 1244–77.

¹⁰⁰ Oliver Mac Donagh, 'The politicisation of the Irish Catholic bishops 1800–1850', in *Hist. Jn.*, xviii, 37–53; K. B. Nowlan,' 'The Catholic clergy and Irish politics in the eighteen thirties and forties', in J. G. Barry (ed), *Historical Studies, IX* (Belfast 1974), 119–35.

¹⁰¹ C. J. Woods, 'Ireland and Anglo-Papal relations 1880–85' in *I.H.S.* xviii, 29–60; 'The politics of cardinal McCabe, archbishop of Dublin, 1879–85', in *Dublin Hist. Rec.*, xxvi, 101–110.

¹⁰² But see also Patirck O'Donoghue, 'The holy see and Ireland 1780–1803', in *Archiv. Hib.*, xxxiv, 99–108.

¹⁰³ Mark Tierney, *Croke of Cashel: the life of Archbishop Thomas William Croke 1823-1902.* (Dublin 1976).

¹⁰⁴ Kieran O'Shea, 'David Moriarty 1814–77', in *Kerry Arch. Soc. Jn.*, iii, 84–98, iv, 106–126, v, 86–102, vi, 131–42. See also, O. F. Traynor, 'Dr. James Magauran, bishop of Ardagh, 1815–29' in *Breifne*, iv, 336–44; Moira Lysaght 'Daniel Murray, archbishop of Dublin, 1823–52' in *Dublin Hist. Rec.*, xxvii, 101–108; Brendan Hoban, 'Dominick Bellew 1745–1812: parish priest of Dundalk and bishop of Killala' in *Seanchas*

Ardmhacha, vi, 333–71; M. Coen, 'The election of Oliver Kelly', in *Galway Arch., Hist. Soc. Jn.*, xxxvi (1979).

105 W. M. O'Riordan, 'Succession lists of parish priests in the archdioces of Dublin, 1771–1966', in *Repertorium Novum*, iv, 33–41; P. Ó Gallachair, 'Clogherici: a dictionary of the Catholic clergy of Clogher, 1534–1835', in *Clogher Rec.*, vii, 514–28; Pilib Ó Mordha, 'Some priests and parsons of the Clones area, 1620–1840, with notes on some families of the period' in *Clogher Rec.*, 1x, 232–60; T. P. Cunningham, 'Students of Kilmore Academy 1839–1874', in *Breifne*, v, no. 18, 278–93; Francis J. McKiernan, 'Parish priests of Kilmore', in *Breifne*, iv, 370–405.

106 e.g. Fred Heatley, *St. Joseph's centenary, 1872–1972: story of a dockside parish* (Belfast 1972); Joseph Duffy (ed), *Clogher Record Album: a diocesan history* (Enniskillen 1975); Canice Mooney, *The Friars of Broad Lane: the story of a Franciscan friary in Cork, 1229–1977*. (Cork 1977); Patrick Conlan, *Franciscan Ireland* (Dublin 1978); ibid., 'The Franciscan Friary, Killarney 1860–1902', in *Kerry Arch. Soc. Jn.*, x, 77–110; P. J. Campbell, 'Towards a history of the parish of Togher', in *Seanchas Ardmhacha*, ix, 128–150; J. Coombes, 'Catholic churches of the 19th century: some newspaper sources', in *Cork Hist. Soc. Jn.*, lxxx, 2–12.

107 E. Larkin, 'The devotional revolution in Ireland, 1850–75' in *A.H.R.*, lxvii, 625–52.

108 Sr. M. A. Bolster, 'Insights into fifty years of episcopal elections, 1774–1824', *Kerry Arch. Soc. Jn.*, v, 60–76; P. J. Murphy, 'The papers of Nicholas Archdeacon, bishop of Kilmacduagh and Kilfenora 1800–23; in *Archiv Hib.*, xxxi, 124–31; Kieran O'Shea, 'Three early 19th century diocesan reports', in *Kerry Arch. Soc. Jn.*, x, 55–76; John Ainsworth (ed), 'Two letters from the Eaneas McDonnell MSS', in *Archiv. Hib.*, xxxi, 95–101.

109 See, for example, Maureen Purcell, *The story of the Vincentians* (Dublin 1973); Evelyn Bolster, *The Knights of Columbanus* (Dublin 1979); Raymond McGovern, 'Father Tom Maguire: polemicist, popular preacher and patriot', in *Breifne*, v, 279–88; Joseph P. Kelly, 'Rev. Thomas MacNamara', in *Riocht na Midhe*, v, no. 4, 60–70. For difficulties in collecting data see P. de Brún, 'A census of the parish of Ferriter, Jan 1835', and 'A census of the parishes of Prior and Killemlagh', in *Kerry Arch. Soc. Jn.*, vii, 37–70, viii, 114–35; also, Malcolm P. A. Macourt, 'The religious enquiry in the Irish census of 1861', in *I.H.S.*, xxi, no. 82, 168–87.

110 P. J. Corish, 'Gallicanism at Maynooth: Archbishop Cullen and the

Royal Visitation of 1853', in Cosgrove and McCartney (ed), *Studies in Irish History* (Naas 1979), 176–189. See, also, J, Newman, *Maynooth and Georgian Ireland* (Galway 1979).

[111] For a recent example see Karl Woste, *Englands Staats - und Kirchenpolitik in Irland 1795-1869* (Bonn 1976). For an essay which places this whole problem in a wider context see, Hilary Jenkins, 'The Irish dimension of the British Kulterkampf: Vaticanism and Civil Allegiances 1870–75', in *Jn. of Eccl. Hist.*, xxx, no. 3 (1979), 353–377.

[112] S. J. Connolly, 'Catholicism and Social Discipline in pre-famine Ireland', (Thesis abstract, D. Phil., New Univ. Ulster 1977) in *Ir. Econ. Soc. Hist.*, iv, 74–6; also, S. J. Connolly, 'Illegitimacy and pre-nuptial pregnancy in Ireland before 1864: the evidence of some Catholic parish registers', in *Ir. Econ. Soc. Hist.*, vi, 5–23.

[113] David Dickson, 'Aspects of the rise and decline of the Irish cotton industry', in Cullen and Smout (ed), *Aspects of Scottish and Irish Economic and Social history 1600-1900*. (Edinburgh 1977). For exceptions see, e.g. D. S. Jacobson, 'The political economy of industrial location: the Ford Motor Company at Cork 1912–26', in *Ir. Econ. Soc. Hist.*, IV (1977), 36–55; A. C. Davies, 'Roofing Belfast and Dublin 1896–8', in *Ir. Econ. Soc. Hist.*, IV (1977), 26–35; H. G. Bass, *Boyd's of Castle Buildings, Lisburn: a short history of an old family firm*. (Lisburn 1977); Also, P. Bottomley, *The Ulster Textile Industry: a Catalogue of Business Records in P.R.O.N.I. relating principally to the Linen industry in Ulster* (Belfast 1978); F. B. McGuire, *Irish Whiskey: a history of distilling, the spirit trade and excise controls in Ireland* (Dublin 1973); Robert Shipkey, 'Problems in Alcoholic production and controls in early 19th century Ireland', in *Hist. Jn.*, xvi (1973), 291–302.

[114] But see J. S. Donnelly, 'Cork market: its role in the nineteenth century butter trade', in *Studia Hibernica*, II (1971), 30–63; and Liam Kennedy, 'The decline of the Cork butter market: a comment', in *Studia Hibernica*, 16 (1976), 175–77.

[115] There is a stimulating discussion of the problem in J. Lee, *The modernisation of Irish society 1848-1918*. (Dublin 1973), 1–35; there are also some tantalisingly brief comments on the problem in Liam Kennedy, 'Traders in the Irish rural economy 1881–1901', in *Econ. H.R.*, xxxii, no. 2, 201–210, and also in the articles cited in n. 114 above.

[116] On banking and credit, see also Lennox Barrow, 'The use of money in mid-nineteenth century Ireland', in *Studies*, 1ix, 81–8; G. L. Barrow, 'Justice for Thomas Mooney', in *Dublin Hist. Rec.*, xxiv, 173–188; A valuable case-study is J. B. O'Brien, 'Sadlier's Bank', in *Cork Hist. Soc.*

Jn., lxxxii, 33–8; N. Simpson, *The Belfast Bank 1827-1970* (Belfast 1975)

117 See, H. C. Casserly, *An Outline of Irish Railway History* (Newton Abbot 1974). Also, A. A. Horner, 'Planning the Irish transport network: parallels in nineteenth and twentieth century proposals' in *Ir. Geog.*, x, 44–57; Jack Johnston, 'Communications in the Clogher Valley, 1700–1900', in *Clogher Rec.*, ix, no. 3,310–25; Patrick F. Wallace, 'The organisation of pre-railway public transport in Limerick and Clare', in *Nth Munster Antiq. Jn.*, xv, 35–58.

118 Peter M. Solar, 'The Agricultural Trade Statistics in the Irish Railway Commissioners' Report', in *Ir. Econ. Soc. Hist.*, VI, 24–40; J. B. O'Brien, 'Agricultural prices and living costs in pre-famine Cork' in *Cork Hist. Soc. Jn.*, xxxii, 1–10.

119 Joseph Lee, 'The Dual Economy in Ireland 1800–1850', in T.D. Williams (ed), *Historical Studies*, VIII (1971), 191–201; James H. Johnson 'The two Irelands at the beginning of the nineteenth century', in N. Stephens & R. E. Glascock (ed), *Irish geographical studies in honour of E. E. Evans*.

120 Liam Kennedy, 'A skeptical view of the re-incarnation of the Irish "gombeenman" ', in *Econ. & Soc. Rev.*, VIII, 3, pp 213–22; 'Retail markets in rural Ireland at the end of the nineteenth century', *Ir. Econ. Soc. Hist.* V, 46–63; 'The early response of the Irish Catholic clergy to the Co-operative movement', in *I.H.S.*, xxi, no. 81, 55–74; 'The Roman Catholic Church and economic growth in 19th century Ireland', *Econ. & Soc. Rev.*, X, no. 1, 45–60; see also n. 115 above.

121 P. Gibbon & M. D. Higgins, 'Patronage, tradition and modernisation: the case of the Irish "gombeenman" ', in *Econ. & Soc. Rev.*, VI, no. 1 (1974); 'The Irish gombeenman: re-incarnation or rehabilitation?', in *Econ. & Soc. Rev.*, VIII, no. 4. (1977).

122 A recent full-length study of the co-operative movement is, Patrick Bolger, *The Irish Co-operative movement: its history and development.* (Dublin 1977);

123 See, for example, Brendan M. Walsh, 'Marriage rates and population pressure Ireland 1871 and 1911', in *Econ. Hist. Rev.*, xviii, 148–62; Valerie Morgan, 'A case study of population change over two centuries: Blaris, Lisburn, 1661–1848', in *Ir. Econ. Soc. Hist.*, iii, 5–16; G. S. L. Tucker, 'Irish fertility rates before the famine', in *Econ. Hist. Rev.*, xxxi, no. 2, 238–56 Robert E. McKenna, 'Age, religion and marriage in post-famine Ireland: an empirical examination', in *Econ. Hist. Rev.*, xxxi, no. 2, 238–56 Robert E. Kennedy, *The Irish: emigration, marriage and fertility.* (Berkeley 1973); Michele Brahimi, 'Nuptualité et Fécondite en

Irlande: Des marriages en Irlande', in *Population,* xxxiii, no. 3, 663–703. A valuable reference work just recently published is, W. E. Vaughan and A. J. Fitzpatrick (ed), *Irish Historical Statistics: Population 1821-1971.* (Dublin 1978).

[124] F. J. Carney, 'Pre-famine Irish population: the evidence from the Trinity College Estates', in *Ir. Econ. Soc. Hist.,* II (1975), 35–45.

[125] Cormac Ó Gráda, 'Seasonal migration and post-famine adjustment in the west of Ireland', *Studia Hibernica,* no. 13, 47–76; 'Some aspects of nineteenth-century Irish emigration', in Cullen & Smout (ed), *Comparative aspects of Scottish and Irish economic & social history 1600-1900* (Edinburgh 1977); 'A note on nineteenth century Irish emigration statistics', in *Population Studies,* xxix, 143–9.

[126] M. Beames, 'Cottiers and conacre in pre-famine Ireland', in *Jn. of Peasant Studies,* 2, no. 3 (1975); 'Peasant movements: Ireland 1785–95', in *Jn. of Peasant Studies,* 2, no. 4 (1975); 'Rural conflict in pre-famine Ireland: Peasant assassinations in Tipperary 1837–1847' in *Past & Present,* LXXXI, 75–91. But on this last point see, J. Lee, 'Ribbonmen' in T. D. Williams (ed), *Secret Societies in Ireland* (Dublin 1973) and James W. Hurst, 'Disturbed Tipperary 1831–60', in *Eire-Ireland,* ix, no. 3, 44-60. For definitions of the peasantry see also Margaret MacCurtain, 'Pre-famine peasantry in Ireland: Definition and theme' in *Irish Univ. Rev.,* iv, 188–98.

[127] P. Gibbon & C. Curtin, 'The Stem Family in Ireland', in *Comparative Studies in Society and History,* XX, no. 3, 429-53.

[128] The main contributions have been: Samuel Clark, *Social Origins of the Irish Land War* (Princeton 1979); Paul Bew, *Land and the National Question in Ireland 1858-82.* (Dublin 1978); J. S. Donnelly, *The Land and People of Nineteenth century Cork* (London & Boston 1975); B.L. Solow, *The Land Question and the Irish Economy, 1870-1903* (Cambridge, Mass. 1971); Joseph Lee, *The modernisation of Irish society 1848-1918.* (Dublin 1973); C. Ó Grada, 'Agricultural Head-Rents, Pre-Famine and Post-Famine', in *Econ. & Soc. Rev.,* V, no. 3 (1974); 'The investment behaviour of Irish landlords, 1850–75', in *Agric. Hist. Rev.,* XXXIII, Part 2 (1975); 'The beginnings of the Irish creamery system 1880–1914', in *Econ. Hist. Rev.,* XXX, no. 2, 284–305; W. A. Maguire, *The Downshire Estates in Ireland, 1801-45.* (Oxford 1972); W.E. Vaughan, 'Landlord and Tenant relations in Ireland between th Famine and the Land War', Thesis abstract, *Ir. Econ. Soc. Hist.,* I (1974); 'Landlord and Tenant relations in Ireland between the Famine and the Land War, 1850–78', in Cullen & Smout (ed), *Comparative Aspects.* (Edinburgh 1977). See also,

R. W. Kirkpatrick, 'Landed Estates in Mid-Ulster and the Irish Land War 1879-85', Thesis abstract, *Ir. Econ. Soc. Hist.*, V, 73–75; John B. O'Brien, 'The land and people of 19th century Cork', in *Cork Hist. Soc. Jn.*, lxxx, 95–101; *General Report on the gosford Estates in Co. Armagh, 1821 by William Greig*, with an introduction by F. M. L. Thompson and D. Tierney (Belfast 1976); G. E. Christianson, 'Landlords and land tenure in Ireland 1790–1830', *Éire-Ireland*, 9, no. 1, 25–58; J. S. Donnelly, 'The Irish Agricultural depression of 1859–64', in *Ir. Econ. Soc. Hist.*, 3, 33–54; For the Encumbered Estates Act and its effect see, Pádraig G. Lane, 'The Encumbered Estates Court, Ireland: 1848–49, in *Econ. and Soc. Rev.*, 3, no. 3 (1972); 'The management of estates by financial corporations in Ireland after the famine,' in *Studia Hibernica*, 14, pp 67–89; 'The general impact of the Encumbered Estates Act of 1849 on Counties Galway and Mayo', in *Galway Arch. Hist. Soc. Jn.*, 33 (1972).

[129] But, for seeds of optimism see, Peter Connell, *Changing Forces shaping a Nineteenth century Irish town: A case study of Navan* (Maynooth 1978). Also, M. E. Crowley, 'A social and economic study of Dublin 1860–1914', Thesis abstract, *Ir. Econ. Soc. Hist.*, I (1974), 63–65. But for a sensitive study of a community see, D. H. Akenson, *Between Two Revolutions - Islandmagee, Co. Antrim 1798-1926* (Ontario 1979); For a useful contribution on housing, see Alan Gailey, *Rural Housing in Ulster in the mid-nineteenth century* (Belfast 1974). Patrick Shaffrey, *The Irish Town: an approach to survival* (Dublin 1975); L. M. Cullen, *Towns and Villages of Ireland* (Dublin 1979).

[130] Arthur Mitchell, *Labour in Irish Politics 1890-1930* (Dublin 1974); See also, A. Mitchell, 'William O'Brien 1881–1968 and the Irish Labour movement', in *Studies*, 1x, 311–31; Frank Robbins, *Under the starry plough.* (Dublin 1977); M. Gallagher, 'Socialism and the nationalist tradition in Ireland, 1798–1918', in *Éire-Ireland*, 12, no. 2, 63–102; Maura Murphy, 'Fenianism, Parnellism and the Cork Trades 1860–1960', in *Saothar 5*, 27–38; S. U. Larsen & O. Snoddy, '1916–a workingmens revolution: an analysis of those who made the 1916 revolution in Ireland', in *Social Studies*, ii, 377–98.

[131] Charles McCarthy, *Trade Unions in Ireland 1894-1960* (Dublin 1977); A more general account is Andrew Boyd, *The rise of the Irish trade unions 1729-1970* (Tralee 1972); From the extensive literature on labour supply, labour organisation and disputes, see Joseph Lee, 'Railway labour in Ireland 1833–56', in *Saothar 5*, 7–26; Pamela Horn, 'The Agricultural Labourers Union in Ireland, 1873–79', *I.H.S.*, xvii, 340–52; W.

Moran, 'Dublin Lockout 1913', in *Soc. Study Lab. Hist. Bull.*, no. 27, 10–1. There are several short pieces on the impact of the 'new unionism' on Ireland in *Soc. St. Lab. Hist. Bull*, 35; J. McHugh, 'Belfast Labour disputes and riots, 1907', in *Int. Rev. Soc. Hist.*, xxii, 1–20; Emily Boyle, 'The Linen Strike of 1872', in *Saothar 2*, 12–22; Joseph J. Lecky, 'The Railway servants strike in county Cork, 1898, in *Saothar 2*, 39–44; Gordon McMullan, 'The Irish Bank "Strike" in 1919, in *Saothar 5*, 39–49; D. Keogh, 'Michael O'Lehane and the organisation of linen drapers' assistants', in *Saothar 3*, 33–43, and also several pieces by the same author on 'new unionism', in *Capuchin Annual* 1975, 1976, 1977.

[132] For a vivid, detailed account, see Seán Daly, *Cork, a city in crisis: a history of labour conflict and social misery 1870-72* (Cork 1978); also M. McCaughan, 'An account of life in late 19th century East Belfast', in *Ulster Folklife*, no. 19, 68–72.

[133] The history of women in Irish society has only begun to be written, but see Margaret MacCurtain & Donncha Ó Corráin (ed), *Women in Irish Society: the Historical Dimension.* (Dublin 1978) for an introduction.

[134] Stephen Thernstrom, *The other Bostonians: poverty and progress in American metropolis 1880-1970* (Cambridge Mass. 1973). Also, Thernstrom & R. Sennett (ed), *Nineteenth century cities* (New Haven 1969).

[135] The following is only a selection: D. H. Akenson, *The United States & Ireland* (Cambridge, Mass. 1973); Lawrence J. McCaffrey, *The Irish diaspora in America* (Bloomington 1976) and *Irish nationalism & the American contribution* (New York 1976); James B. Walsh (ed), *The Irish — America's political class* (New York 1976); Thomas M. Henderson, *Tammany hall and the new immigrants: the progressive years* (N.Y. 1976); Michael F. Funchion, *Chicago's Irish nationalists 1881-90* (N.Y. 1976); Grace McDonald, *History of the Irish in Wisconsin in the 19th century* (N.Y. 1976); Earl F. Niehaus, *The Irish in New Orleans, 1800-60* (N.Y. 1976); R.A. Burchell, *The San Francisco Irish 1840-80* (Manchester 1979); Jo Ellen Vinyard, *The Irish on the urban frontier: Detroit 1850-80* (N.Y. 1976); Jay P. Dolan, *The immigrant Church: New York's Irish and German Catholics, 1815-65* (Baltimore 1975); Thomas N. Brown, 'The United States of America: the Irish layman', in P. J. Corish (ed), *History of Irish Catholicism*, VI, fasc. 2 (Dublin 1970); A. M. Greeley, *The most distressful nation* (Chicago 1972); Robert F. Hueston, *The Catholic press and nativism 1840-60* (N.Y. 1976); J. E. Cuddy, *Irish-America and national isolation 1914-20* (N.Y. 1976); David N. Doyle *Irish Americans: native rights and national empires: the structures, divisions and attitudes of*

the Catholic minority in the decade of expansion 1890–1901 (N.Y. 1976); John P. Buckley, *The New York Irish their view of American foreign policy, 1914-21* (N.Y. 1976); W. L. Joyce, *Editors and Ethnicity: a history of the Irish-American press 1848-83* (New York 1976)

[136] e.g. S. M. Ingham, *Enterprising migrants: an Irish family in Australia* (Melbourne 1975); James Waldersee, *Catholic Society in New South Wales 1788-1860* (Sydney 1974); G. Rudé, *Protest and punishment: the story of the social and political protesters transported to Australia 1788–1868*. (Oxford 1978); Oliver MacDonagh, 'The Irish in Victoria 1851-91: a demographic essay', in T. D. williams (ed), *Historical Studies*, VIII (1971), 67–92.

[137] Richard P. Davis, *Irish issues in New Zealand Politics 1868-1922* (Dunedin 1974).

[138] e.g. John J. Mannion, *Irish settlements in eastern Canada: a study of cultural transfer and adaption* (Toronto 1975); William J. Smyth, 'The Irish in mid-19th century Ontario', in *Ulster Folklife*, xxiii, 97–105.

[139] See, e.g., Sheridan Gilley, 'English attitudes to the Irish in England', in C. Holmes (ed), *Immigrants and Minorities in British Society.* (London 1978) and the works cited therein; J. Handley *The Navvy in Scotland* (Cork 1970); Lynn Lees, *Exiles of Erin: Irish Migrants in Victorian London* (Manchester 1979) and the works cited therein; Brenda Collins, 'Aspects of Irish immigration into two Scottish towns during the 19th century', Thesis abstract, in *Ir. Econ. Soc. Hist.*, VI, 71-73.

[140] See, especially, Patrick O'Farrell, 'Emigrant attitudes and behaviour as a source for Irish history', in G. A. Hayes-McCoy (ed), *Historical Studies, X,* 109–31 (Conamara 1976).

[141] On the social history of the language change, see Brian Ó Cuiv (ed), *A view of the Irish language* (Dublin 1969); Seán Ó Tuama (ed), *The Gaelic League Idea* (Cork 1973); Caoimhín Ó Danachair, 'The Irish language in county Clare in the 19th century', in *Nth. Munster Atriq. Jn.* xiii, 40–52; G. B. Adams, 'Language in Ulster 1820–1850', in *Ulster Folklife,* xix, 50–55; 'The 1851 census in the north of Ireland', in *Ulster Folklife,* xx, 65–70. For the social and intellectual provenance of literature, the following are noteworthy: Oliver MacDonagh, *The nineteenth century novel and Irish social history: some aspects* (Dublin 1971); D. H. Akenson, & W. H. Crawford (ed), *Local poets and social history: James Orr, Bard of Ballycarry* (Belfast 1977); Tomás Ó Fiaich & L. Ó Caithnia (ed), *Art Mac Bionaid: Dánta* (Dublin 1979); Seosamh Ó Duibhginn (ed), *Séamas Mac Giolla Choille, c. 1759-1828* (Dublin 1972); P. Ó Fiannachta (ed), *Léachtaí Cholm Cille,* I, III, VII (Maynooth 1970, 1972,

1976); Malcolm Brown, *The politics of Irish literature from Thomas Davis to W. B. Yeats.* (London 1972). Robert O'Driscoll (ed), *Theatre and nationalism in twentieth century Ireland* (London 1971); Peter Costello, *The heart grown brutal: the Irish revolution in literature from Parnell to the death of Yeats.* (Dublin 1977).

[142] e.g. Donal McCartney, 'James Anthony Froude: a historiographical controversy of the nineteenth century', in *Historical Studies,* VIII (1971), 171–90; Leon Ó Broin, *An Maidineach: Staraí na nÉireannach Aontaithe* (Dublin 1971); F.S.L. Lyons, 'The Dilemma of the Irish contemporary historian', in *Hermathena,* CXV, 45–56; T. W. Moody, 'Irish history and Irish mythology', in *Hermathena,* CXXIV, 7–24; David W. Harkness, *History and the Irish* (Belfast 1976); Ned Lebow, 'British historians and Irish history', in *Eire-Ireland,* viii, no. 4, 3–38; P. J. McGill, 'Five Donegal historians of the last century', in *Donegal Annual,* XI, 53–65.

[143] e.g. Barbara Hayley, 'Irish periodicals from the Union to the "Nation"', in *Anglo-Irish Studies, II,* 83–108; Virginia E. Glandon, 'Index of Irish newspapers 1900–22', Two parts: *Eire-Ireland,* xi, no. 4, 84–121; xii, no. I, 86–115; Aiken McClelland, 'The Ulster Press in the eighteenth and nineteenth centuries', in *Ulster Folklife,* XX, 89–99; for intellectual influences see, Patrick O'Neill, 'The reception of German literature in Ireland 1750–1850', 2 parts, in *Studia Hibernica* nos. 16 and 17/18, pp. 122–139, 91–106; W. B. Stanford, 'Towards a history of Classical influences in Ireland', *R.I.A. Proc,* 1xx, C, No. 3, 14–91.

[144] e.g. E. E. Evans, *The personality of Ireland: habitat, heritage and history* (London 1973); Frank Mitchell, *The Irish landscape* (London 1976); F. H. A. Aalen, *Man and the Landscape in Ireland* (London 1978). Also, Eileen McCracken, *The Irish Woods since Tudor times: distribution and exploitation* (Newton Abbot 1971); William Nolan, *Fassadinan: Land settlement and society in south-east Ireland 1600-1850.* (Dublin 1979) is an interesting example of a 'geographer's perspective. See, also, W. J. Smyth, 'Estate records and the making of an Irish landscape: an example from County Tipperary' in *Irish Geography,* ix, 29–49.

[145] Art Byrne & Sean McMahon, *Faces of the West, 1875-1925* (Belfast 1976); *Faces of Munster* (Belfast 1977); G. Morrison (ed), *An Irish Camera* (London 1979); M. Gorham, *Dublin from old Photographs.* (London 1972); K. Hickey, *The light of other days.* (London 1973); B. M. Walker, *Faces of the Past: a photographic and literary record of Ulster Life 1800-1915* (Belfast 1974); P. Hamilton, *Up the Shankill* (Belfast 1979).

[146] e.g. Thomas J. Walsh, *Opera in Dublin* (Dublin 1973); Eugene Waters & M. Murtagh, *Infinite Variety: Dan Lowry's Music Hall, 1879-97.* (Dublin 1975); Breandán Breathnach, *Folk Music and Dances of Ireland* (Dublin 1971); J. C. Conroy (ed), *Rugby in Leinster 1879-1979* (Dublin 1979); Raymond Smith, *The clash of the ash* (Dublin 1972); Mark Tuohy, *Belfast Celtic* (Belfast 1978); Sam Hanna Bell, *The Theatre in Ulster* (Dublin 1972).

Ireland Since 1921

*Professor David W. Harkness,
Department of Modern History, Queen's University, Belfast*

Helen Mulvey, surveying the bulk of this period a decade ago,[1] lamented the absence of any overall account which gave in consecutive detail the history and character of Ireland in the twentieth century. Historians have since responded to supply a number of works of at least outline coverage, while there has been an encouraging growth of studies of particular themes. In organising this essay, therefore, it has seemed appropriate to discuss first the general histories and then to tackle particular themes, taking these in chronological order where that approach is appropriate, but only after considering those which either run throughout the period or through a substantial part of it. In this context it will be observed immediately that the outstanding feature of the historiography of Ireland since 1921 has been dictated by partition. Very few works now treat of the island as a whole. The experiences of the peoples, north and south, have drawn apart and even if the attempt is made to encompass both in the same book, they are perforce examined separately. By and large this fact of life is simply accepted and the subject matter, be it broad outline, particular event or general theme, is confined to the twenty-six counties or the six. Bibliographical discussion necessarily here follows the same pattern, with final comment being preceded by a brief reference to works of biography.

The most complete account of Ireland, north and south, to emerge in the seventies, is contained in Dr. F. S. L. Lyons's[2] magisterial history of *Ireland since the Famine* (London, 1971, with extended paperback edition, 1973), almost half of its 800 pages being devoted to the post-1921 era. Wise, balanced, informed and still remarkably fresh in its scholarship after ten years, this must remain not only one of the outstanding achievements of the decade but also the fullest guide for the student of modern Irish history. No less balanced and judicious, though with a much tighter limitation of space, is Professor John A. Murphy's *Ireland in the Twentieth Century* (Dublin, 1975), the concluding volume of the excellent Gill and Macmillan paperback history of Ireland. Running from 1919 it presents the experience of independent Ireland in six chapters, after an introductory account of 'the Independence struggle, 1919–21', and with a concluding chapter devoted to Northern Ireland. Professor Oliver MacDonagh's scintillating essay *Ireland* (Englewood Cliffs, N.J., 1968), revised, enlarged and re-titled *Ireland: the union and its aftermath* (London, 1977) continues to offer insights into post-independence Ireland, with profound new reflections upon the contributions of past behaviour, ideology and policy to an understanding of the current northern crisis. No other general account approaches these three, though useful perspectives are advanced by E. Rumpf and A. C. Hepburn in *Nationalism and Socialism in twentieth century Ireland.* (Liverpool, 1977). Erhard Rumpf's original Ph.D. thesis, completed in the early sixties, has been expanded and up-dated as well as being translated and re-written in places by Dr. Hepburn. It offers a structural analysis of Irish nationalism and republicanism, and of the politics of Northern Ireland, protestant, catholic and non-sectarian, since 1920. From a more particular point of view, D. R. O'Connor Lysaght provides a stimulating socialist perspective in his *The Republic of Ireland* (Cork, 1970), incorporating the tools of the political scientist as well as the historian, while Sean Cronin's *Ireland since the Treaty* (Dublin, 1971) gives a brief, left-wing survey of the ills of the 1921 settlement, fifty years on.

A number of other books have given insight into the development of twentieth century Ireland while traversing a broad canvas. Of these, mention may be made of Garret FitzGerald's *Towards a new Ireland* (London, 1972, Dublin, 1973), which considers the impact of partition upon Ireland, north and south, and Conor Cruise O'Brien's *States of Ireland* (London, 1972), in which autobiography is mixed with historical and political analysis. Both books, by working politicians, are concerned also with future political developments and both have been influential in moulding opinion. On a different note, Professor Kevin Nowlan's chapter 'modern Ireland: the birth and growth of the new state' in Brian de Breffny (ed) *The Irish World* (London, 1977), a coffee-table production of unusually high quality, shows well how the challenge of compression can be met.

Turning to significant themes and taking first those concerning independent Ireland, the outstanding work, throwing light on many crucial areas of Irish and indeed Anglo-Irish affairs, is Ronan Fanning's *The Irish Department of Finance, 1922-58* (Dublin, 1978). Dr. Fanning is especially helpful on the problems of establishing the new state, but with unique access to departmental records he is able to quote and analyse a mass of official papers throughout his period. No student of the history of the Irish republic can afford to overlook this study of so central an institution of government, with its decisive influence on so many others, from domestic development through, for example, industry and commerce, and agriculture, to external relations, particularly relations between Ireland and Britain. Dr. Fanning adds a most perceptive chapter on events since 1958, while his bibliography includes important articles by T. K. Whitaker[3] describing the breakthrough to economic planning. In the area of finance, note may also be taken of Maurice Moynihan's *Currency and Central Banking in Ireland 1922-60* (Dublin, 1975).

Another theme well developed in the past decade has been that of external relations. Here the pioneer has been Patrick Keatinge, whose *Formulation of Irish foreign policy* (Dublin, 1973) sets down not only the historical record of Irish foreign policy but also the nature of the policy-making process. In numerous articles[4] and in his *A place amongst the nations: issues of Irish foreign policy* (Dublin, 1978), which examines such specific concerns as independence and identity, security, unity, and prosperity, and gives reference to his other writings, he has both tackled the external relations problems inherent in the Irish system of government and argued the necessity of greater public knowledge of, and response to, international affairs.

Specifically Anglo-Irish relations in this period are touched upon at the tail end of Patrick O'Farrell's *Ireland's English Question* (London, Oxford, New York, 1975). Truly has he remarked that understanding of Irish history is impossible without knowledge of the decision-making process on the neighbouring island, and no finer illustration of this could be given than by the inside observations of Thomas Jones, whose *Whitehall Diary* iii *Ireland, 1918-25* (edited by Keith Middlemas, London, New York, Toronto, 1971) stretches into this period. The present author's article 'Mr de Valera's Dominion: Irish relations with Britain and the Commonwealth, 1932-8'[5] examines some of the constitutional issues at stake in a period recently given comprehensive treatment by Dr. Deirdre Macmahon.[6] Much valuable comment of Irish interest in this period is also contained in Professor P. N. S. Mansergh's *Commonwealth experience* (London, 1969) and Duncan Hall's monumental *Commonwealth: a history of the British Commonwealth of nations* (London, 1971); while Ged Martin attacks the present author's thesis on the contribution of the Irish Free State to Commonwealth development in chapter ten of R. Hyam and G. Martin, *Reappraisals in British Imperial History* (London, 1975). A contribution to Anglo-Irish relations in the seventies is contained in retired British ambassador John Peck's *Dublin from Downing St.* (Dublin, 1978).

In broader, bilateral terms, Irish-American relations have not been of notable interest to scholars in this decade, but the multifarious activities of Irish immigrants in America, including some in the post-1921 period, are referred to in David Doyle's 'Irish America: a regional bibliography, 1830-1930' in *Irish Historical Studies* (forthcoming). Arthur Mitchell's 'Ireland and the Soviet Union' in *Capuchin Annual* (1975) briefly surveys the limited contact between these two states up to the exchange of diplomatic representation in 1974.

The evolution of politics is another theme well treated in books and articles in this decade. The Gill and Macmillan series 'Studies in Irish political culture' has produced three valuable short monographs: Brian Farrell's *Chairman or chief: the role of Taoiseach in Irish government*, (Dublin, 1971), discussing the office and then each practitioner in turn, and adding useful cabinet lists from 1922; Maurice Manning's *Irish political parties: an Introduction* (Dublin, 1972), dealing with the parties in turn,[7] with an analysis of the 1969 Gallup survey of the electorate; and Al Cohen's *The Irish political elite*[8] (Dublin, 1972), analysing its identification and social composition, comparison with revolutionary and post-revolutionary elites, and its recruitment. Dr. Cornelius O'Leary's *Irish elections 1918-77: parties, voters and proportional representation* (Dublin, 1979) provides a most useful record as well as an analysis of the electoral machinery, while Basil Chubb's *The constitution and constitutional change in Ireland* (Dublin, 1978) revises his *The Constitution of Ireland* (Dublin, 1963), analysing successive constitutions and amendments into the E.E.C. era. His *Cabinet government in Ireland* (Dublin, 1974) offers an historical treatment of the subject from 1919, but see also Alan J. Ward's trenchant 'Parliamentary procedures and the machinery of government in Ireland' in *Irish University Review*, iv, (autumn, 1974) pp 222–43, which examines the degree to which the limited powers and partisan nature of the Dail have so far inhibited good government. T. J. Barrington's *From big government to local government: the road to decentralisation* (Dublin, 1975) is a collection of fifteen of his papers supporting the theme that government is lost in bureaucratic complexity and ought to devolve what it can to the localities. Sean Nolan in a 46 page pamphlet, *Communist Party of Ireland: an outline history* (Dublin, 1975), gives a brief historical sketch of that organisation from within, while the splintered extreme left of the political spectrum, in the period up to the outbreak of the Spanish Civil War, is recorded in Donal Nevin's 'Radical movements in the Twenties and Thirties' in T. Desmond Williams (ed) *Secret Societies in Ireland* (Dublin, 1973).[9]

On the theme of Labour, the most interesting development, perhaps, has been the founding of *Saothar,* journal of the Irish Labour History Society, issued annually in May, from 1975. This admirable publication provides a vehicle for articles in what has been a neglected area and must be welcome, provided it is not accepted that history is to be compartmentalised further into exclusive areas of interest. A number of books spanning a longer period have relevance: P. Beresford Ellis devotes three out of sixteen chapters to post-1922 events in his *A history of the Irish working class* (London, 1972); Andrew Boyd two of thirteen in *The Rise of the Irish Trade Unions, 1729-1970* (Tralee, 1972); while C. McCarthy's *Trade Unions in Ireland, 1894-1960* (Dublin, 1977) is largely concerned with this period. See also his *The Decade of upheval: Irish Trade Unions in the 1960's* (Dublin, 1973).

Church – state relations are the subject of one of the best books produced early in the decade. J. H. Whyte's *Church and state in modern Ireland* (Dublin, 1971) provides a forceful and scholarly examination of a delicate topic and gives the best available record of the 1951 mother-and-child scheme clash. A number of other works giving a general account of Catholicism and Anglicanism over an extended period add little to illumine this period, though R. B. McDowell's *The Church of Ireland, 1869-1969* (London and Boston, 1975), celebrating a hundred years of disestablishment, includes chapters on 'The church and Irish politics' and 'The church in the twentieth century'. Of more immediate relevance and greater significance is Jack White's *Minority Report* (Dublin, 1975), which analyses the fate of the protestant community in independent Ireland. Here indeed is an invaluable social commentary. In a number of areas parish histories are now being written, centenaries being the spur to some. While it is not necessary to list these here, the trend should perhaps be noted.

The main denominations were themselves responsible for publishing *Violence in Ireland* (Belfast, 1976), which, though inspired by events in the north, rightly emphasises responsibilities more widely shared. Under law and order, as a general theme, there is C. Brady's *Guardians of the Peace* (Dublin, 1974) which concentrates largely on the period 1922-45, though the author was misled while going to press into a discussion of the likely repercussions for the Garda Siochana of the abortive Sunningdale Agreement, a warning against topicality in the writing of history. Almost half of S. Breathnach's *The Irish police: from earliest times to the present day* (Dublin, 1974) is on post-1922 policing, with a chapter on the R.U.C. for good measure.

The history of education in the period has also come under scrutiny. Donald Akenson (a pioneer in the north also, see below), in his *A mirror to Kathleen's face: education in independent Ireland, 1922-60* (Montreal and London, 1975) has succeeded in presenting the inter-relation of educational institutions and society, thereby revealing much of the character of the latter. E. Randles, in *Post-primary education in Ireland, 1957-70* (Dublin, 1975) gives an account of educational issues and developments, year by year, which, though not indexed, is clearly enough arranged for reference purposes.

Of communication in the widest sense, there are somewhat inconsequential reminiscences in L. McRedmond (ed), *Written on the wind: personal memories of Irish radio, 1926-76* (Dublin, 1976). D. Fisher's *Broadcasting in Ireland* (London, 1978) is more analytical. P. H. Butler briefly chronicles flying developments in *Irish aircraft: a history of Irish aviation* (Liverpool, 1972); M. H. C. Baker provides a nostalgic glimpse of another form of transport in *The railways of the republic of Ireland, 1925-75: a pictorial survey of the G.S.R. and C.I.E.* (Truro, 1975); while H. C. Casserly's *Outline of Irish railway history* (Newton Abbot, London and Vancouver, 1974) is self-explanatory. But it is in the literature of the period that some of the best insights may be obtained and here two general surveys deserve mention: R. Fallis's *The Irish renaissance: an introduction to Anglo-Irish literature* (Syracuse, N.Y., 1977, Dublin, 1978), and P. Costello's *The heart grown brutal: the Irish revolution in literature, from Parnell to the death of Yeats, 1881-1939* (Dublin and Totowa, N.J., 1977). S. Macmahon's *Best from the Bell* gives the full flavour of the literary world of 1940-45, as expressed in that invaluable journal, which is itself the subject of H. Butler's 'The Bell; an Anglo-Irish review' in *Irish University Review,* vi, (spring, 1976) pp 66–72, in which tribute is paid to its principal editor, Sean O'Faolain.[10] David Thomson's experiences of life in inter-war and wartime Connacht are charmingly evoked in his *Woodbrook* (London, 1974): social commentary on a narrow front, perhaps, but instructive as well as a delight to read.

Finally, in this general survey section, two other works must be noted. Hugh Brody's *Inishkillane: change and decline in the West of Ireland* (London, 1973) charts eloquently the atrophy and demoralisation of the smaller western communities experiencing social and cultural destruction as well as demographic loss. Some of the latter phenomenon is charted, if not explained, in an important ancillary volume of the New History of Ireland project: W. E. Vaughan and A. J. Fitzpatrick's *Irish Historical Statistics: population, 1821-1971* (Dublin, 1978) which provides a mass of tables, area by area, period by period, over this significant span.

Turning to the rather random particular events treated by historians of the last decade, in chronological sequence, it will be seen that one of the growth areas has been the period of the second world war. But first, in point of time, comes the civil war period, and the elaborate attempts made in the early months of 1922 to heal the rift before it widened irrevocably. Four articles tackle in different ways this constitutionally uncertain period, all drawing on recently released official papers: Kevin Boyle's 'The Tallents report on the Craig-Collins pact of 30 March 1922' in *The Irish Jurist,* xii, (new series) part 1, (summer, 1977) pp. 148-75, reproduces a fascinating investigative document, hitherto unknown, and sets this abortive agreement in context; Thomas Towey's 'Hugh Kennedy and the constiutional development of the Irish Free State, 1922–3' in *ibid.,* part 2, (winter, 1977) pp. 355–70, stresses the role of the new dominion's first Attorney General in its creation and constitutional development; D. H. Akenson and J. F. Fallin's long, three-part 'The Irish Civil War and the drafting of the Free State constitution' in *Eire-Ireland,* v, no. 1, pp. 10–26, no. 2, pp. 42–93, no. 4, pp. 28–70 (spring, summer and winter, 1970), contains a wealth of documentary evidence in emphasising the significance and complexity of the Provisional Government's attempt to achieve a broadly acceptable constitution; while J. M. Curran's 'The issue of external relations in the Anglo-Irish negotiations of May-June 1922' in *Eire-Ireland,* xiii, no. 1, (spring, 1978) pp 15–25, throws interesting light on the weakness of the United Kingdom's position, hinting that British bluff might profitably have been called. The anti-Treaty view of the war itself is illuminated by the posthumously published memoirs of that able but instransigent soldier, Ernie O'Malley. *The singing flame* (Dublin, 1978) takes his story, so well begun in *On another man's wound* (London, 1936), through the Treaty and its rejection and the occupation and destruction of the Four Courts, to his eventual capture and imprisonment, and finally his release in mid-1924. The closing years of the I.R.B., for which the civil war was a crucial event, are discussed in two works: the latter chapters of Leon Ó Broin's *Revolutionary underground: the story of the Irish Republican Brotherhood, 1858-1924* (Dublin, 1976); and John O'Beirne-Ranelagh's 'The I.R.B. from the treaty to 1924' in *Irish Historical Studies,* xx, no. 77, (March, 1976) pp 26–39.

The immediate political fortunes of the republican party are dealt with by Thomas P. O'Neill's 'In search of a political path: Irish republicanism 1922–27' in *Historical Studies X,* (Dublin, 1976) pp 147–71, and in three articles by Peter Pyne: 'The politics of parliamentary absenteeism: Ireland's four Sinn Fein parties, 1905-26' in *The journal of Commonwealth and comparative politics*, xii, no 2 (July, 1974), pp 206-27; 'the third Sinn Fein party, 1923-26' (in two parts) in *Economic and Social Review*, i, nos 1 and 2, (October, 1969 and January, 1970) pp 29-50 and pp 229-57; and 'The new Irish state and the decline of the Republican Sinn Fein party, 1923-6' in *Eire-Ireland* xi, no. 3, (autumn, 1976) pp 33-65 (an extended version of the previous article). Arthur Mitchell, in 'The Irish government that never was', *Capuchin Annual* (1973), pp 55-60, discusses the stillborn attempt to form a coalition of Labour, National League and Independents, with Fianna Fail backing, in 1927. Further aspects of the Cosgrave regime are treated by T. K. Daniel's 'Griffith on his noble head: the determinants of Cumann na nGaedheal economic policy, 1922-32', in *Irish Economic and Social History*, iii, (1976) pp 55-65, a clear case of economics and politics overlapping; in P. Mair's 'Labour and the Irish party system revisited: party competition in the 1920s' in *Economic and Social Review*, ix, no 1, (October, 1977) pp 59-69; and in David Fitzpatrick's 'Yeats in the Senate' in *Studia Hibernica*, xii, (1972) pp 7-26, which charts the poet's often outrageous contributions to the debates of the 'twenties.

The outstanding book on the 1930s, with many historical and political insights, is Maurice Manning's *The Blueshirts* (Dublin, 1970), but note also F. Munger's booklet *The legitimacy of opposition: the change of government in Ireland in 1932* (London, 1975).

The Second World War has attracted a number of works, with more in the pipeline.[11] Joseph T. Carroll's *Ireland in the war years, 1939-45* (Newton Abbot and New York, 1975), the first to make use of the official British records, gives a lively narrative of the period, but by its own admission and by the evidence of what Ronan Fanning has produced from the Irish Finance archives, this can be only a beginning. Bernard Share, in his *The emergency: neutral Ireland* (Dublin, 1978), successfully captures, in picture, cartoon and text, the social atmosphere of wartime Ireland, while Carolle J. Carter up-dates previous accounts of spying activity by making full use of the German records in her *The Shamrock and the Swastika: German espionage in Ireland in World War Two*[12] (Palo Alto, Calif., 1977). T. Ryle Dwyer, drawing extensively on both the Roosevelt papers and those of David Gray, U.S. Ambassador to Ireland in the war years, gives wide, though one feels not yet complete, coverage to the transatlantic relationship in his *Irish neutrality and the U.S.A., 1939-47* (Dublin, 1977). J. L. Rosenberg's rather tendentious 'Irish conscription crisis, 1941' in *Eire-Ireland*, xiv, no 1, (spring, 1979) pp 16-25, refers to events in Northern Ireland but presents them in terms of Dublin victories over Belfast and London. Unfortunately it neglects the mass of material in the Northern Ireland Public Record Office.

Economic take-off and EEC entry as yet lack specific monographs, but the impact of the northern crisis on the Republic has produced several narratives, most notably on the Cabinet crisis of 1970. Tom MacIntyre's *Through the Bridewell gate: a diary of the Dublin arms trial* (London, 1971) shows how remarkable it was that the government of the day survived a notable scandal, while Kevin Boland's *Up Dev!* (Dublin, 1978) explains why it should not have been allowed to do so, and James Kelly's *Orders for the Captain* (Dublin, 1971) gives a participant's own racy account of events. The Irish premier's not always sensitive or well-timed responses to successive northern events are contained in J. Lynch *Speeches and statements: Irish unity; Northern Ireland; Anglo-Irish relations. August 1969-October 1971* (Dublin, 1971).

Other glimpses of Ireland to-day may be found in T. P. Coogan's *The Irish, a personal view,* (London, 1975), and in Jill and Leon Uris's *Ireland, a terrible beauty: the story of Ireland to-day,* of which the pictures (Jill's) are largely beautiful and the text (Leon's) sometimes terrible. Though it is not easy to recommend anything connected with the author of *Trinity,* (London, 1976), that luridly inventive novel that is so widely misunderstood to relate to real events in Ireland, the Uris's have provided a fine pictorial record of the island of the 'seventies, north and south.

Turning now to Northern Ireland, it is apparent that the overwhelming bulk of writing on Irish affairs of the last decade has been devoted one way or another to the northern crisis. There is therefore a risk that bibliographical discussion of one short period of part of the island might overshadow all other aspects. This may be countered in two ways: firstly by giving due attention to books relating to other periods and events in Northern Irish history; secondly by concentrating on those books and articles which themselves tackle the problem of sifting the scholarly wheat from the pot-boiling chaff.

No single, simple outline history of Northern Ireland from 1920, drawing on official records and standing aloof from partisan commitment, has yet been published though the Educational Company of Ireland, aiming to produce a multi-volume history of Ireland comparable to that of Gill and Macmillan, has at last commissioned such a study. The best overall survey is still contained in *Ireland since the Famine* (see the extended paperback edition, 1973) but two new works, drawing heavily on the recently released Belfast government archives, will be of interest to the historian. Patrick Buckland's *The Factory of grievances: devolved government in Northern Ireland, 1921–39* (Dublin and New York, 1979) covers with perception the formative years of the Unionist regime. The title is taken from a comment by Wilfred Spender, chief civil servant for almost all of this period, but Dr. Buckland has drawn widely on official sources as well as the voluminous diary kept, especially in the 1930s, by that often disapproving figure. Some of the less savoury aspects of unionist control are seen to have developed by accident from the turmoil surrounding the birth of the state, though discrimination in justice, education, housing and local representation later proved too useful to be discarded. There is much here on the financial shortcomings of the Belfast-London relationship,[13] on the workings of regional government itself, and upon the whole range of social policies. The inter-war years were hard, not only in Northern Ireland and the U.K. as a whole, but globally, not ideal for constitutional experiment. Even so, Dr. Buckland concludes firmly that the Unionist state proves the un-wisdom of parliamentary, as opposed to administrative, devolution from Westminister. Paul Bew, Peter Gibbon and Henry Patterson's *The state in Northern Ireland 1921–72: political forces and social classes* (Manchester, 1979), adopts a different perspective. Opening with an essay on 'Marxism and Ireland' it then spans briefly the lifetime of the devolved northern government, offering insights at selected points. It diminishes its usefulness, however, by applying too dogmatic a classification of men and events and by concentrating too exclusively on the inherent contradictions detected in the Unionist camp.

Two other general accounts were written before the archives were opened in 1976, namely Martin Wallace's *Northern Ireland — 50 Years of self-government* (Newton Abbot, 1971), which is concise, clear and balanced; and Michael Farrell's *Northern Ireland: the Orange State* (London, 1976), which is perhaps too committed to furthering the workers' revolution to be regarded as impartial. Its standpoint is unconcealed, if ill-defined, and its pages contain a deal of information not available elsewhere.[14] Students anxious to explore Northern Irish history, however, will facilitate their task considerably by consulting Richard R. Deutsch's *Northern Ireland 1921-1974: a select bibliography* (New York and London, 1975), which contains a wide range of titles, well categorised, and an outline chronology which becomes detailed from 1969.[15] Arthur Maltby's *The Government of Northern Ireland 1922-72: a catalogue and breviate of parliamentary papers* (Dublin, 1974) provides another obvious service, as does the Public Record Office of Northern

Ireland's *Northern Ireland in the Second World War: a guide to official documents in PRONI* (Belfast, 1976), a booklet prepared to coincide with the implementation of the thirty-year rule.

Other valuable accounts spanning much of Northern Ireland's history include Ian Budge and Cornelius O'Leary's *Belfast: approach to crisis: a study of Belfast politics, 1613-1970* (London, 1973), over two-thirds of which applies post-1921 with considerable emphasis on the politics of the 1960s, and all of it to the current home of more than a quarter of Northern Ireland's population. J. F. Harbinson's *The Ulster Unionist Party, 1882-1973: its development and organisation* (Belfast, 1973) is a mine of information, as is Sydney Elliott's carefully compiled, edited and indexed *Northern Ireland parliamentary election results 1921-72* (Chichester, 1973).[16] D. H. Akenson's *Education and enmity: the control of schooling in Northern Ireland 1920-50* (Newton Abbot and New York, 1973) is dominated by the problem of segregated schooling and must in time be overtaken by a study based upon the extensive official files now available, as will, no doubt, Sir Arthur Hezlet's *The 'B' Specials: a history of the Ulster Special Constabulary* (London, 1972), a reasoned defence of a much maligned force by an author who makes his position clear at the outset. N. MacNeilly's *Exactly fifty years: the Belfast education authority and its work, 1923-73* (Belfast, 1975) gives a factual record of the nineteen twenties, the Depression, the War years, effort and expansion after the 1947 Act, and of subsequent consolidation of the Belfast educational system after 1960. In different vein, Nancy Kinghan's *United we stood: the official history of the Ulster women's Unionist Council, 1911-74* (Belfast, 1975), though brief, gives an insight into the background of those involved. Paul Bew and Christopher Norton's 'The Unionist state and the outdoor riots of 1932', in *Economic and social review*, x, no 3, (April, 1979) pp 255-65, focuses on one of the high points in working-class solidarity across the religious divide in the face of common exploitation, and is evidence of the considerable amount of labour history research currently being pursued. It also elaborates a theme of populist and anti-populist division within the Northern Ireland state apparatus, the two wings of which centred upon James Craig, J. M. Andrews and R. Dawson Bates and upon H. M. Pollock and Wilfred Spender respectively. The present author's 'The difficulties of devolution: the post-war debate at Stormont', in *The Irish Jurist*, xii, part 1, (summer, 1977) pp 176-86, glimpses the Brooke Cabinet's misgivings regarding socialist legislation under Labour, 1945-7.

The move from general studies, or those concerned with limited themes of Northern Irish history, to the particular crisis of the late 'sixties and 'seventies can be effected in a number of different ways. Two books of major importance, spanning the history of the protestant population from its roots, both written (and very well written) very much with the current 'troubles' in mind, may be used as avenues of approach. The first is A. T. Q. Stewart's *The Narrow Ground: aspects of Ulster, 1609-1969*[17] (London, 1977). Illustrating five major elements of the Ulster experience – plantation and its reinforcement, wars and rebellions, presbyterianism, recurrent violence, and 'modes of minority' – this book emphasises the ancient integrity of the present quarrel. The second is David W. Miller's *Queen's rebels: Ulster loyalism in historical perspective* (Dublin and New York, 1978) which elaborates, with a degree of success that will be debated, a contractarian basis of Ulster loyalism that sets the Ulster protestant apart, not alone from Irishmen, but also from other Britons. With scholarly verve Dr. Miller sweeps from the seventeenth to the twentieth century stressing, as does Dr. Stewart, the inadequacy of interpretations based merely on the recent past.

Alternatively, biographical and autobiographical works, spanning the longer period but moving inevitably into the crisis phase, can be utilised. Here it is the accounts of the principal actors which must be of most interest: O'Neill's *Autobiography of Terence O'Neill* (London, 1972) and Brian Faulkner's *Memiors of a statesman* (London, 1978). The former, backed by the same author's *Ulster at the crossroads* (London, 1969) – a collection of speeches with an historical introduction by John Cole – gives a good insight into Northern Ireland's first modern premier who lacked the common touch; the latter relates the political career and milieu of the more flexible and realistic of his successors. Both inform of the post-war economic and social adjustments of the province, in which they played a part, and their evidence may be usefully supplemented by John Oliver's autobiography *Working at Stormont* (Dublin, 1978), which, for all its omissions and general discretion, gives an invaluable insight into northern government by one of the abler of its civil servants, from the late 'thirties to the mid-seventies.[18] Two brief lives have also been written of Brian Faulkner, David Bleakley's *Faulkner: conflict and consent in Irish politics*[19] (London and Oxford, 1974) being more sympathetic than Andrew Boyd's *Brian Faulkner and the crisis of Ulster unionism* (Tralee, 1972) which, though informative, is perhaps too hostile to Unionists in general to be fair to this one in particular. P. Marrinan's *Paisley, man of wrath* (Tralee, 1973) is an assessment of a man who bears a heavy responsibility, by a thoughtful christian opponent.

A third method of transition is to consider those articles, some written with the benefit of hindsight, which set out to examine the last peaceful years of the 1960s, for example Desmond Wilson's 'The 'sixties, the years of opportunity' in *Aquarius,* no 6, (1973) pp 7–16, which reviews the wasted ecumenical and other opportunities for reconciliation in Northern Ireland during the decade.[20]

The best way of apporaching the massive literature of the crisis itself, however, is through bibliographical or bibliographically-oriented books and articles, of which that by Richard Deutsch (above) is perhaps the foremost, with J. W. Gracey and P. Howard's 'Northern Ireland political literature 1968-70: a catalogue of the collection in the Linen Hall Library' in *Irish Booklore,* i, no 1, (1971) pp 44–82, a valuable but all too brief and isolated list, particularly of the ephemeral literature of the times. A series of attempts to keep readers abreast of current analyses was made by a number of journals and in succession the best from these can be listed: Cornelius O'Leary's 'The Northern Irish crisis and its observers' in *Political Quarterly* xlii, no 3, (July/Sept, 1971) pp 255–68; J. Bowyer Bell's 'The chroniclers of violence in Northern Ireland: the first wave interpreted' in *Review of Politics,* xxxiv, no 2, (April, 1972) pp 147–57 and 'The chroniclers revisited: the analysis of tragedy in *ibid.,* xxxvi, no 4, (October, 1974) pp 521–43;[21] Richard Rose's 'Ulster politics: a select bibliography of political discord' in *Political Studies,* xx, (June, 1972) pp 206–212; Arend Lijphart 'The northern Ireland problem: cases, theories and solutions' in *British Journal of political science,* v, no 1, (January, 1975) pp 83–106; and finally John Whyte's careful categorisation of analyses across the political spectrum, 'Interpretations of the Northern Ireland problem: an appraisal' in *Economic and social review,* ix, no 4, (July, 1978) pp 257–282.[22] Alternatively, one of the best guides to the student is provided by John Darby in his *Conflict in Northern Ireland: the development of a polarised community* (Dublin and New York, 1976), which describes the course of events and the province's political and social characteristics, but above all contains an impressive bibliography of books, articles, pamphlets, theses and government publications,[23] attached to a thoughtfully arranged bibliographical chapter, drawing not least upon the Northern Ireland Community Relations Commission's *Register of completed and ongoing research into the Irish Conflict* (Belfast, 1972) for which Darby had responsibility as the Commission's research officer. If there is a deficiency in Darby's consideration of socialist analyses, then this is well made up by Belinda Probert in her *Beyond Orange and Green: the political economy of the Northern Ireland crisis* (Dublin, 1978), a work devoted to just such a purpose.[24] One of the most balanced and scholarly introductions to the crisis, also with a useful bibliography, is T. W. Moody's *The Ulster Question 1603-1973* (Dublin & Cork, 1974) which concentrates on the years from 1968, but places them firmly in historical context. There is also a deal of wisdom and perception in an essay by that other northern doyen of Irish historical scholarship, J. C. Beckett: 'Northern Ireland' in the *Journal of Contemporary History,* vi, no 1, (1971) pp 121–34.

With many general accounts and a plethora of analytical attempts thus allocated to periodic surveys, it remains to mention some books describing particular themes or landmarks of the last troubled decade. Richard Rose's *Governing without consensus* (London and Boston, 1971), based upon survey data completed just before the crisis broke, remains valuable, while his *Northern Ireland: a time of choice* (London, 1976) admirably details the summoning, election and operation of the Constitutional Convention, 1975. Ian McAllister's *The Northern Ireland Social Democratic and Labour Party: political opposition in a divided society* (London, 1977) not only relates the experience of the major opposition party in Northern Ireland, from 1970-76, but also gives a good account of the post-war circumstances out of which it materialised. In 'Bi-confessionalism in a confessional party system: the Northern Ireland Alliance Party', (with Brian Wilson) in *Economic and Social Review,* ix, no 3, (April, 1978) pp 207–225, he extends his analysis of northern political parties, and draws upon a questionnaire sent to Alliance candidates in the 1973 general election.[25] The other worthwhile study of a particular party is Paul Arthur's *The peoples democracy 1968-73* (Belfast, 1974), a remarkably successful analysis of a movement of which the author was himself a member.

Rosemary's Harris's *Prejudice and tolerance in Ulster* (Manchester and Totowa, N.J., 1972) is a study of the nature of prejudice in Ulster based upon a small border community, and although the result of research in the 1950s, was a perceptive eye-opener when published and remains an outstanding contribution. The same stature cannot be accorded to Rona Fields' *A society on the run: a psychology of Northern Ireland* (Harmondsworth, 1973). A badly produced book, later withdrawn, it posited a provocative, anti-British view with some interesting data. *The Sunday Times' Insight Team's Ulster* (Harmondsworth, 1972), which went through three editions in its year of publication, gives a vivid rendering of the years up to 1972; John MacGuffin, inspired no doubt by his own brief internment on the introduction of that policy on 9 August 1971, describes this and the twentieth century use of the internment weapon in Ireland in *Internment* (Tralee, 1973); David Boulton's *The U.V.F., 1966-73: an anatomy of loyalist rebellion* (Dublin, 1973) outlines the emergence of this protestant paramilitary group.

The problem of containing paramilitary activity, with substantial reference to Northern Ireland, is discussed in F. Kitson, *Low intensity operations: subversion, insurgency and peacekeeping* (London, 1971); R. Clutterbuck, *Protest and the urban guerrilla* (London, 1973); and R. Evelegh, *Peacekeeping in a democratic society: the lessons of Northern Ireland* (London, 1978); while some of the legal characteristics of Northern Ireland are described in T. Hadden and P. Hillyard, *Justice in Northern Ireland, a study in social confidence* (London, 1973), a Cobden Trust pamphlet charting judicial bias against Roman Catholics, and K. Boyle, T. Hadden[26] and P. Hillyard, *Law and state: the case of Northern Ireland* (London, 1975), an examination of civil rights, emergency powers, courts and the administration of justice, and international proceedings. Contrasting aspirations are presented in the Official IRA's *In the 70's the IRA speaks* (no venue, 1970); the Provisional IRA's *Freedom struggle* (no venue, 1973); *Administration,* xx, no 4, (winter, 1972) which is sub-titled 'The Irish dimension' and is devoted to a series of articles contemplating the future possibilities for Northern Ireland, providing a good cross-section of the thinking of the time; and T. E. Utley's *Lessons of Ulster* (London, 1975), a right wing, conservative and unionist condemnation of British dithering and policy confusion, and a forecast that the integration of Northern Ireland into the United Kingdom was the only viable option then remaining. The observations of prominent British politicians during this whole period should not be overlooked, and some of the comments of Harold Wilson, in *The Labour Government 1964-70: a personal record* (London, 1971), James Callaghan, in *A House divided: the dilemma of Northern Ireland* (London, 1973), and Richard Crossman, in *Diaries of a Cabinet Minister* (3 vols, London, 1975-7), are especially revealing, of attitudes as well as actions.

Finally in this section, two books of selected documents, neither comprehensive but both providing an introductory background and a representative cross-section of views, may be mentioned: John Magee's *Northern Ireland: crisis and conflict,* (London and Boston, 1974) which devotes thirty-two out of fifty extracts to events leading up to the current period, and Charles Carleton's *Bigotry and Blood: documents on the Ulster Troubles* (Chicago, 1977), which allocates eighty out of one hundred and fifty pages to events before 1968.

If biographical works are discussed together, at this point, it is partly because they can help to re-impose a sense of oneness upon the subject of Irish history, though, it has to be admitted, a number of northern lives have already been treated separately above. Of the leading individuals written about, who grew up in an all-Ireland context, the outstanding example is Eamon de Valera, the subject of an all too brief and unquestioning semi-official biography, which is even so, absorbing and valuable: Thomas P. O'Neill and Lord Longford's *Eamon de Valera* (London, 1970). To this may be added the text and pictures of two other tributes: C. Fitzgibbon and G. Morrison's *The Life and times of Eamon de Valera* (Dublin, 1973) and the *Irish Times* collection of contributions *Eamon de Valera 1882-1975: the controversial giant of modern Ireland* (Dublin, 1976). Alexis FitzGerald's 'Eamon de Valera' in *Studies*, lxiv, (autumn, 1975) pp 207–14 is a generous, brief assessment by a political opponent to mark the elder statesman's death. F. X. Martin and F. J. Byrne's edition of essays on another pioneer of Irish independence, *The Scholar Revolutionary: Eoin MacNeill, 1867-1945 and the making of the new Ireland*, (Dublin, 1973) is uneven but in the context of this essay is distinguished by a long and useful account by Geoffrey Hand of 'MacNeill and the Boundary Commission'. Henry Summerfield's *That myriad minded man: a biography of George William Russell, 'AE', 1867-1935* (Gerard's Cross, 1975) naturally has much prior to our period, but if his two volumes of *Selections from the contributions to the Irish Homestead by G. W. Russell* (Atlantic Highlands, N.J., 1978) are indeed followed as promised by a similar selection from *The Irish Statesman* (1923–30), then historians will be deeply in his debt both for the biography and for the wonderful fund of raw material by which to assess Ireland's economic and social development, as well, latterly, as the political development of the Free State. Other literary and political figures have had worthwhile biographies written: T. O'Keeffe's *Myles: portrait of Brian O'Nolan* (Cranbury N.J., 1973) discusses that wittiest of social commentators; G. Freyer's *Paedar O'Donnell*[27] (Lewisburg, 1973) is a brief life of an indefatigable republican and novelist, whose record can be amplified by M. McInerney's *Peadar O'Donnell: Irish social rebel* (Dublin, 1974), based largely upon that journalist's protracted interviews. Edward MacLysaght, republican, genealogist, author and farmer, gives his own idiosyncratic and interesting self-portrait in *Changing Times: Ireland since 1898* (Gerards Cross, 1978); H. Montgomery Hyde's family history, *The Londonderry's: portrait of a noble family* (London, 1979) includes an insight into the seventh Marquess, first Minister for Education in the Northern Ireland government; Calton Younger's *A state of disunion* (London, 1972) offers concise portraits of Eamon de Valera and James Craig, as well as Arthur Griffith and Michael Collins.

The need is for a fuller selection of lives, so that the founders and builders of modern Ireland, their motivation as well as their achievement, may be assessed in context and in interrelation. Happily some work is under way, and in the meantime a number of articles help to expand the picture. Arthur Mitchell's 'William O'Brien 1881-1968 and the Irish labour movement' in *Studies* 1x, (autumn/winter, 1971) pp 311–31, supplies many biographical details of the trade union leader lacking in Edward MacLysaght's *Forth the banners go: reminiscences of Wm. O'Brien* (Dublin, 1969), which is largely based on tape recordings; Leon Ó Broin portrays independent Ireland's outstanding civil servant in 'Joseph Brennan, civil servant extraordinary' in *Studies,* 1xvi, (spring, 1977) pp 25–37, a foretaste, it is to be hoped, of a complete biography to come; Nollaigh O'Gadhra assesses Ernest Blythe in 'Earnan de Blaghd 1880 (sic) – 1975' in *Eire-Ireland,* xi, no 3, (autumn, 1976) pp 93–105, the first date being a misprint for the 1889 correctly used in the text; while the present author has given some account of the international contribution of one of Ireland's ablest and most versatile government ministers in 'P. McGilligan, man of Commonwealth', in *Journal of Imperial and Commonwealth History,* viii, no 1, (October, 1979) pp 117–34.

Finally, it is the bibliographer's privilege, if precedent is a guide, to conclude with a brief reflection on what it would be pleasant to record in ten years time. Occasional footnote reference has already been made to research completed or well in hand, and certainly it is to be hoped that the best of what our young scholars are producing will not lack publishers, despite rising costs and a market that does not increase. The modern volume of the multi-contributor *New History of Ireland* is anticipated in 1982, and with the completion of this splendid project, with its additional ancillary volumes, it would be appropriate if the energies of historians could be directed towards a fully comprehensive Irish Dictionary of National Biography, a project being widely discussed, and one in no way satisfied by Henry Boylans's shot across the bows, *A Dictionary of Irish biography* (Dublin, 1978).

The *New History* and an Irish DNB represent co-operative projects on the grand scale. Individual research will continue, perhaps tilling such neglected fields as business history, perhaps filling out the twentieth century record with more detailed regional studies (along lines such as those pursued, for example, for nineteenth century Cork by James Donnelly and Ian d'Alton). Emigration studies have had a nineteenth century resurgence, and this is another topic which could be carried forward into the twentieth century with profit, while the neglected role of women in society is already attracting attention.[28] In Northern Ireland, in particular, historians are responding to the condition of their society, attempting to attack the mythologisers upon whose black-and-white, one-side-right-and-the-other-side-wrong accounts men of violence prosper. Those who enjoy formal instruction in history already have admirable textbooks. Now those who do not, for example the primary school children for whom history as such is not taught, are being encouraged through local or environmental studies or even through history projects to learn the value of discipline and the pursuit of objectivity.[29] In this context there is room for such teaching aids as the notable P.R.O.N.I. educational facsimile packs,[30] which as yet span only the early seventeenth to the early twentieth centuries, to be extended up to and perhaps beyond the Second World War.

That historical scholarship is flourishing is not in doubt. New publishing houses and new journals have come into being in the past decade; the public interest has never been higher. The proposal floated to established an institute of historical research, a central facility for scholars, with modern amenities and the potential to assist in co-ordinating the undoubted energy present in and beyond a university system which is itself undergoing dynamic change, should surely be welcomed. In wishing such a proposal well the bibliographer can rest confident that its success would certainly ensure the review of a considerable historiography of the 1980s.

[1] See Helen F. Mulvey 'Twentieth century Ireland, 1914–70' in T. W. Moody (ed), *Irish Historiography, 1936-70* (Dublin, 1971), pp 103–36. Professor Mulvey provides much invaluable comment on books covering this period and no student beginning a study of it should neglect her essay. What follows above is intended only to bring that essay up to date. Like it, this chapter relies heavily upon the annual lists of 'Writings on Irish history' published in the September issue of *Irish Historical Studies;* like it, too, a debt is acknowledged to the review columns of several journals, in this case including *Irish Historical Studies, Studies, Eire-Ireland, Irish Economic and Social History* (from 1974), *Saothar* (from 1975), *Economic & Social Review* and *Books-Ireland* in particular. Unlike Professor Mulvey's essay, however, this account ignores that vital area of economic affairs, given separate treatment by Professor Lee in chapter 7.

[2] See also his *Culture and Anarchy in Ireland 1890-39* (Oxford & London, 1979), the Ford Lectures, 1978.

[3] See for example T. K. Whitaker, 'From protection to free trade: the Irish experience' in *Social and Economic Administration,* viii, no 2, (1974) pp 95–115. Others may be found in *Administration,* vols ii, iv, ix, xiv.

[4] See, for example his 'The formative years of the Irish diplomatic service in *Eire-Ireland,* vi, no 3, (autumn, 1971) pp 57–71, and 'Ireland and the League of Nations' in *Studies,* lix, (summer, 1970) pp 133–47.

[5] *Journal of Commonwealth political studies,* viii, no 3, (1970) pp 206–28.

[6] See her two unpublished theses: 'Malcolm MacDonald, and Anglo-Irish relations 1935–38' (M A Univ. Coll. Dublin, 1975) and 'Anglo-Irish relations 1932-1938' (PhD Cambridge University, 1979).

[7] Arthur Mitchell takes the story of the Labour Party up to 1930 in his *Labour in Irish politics 1890-1930: the Irish Labour movement in an age of revolution* (Dublin, 1974). Informative and thorough, the book is too chronologically structured to permit adequate analysis of the underlying social issues at stake in the period. Note also John Walsh's unpublished thesis 'The decline and resurgence of Fine Gael 1937-54' (MA Univ. Coll. Cork, 1978).

[8] See also his 'Career pattern in the Irish political elite' in *British Journal of Political Science,* iii, Part 2, (1973) pp 213–28.

[9] In the same volume John A. Murphy surveys 'The new I.R.A., 1925-62'.

[10] See also in the same issue Donal McCartney's biographical essay on O'Faolain (pp 73–86).

[11] Robert Fisk, for example, has drawn extensively on official records, north and south, and also in London, for his forthcoming study of Irish neutrality.

[12] See also her 'Ireland: America's neutral ally, 1939-41' in *Eire-Ireland*, xii, no 2, (summer, 1977) pp 5–13.

[13] A useful, near-completed M A study (Univ. Coll. Dublin) 'The relationship between Belfast and London 1926–1938' has been undertaken by Breda M. Howard.

[14] See Paul Bew's article (p 152 n 24) for a fuller review of this book.

[15] For a daily account of the period 1968–73 see Deutsch R & Magowan V, *Northern Ireland 1968-73. A chronology of events*, i, *1968-71* (Belfast, 1973), ii, *1972-3* (Belfast, 1974).

[16] Other psephological and analytical aids are J. Knight and N. Baxter-Moore's *Northern Ireland: the elections of the Twenties* (London, 1972), covering the p. r. elections of 1921 and 1925 and the single member election of 1929: J. Knight, *The elections of 1973* (London, 1974) examining the June election for the Northern Ireland Assembly (p. r. once again); J. Knight and N. Baxter-Moore, *Northern Ireland Local Government elections: 30 May 1973* (London, 1973), and S. Elliott and F. J. Smith, *Northern Ireland local government elections 1977* (Belfast, 1977) which is based upon computer print outs. Paul A. Compton's *Northern Ireland: a census atlas* (Dublin, 1978) is another pioneering work, with maps 'summarising the main spatial characteristics of the population of Northern Ireland and the urban area of Belfast in 1971' based on census data of April of that year and dealing in particular with three main themes: demography of the province, the social and economic characteristics of the people and household data.

[17] Joint winner of the 1978 Ewart Biggs memorial prize.

[18] See also John Oliver's *Ulster to-day and tomorrow* (London, 1978), an analysis of future options, prepared for Political and Economic Planning and appearing as PEP broadsheet No 574.

[19] See also David Bleakley's *Peace in Ulster* (London and Oxford, 1972) which shows the too rarely reported other side of conflict – the interdenominational and ecumenical efforts at reconciliation that are a daily occurance.

[20] See also V. E. Feeney's 'The civil rights movement in Northern Ireland' and 'Westminister and the early civil rights struggle in Ireland' in *Eire-Ireland*, ix, no 2, (summer, 1974) pp 30–40, and xi, no 4, (winter, 1976) pp 3–13, respectively, and his unpublished thesis 'From reform to

resistance: a history of Civil Rights in Northern Ireland' (PhD Univ. of Washington, 1974).

[21] See also the third, extended version of his study of one of the main perpetrators of violence, *The secret army, a history of the IRA 1916-79* (Dublin, 1979), and his 'The chroniclers of violence: the troubles in Northern Ireland interpreted' in *Eire-Ireland,* vii, no 1, (spring, 1972) pp 28-38.

[22] For an absorbing study of how the British newspapers have treated the Northern Ireland crisis see the unpublished thesis of John Kirkaldy 'English newspaper images of Northern Ireland, 1968-73: an historical study in stereotypes and prejudices' (PhD Univ of New South Wales, 1979). An intensive examination of 27 national English newspapers and periodicals it concludes that the present crisis has rekindled much dormant English hostility towards the Irish so that in time the papers themselves have become a factor in the crisis, rather than part of the process of resolving it.

[23] The successive government reports and discussion documents are a particularly fruitful source of information about Northern Ireland in these years.

[24] And see also Paul Bew's 'The problem of Irish Unionism' in *Economy and Society,* vi, no 1, (1977) pp 89-109, a review article which draws upon and lists a valuable set of political and sociological analyses.

[25] See also his 'The legitimacy of Opposition: the collapse of the 1974 Northern Ireland Executive' in *Eire-Ireland,* xii, no 4, (winter, 1977) pp 25-42. The circumstances leading up to the collapse are told in detail and with fairness by Robert Fisk in his *The point of no return: the strike that broke the British in Ulster* (London, 1975), an account of the May 1974 Ulster Workers' Council strike.

[26] See also T. Hadden's 'Interlocking Ulstermen' in *New Society,* 17 February 1972, an examination of the historical and religious preoccupations of the two communities.

[27] See also Grattan Freyer's ' "Big Windows": the writing of Peadar O'Donnell' in *Eire-Ireland,* xi, no 1, (spring, 1976) pp 106-14.

[28] As evinced, for example, by Patricia McCaffrey's 'Women and society in twentieth century Ireland' (PhD thesis being undertaken, University College Cork), and the founding and publication programme of Arlen House, The Women's Press (Dublin).

[29] See for example, The Teachers' Centre, The Queen's University of Belfast's *Teaching History: 8-13* (Belfast, 1979), a stimulating example of how history can be made rewarding to younger children.

[30] There are at present a dozen separate packs each of twenty facsimile documents, devoted to such topics as *Plantations in Ulster, Irish Elections 1750-1832* and *Steps to partition,* all published for the Public Record Office of Northern Ireland by H.M.S.O.

Irish Ecclesiastical History since 1500

Patrick J. Corish

It has been remarked that 'ecclesiastical history' is to some extent an unreal abstraction from 'history', in so far as it may imply that the existence of religious communities is separated, or at least separable, from the other political communities with whom they live intermingled, or that the religious life of an individual exists for him in a compartment separated from his life as a whole. In Ireland, at any rate, there is little possibility of separating 'religion' and 'politics': the traditional advice to visitors to avoid them as topics of conversation is tautological in that to avoid either he must to a large extent avoid both.

Much has been written on problems of 'church and state,' but it remains a real topic, by no means exhausted. A somewhat less real topic is the kind that too often resolves itself into a minute investigation of clerical disputes, not of great importance in themselves, and often, surely, very opaque indeed to the laity (this type of study may have been encouraged by the fact that the administrative sources contain a quite disproportionate amount of material dealing with it).

However, for some time past on the continent, and more recently in England, indications have been multiplying of a break-through into what is really more properly 'ecclesiastical history.' In the catholic communion, these have been associated with the rethinking of the idea of 'the church' that preceded the II Vatican Council and ultimately found expression in its decrees. Similar ideas had been and are fermenting in other christian communions. At the centre of this new thinking is the realisation that 'the church' cannot be equated with 'the clergy': there are laity as well. As John Henry Newman put it at the high tide of nineteenth-century clericalism, 'the church would look foolish without them.'

What this has meant in historical writing is that ecclesiastical history has begun to catch up with the approaches to historical studies in general, paralleling their emphases on such things as social and economic history with corresponding emphasis on the christian community rather than on its ministry. Two examples might be cited which sum up the fruits of a generation of this development. One is the German *Handbuch der Kirchengeschichte* (Freiburg, 1965 ff, in progress). The title of *Handbuch* is possibly inapt as a description of the ten massive volumes, ranging from *c.* 350 to *c.* 700 pages each, with one or two more to come. Furthermore, because of the very bulk of the enterprise the project of an English translation was abandoned after three volumes had appeared. However, the series as a whole shows well the present concern of church historians not just with political issues, but also with cultural factors, daily christian life and the impact of general social structures. A more immediate taste of the new historiography is provided by Jean Delumeau, *Catholicism between Luther and Voltaire: a new view of the counter-reformation* (Eng. tr., London, 1977), which presents a synopsis of the work of French historians over the last generation. The introduction to the English translation is by John Bossy, whose own work, *The English catholic community 1570-1850* (London, 1975), is a brilliantly pioneering work in the religious history of these islands. The challenge it presents to Irish church historians is well exemplified by the fresh questions he has been able to ask of what had begun to appear rather tired evidence in his essay 'The counter-reformation and the people of catholic Ireland' in T. D. Williams (ed.), *Historical Studies VIII* (Dublin, 1971), pp 155-69.

The brief for this survey is Irish ecclesiastical historiography since 1970, with some freedom to range back before that date, and with 'the overwhelming emphasis' on the period since 1500. This must surely allow the inclusion of the two works by the late Kathleen Hughes, *The church and early Irish society* (London, 1966) and *Early christian Ireland: introduction to the sources* (London, 1972). With them may be recorded the earlier fascicules of the unfortunately uncompleted *A history of Irish catholicism*: Ludwig Bieler, *St. Patrick and the coming of christianity* (Dublin, 1967), John Ryan, *The monastic institute* and Patrick J. Corish, *The pastoral mission* (Dublin, 1972), Aubrey Gwynn, *The twelfth-century reform* (Dublin, 1968), Geoffrey Hand, *The church in the English lordship 1216-1307* and Aubrey Gwynn, *Anglo-Irish church life: fourteenth and fifteenth centuries* (Dublin, 1968) and Canice Mooney, *The church in Gaelic Ireland: thirteenth to fifteenth centuries* (Dublin, 1969).

Some other publications have made useful contributions to the later medieval centuries. *Medieval religious houses: Ireland*, by Aubrey Gwynn and R. N. Hadcock (London, 1970) is a comprehensive guide to the source-material of medieval monasticism. Leonard E. Boyle, *A survey of the Vatican and of its medieval holdings* (Toronto, 1972) has a special interest for Irish historians because the author tends to use Irish material for his exemplifications. Charles Burns has published 'Sources of British and Irish history in the "Instrumenta miscellanea" of the Vatican archives' in *Archivum historiae pontificiae*, ix, pp 7-141 (1971). This collection, as miscellaneous as its title indicates, ranging from the ninth to the twentieth century, yielded 394 items of interest, 321 of them pre-1500. More substantial is the first volume of the revived *Calendar of papal letters relating to Great Britain and Ireland:* xv, *Innocent VIII 1484-1492,* ed. Michael J. Haren (Dublin, 1978). No praise can be too high for the editorial presentation, but one is left with a lingering suspicion if this is the best way in these times to explore what is in the Vatican archives down to 1558, when the first published wolume of *Cal. S. P. Rome* begins. The great medieval registers may be changing their character, like the Vatican register, or even dying out as sources, as the Lateran register may possibly be in the sixteenth century. Renewed interest in Irish Tudor history, so far based primarily on a re-evaluation of the P.R.O. material, does seem to demand a more rapid opening up of the Vatican, with the help of modern techniques for the reproduction of documents. Attention might well focus on the role of the 'cardinal-protector' — see especially William E. Wilkie, *The cardinal-protectors of England: Rome and the Tudors before the reformation* (Cambridge, 1974) and, for Ireland, Katherine Walsh, 'The beginnings of a national protectorate' in *Archiv. Hib.*, xxxii, pp 72-9 (1974).

At the local and diocesan level another volume of the Armagh registers has been published: *Registrum Johannis Mey ... archbishop of Armagh 1443-56,* ed. W. G. H. Quigley and E. F. D. Roberts (Belfast, 1972). It is unnecessary to comment that these Armagh documents are scarcely 'registers' in the commonly-accepted sense, but how rich they are as historical sources has been shown by Katharine Simms, 'The archbishops of Armagh and the O'Neills' in *I.H.S.*, xix, pp 35-58 (1974) and 'The concordat between Primate John Mey and Henry O'Neill (1455)' in *Archiv. Hib.*, xxxiv, pp 71-82 (1976-7). Another major contribution in the difficult field of medieval diocesan history is Angela Bolster, *A history of the diocese of Cork from the earliest times to the reformation* (Shannon, 1972).

John Watt, *The church and the two nations in medieval Ireland* (Cambridge, 1970), is a satisfactory and dispassionate study. He broadened his canvass somewhat in his volume of the Gill History of Ireland, *The church in medieval Ireland* (Dublin, 1972). His perceptive probings on lay spirituality just before the reformation are stimulating. However, this volume, like its predecessor, tapers off after the mid-fourteenth century, no doubt by agreement with the author of another volume in this series, K. W. Nicholls, whose *Gaelic and gaelicised Ireland in the middle ages* (Dublin, 1972) confirms the pioneering study by Canice Mooney already noted in a verdict in many respects harsh on the quality of religious belief and practice. The same author has also two useful detailed monographs: 'Medieval Irish chapters' in *Archiv. Hib.*, xxxi, pp 102-11 (1973), and 'Rectory, vicarage and parish in the western Irish dioceses' in *R.S.A.I. Jn.*, ci, pp 53-84 (1971), an attempt to probe the obscurities of the origins of the parish in Gaelic Ireland.

A number of contributions of medieval interest in *Archiv. Hib.* may serve as a reminder that this journal has since 1973 published the papers of the Easter conference of the Irish Catholic Historical Committee: Marie Therese Flanagan, 'Hiberno-papal relations in the late twelfth century' (xxxiv, pp 55-70 (1976-7)), showing that Irish affairs, though linked with English, were a separate issue in the eyes of the papacy; Art Cosgrove, 'Irish episcopal temporalities in the thirteenth century' (xxxii, pp 63-71 (1974)); and Ruth Dudley Edwards, 'Ecclesiastical appointments in the province Tuam 1399-1477' (xxxiii, pp 91-100 (1975)), indicating that in the west the clergy of Norman stock could retain their own characteristics even if as seen from London or even from Dublin they might appear 'more Irish than the Irish themselves.'

The 1970s have proved a quite exciting decade in historical revision in the sixteenth century (the only comprehensive guide, D. M. Loades, J. K. Cameron and D. Baker, *The bibliography of the reform, 1450-1648, related to the United Kingdom and Ireland, 1955-70* (Oxford, 1975), as its title indicates, does not cover these new developments). For a generation the sixteenth century had been in something of a backwater, historians being perhaps daunted by the complexity of the problems and the unsatisfactory nature of the evidence. It might be recalled that the last survey (R. Dudley Edwards and David B. Quinn, 'Sixteenth-century Ireland, 1485-1603' in T. W. Moody (ed.), *Irish historiography 1936-70* (Dublin, 1971), pp 23-42) ended with sense of expectancy rather than of achievement: ' A good body of work has been done: much more important still, a number of students in the field are coming forward who will gradually, and it is believed effectively, fill in the gaps in our specialised knowledge which are still evident, and prepare the way for the major synthesis which can now be seen to be possible.'

That hope has been fulfilled. To what extent may be gauged by glancing back at the now dated-looking contributions to *A history of Irish catholicism* by Canice Mooney, *The first impact of the reformation* and Frederick M. Jones, *The counter-reformation* (Dublin, 1967). New ideas come so quickly that even the work by the late Professor G. A. Hayes-McCoy *(A new history of Ireland*, iii (Oxford, 1976), pp 39-141) also shows signs of dating in its treatment of the religious issues (Professor Hayes-McCoy died on 27 November 1975).

The basic fact of Irish sixteenth-century ecclesiastical history is beyond question: Ireland suffered a war of conquest and when it was over the great majority of her people had not accepted the religion of their civil ruler. This religious outcome had no parallel elsewhere. What had been the widely-accepted lines of interpretation, certainly within catholic historiography, are now under question on almost every point, but as yet no clear alternative explanation has emerged of the failure of the established church and the success of counter-reformation catholicism. It is not surprising, therefore, that the only recent attempt at a survey (R. Dudley Edwards, *Ireland in the age of the Tudors: the destruction of Hiberno-Norman civilisation* (London, 1977)) is slow to commit itself to an overall interpretation, though it is clear the author has moved some distance from the conclusion he had reached in *Church and state in Tudor Ireland* (Dublin, 1935). Among those presently writing on sixteenth-century Ireland it will hardly seem invidious to single out Brendan Bradshaw and Nicholas Canny. What might be described as the first shot came from Bradshaw, 'The opposition to the ecclesiastical legislation in the Irish reformation parliament' in *I.H.S.*, xvi, pp 285-303 (1969). This was followed by 'George Browne, first reformation archbishop of Dublin' in *Jn. Ecc. Hist.*, xxi, pp 301-26 (1970); *The dissolution of the religious orders in Ireland under Henry VIII* (Cambridge, 1974); 'The Edwardian reformation in Ireland, 1547-53' in *Archiv. Hib.*, xxxiv, pp 83-99 (1976-7); 'Sword, word and strategy in the reformation in Ireland' in *Hist.Jn.*, xxi, pp 475-502 (1978). Canny's major contributions are *The formation of the Old English elite in Ireland* (Dublin, 1975), *The Elizabethan conquest of Ireland: a pattern established, 1565-1576* (Hassocks, Harvester Press, 1976) and 'Why the reformation failed in Ireland: une question mal posée' in *Jn. Ecc. Hist.*, xxx, pp 1-28 (1979). Bradshaw's review of *The Elizabethan conquest of Ireland...*(*Studies*, lxvi, pp 38-50 (1977)) should be noted, for here the issue is joined on what is emerging as possibly the basic point demanding explanation: how are we to explain the radical difference between the optimistic, conciliatory programme associated with St Leger and Cusack in the 1540s and the emphasis on the need for conquest and plantation which had certainly developed during the limiting dates of Canny's study? Bradshaw and Canny have each adopted a somewhat different approach to the question. Any attempt at a bald summary could not do justice to the nuanced thought of either of them. What may be taken as quite certain is that the new synthesis, whenever it may emerge, will be heavily indebted to the challenging new insights they both present. It may be that this synthesis will have as a component some reflection on the effect of a spirtuality drawing heavily on the Old Testament, especially on the promise of 'the land', with divine licence, indeed a divine command, to exterminate the Cannanite, the Perezzite and the Jebusite and other breeds who had not the law.

Other contributions to the study of the religious history of the sixteenth century can only be listed. They may not open up such broad perspectives, but they provide detail indispensable for testing new hypotheses. The following might be noted: K. W. Nicholls, 'Visitations of the dioceses of Clonfert, Tuam and Kilmacduagh c. 1565–67' in *Anal. Hib.*, xxvi, pp 144–57 (1970); William O'Neill, 'John Bale, 1495–1563', an unpublished Ph. D. thesis (T.C.D., 1970); Donal F. Cregan, 'Irish catholic admissions to the English inns of court, 1558–1625' with 'Irish recusant lawyers in politics in the reign of James I' in *Ir. Jurist*, v, pp 95–114, 306–20 (1970); Helga Hammerstein, 'Aspects of the continental education of Irish students in the reign of Queen Elizabeth I' in T. D. Williams (ed.), *Historical Studies VIII* (Dublin, 1971); T. J. Walsh, *The Irish continental college movement: the colleges at Bordeaux, Toulouse, Lille* (Dublin, 1973) and Liam Swords (ed.), *The Irish-French connection* (Paris, 1978) – most of both these works concerns post-sixteenth-century topics, but to list them here may help focus attention on the crucial question of the origins of the continental seminaries; Brian Bonner, 'Réamonn O Gallachair, bishop of Derry' [1569–1601] in *Donegal Annual*, xi, pp 41–52 (1974); Colm Lennon, 'Recusancy and the Dublin Stanyhursts' in *Archiv. Hib.*, xxxiii, pp 101–10 (1975), 'Richard Stanihurst (1547–1618) and Old English identity' in *I.H.S.* xxi, pp 121–43 (1978) and 'Reform ideas and cultural resources in the inner pale in the mid-sixteenth century' in *Stair*, ii, pp 3–9 (1979) are perceptive studies deriving from an M. A. thesis (U.C.D.) of 1975. Two other published works springing from postgraduate dissertations are Flannan Hogan, 'The last monks and abbots of Bective' in *Riocht na Midhe*, vi, 3–15 (1976) (Maynooth M.A., 1972) and Thomas Morrissey, *James Archer of Kilkenny* (Dublin, 1979) (U.C.D. M.A., 1970). Finally, there is an aptly-titled study by F. X. Martin of a bishop who lived in very uncertain years, 'Confusion abounding: Bernard O'Higgin, O.S.A., bishop of Elphin 1542–61' in Art Cosgrove and Donal McCartney (eds.), *Studies in Irish history presented to R. Dudley Edwards* (Dublin, 1979), pp 35–84.

The seventeenth century is more trodden ground than the sixteenth, with less scope for radical reinterpretation. The only fascicules to appear in *A history of Irish catholicism* were Benignus Millett, *Survival and reorganisation 1650-95* and Patrick J. Corish, *The origins of catholic nationalism* (Dublin, 1968). In the nature of things, most of the contributors to *A new history of Ireland,* iii (Oxford, 1976) treated of church affairs. This holds true of the writers of the 'primary narrative' – Aidan Clarke (1603–41, pp 184–288), Patrick J. Corish (1641–60, pp 289–386) and the late J. G. Simms (1660–91, pp 420–53, 478–508), and even more of some of the contributors to the 'complementary structue' – Brian Ó Cuív, 'The Irish language in the early modern period' (pp 509–45), Benignus Millett, 'Irish literature in Latin, 1550–1700' (pp 561–86) and John J. Silke, 'The Irish abroad in the age of the counter-reformation' (pp 587–633).

In the early seventeenth century a considerable addition to the source-material for the catholic church appears with the foundation of the Roman congregation *de propaganda fide* in 1622. A general survey of its holdings has been published, *Sacrae congregationis de propaganda fide memoria rerum* (Rome, 1972 ff). The material for Great Britain and Ireland has been surveyed by Dominic Conway, 'The anglican world: problems of co-existence during the pontificates of Urban VIII and Innocent X, 1623–1655' (i, pt 2 (1972)), pp 149–62, John Hanly, 'From Alexander VII to Alexander VIII' [1655–91], ibid., pp 176–87 and Hugh Fenning, 'The three kingdoms: England, Ireland and Scotland' [eighteenth century], ibid., ii (1974), pp 604–29. However, because by and large it was contentious issues that tended to be referred for a Roman decision, the relative abundance of material can prove deceptive: it tends to be heavily 'clerical', recording those disputes among the clergy that it has already been suggested provide the least interesting and least rewarding aspects of ecclesiastical history. Nevertheless it also contains a great deal of material of the highest importance. Laudably, interest is switching from printing the full texts of documents to providing adequate guides to the material available on microfilm in N.L.I.

It may help to put some order on what follows if it is noted that Irish affairs might be discussed at a 'congresso', the routine meeting of the permanent officials of Propaganda, or, if judged more important (administratively but not necessarily historically), at a 'congregazione generale', the full meeting of all the cardinals of the congregation, or, if judged to need very special attention, by a sub-committee of these cardinals at a 'congregazione particolare'. The documents tabled at these meetings were filed under the respective heads. The archives are not in good order until about 1660, and down to this date Irish material is very scattered. Benignus Millett has been cataloguing it in *Collect. Hib.,* viii (1965), x (1967), xi (1968) and xii (1969). His last contribution was a

'Catalogue of Irish material in vols 140–143 of the *Scritture originali riferite nelle congregazioni generali* in Propaganda archives' in *Collect. Hib.*, xiii, pp 21–60 (1970). He has since turned his attention to the 'congressi': 'Calendar of volume i (1625–68) of the *Scritture riferite nei congressi, Irlanda* in Propaganda archives', ibid., vi–vii, pp 18–211 (1963–4), 'Calendar of volume ii (1669–71) . . .', ibid., xvi, pp 7–47 (1973), xvii, pp 17–68 (1974–5), 'Calendar of volume iii (1672–5) . . .' pt i, ibid., xviii–xix, pp 40–71 (1976–7). Cathaldus Giblin has published 'A *congregatio particularis* on Ireland at propaganda fide, May, 1671', ibid., xviii–xix, pp 19–39 (1976–7), and fourteen documents from the Propaganda archives under the title 'St Oliver Plunkett, Francis McDonnell, O.F.M., and the mission to the Hebrides', ibid., xvii, pp 69–102 (1974–5). Though most of the material in his more recent contributions (ibid., xiii, pp 61–99 (1970), xiv, pp 36–81 (1971), xv, pp 7–55 (1972)) deals with the eighteenth century, his 'Catalogue of material of Irish interest in the collection *Nunziatura di Fiandra,* Vatican archives', which has been running since the first (1958) number of *Collect. Hib.* may also be noted here, together with his guide to 'Vatican archives: *lettere di particolari'* in *Archiv. Hib.,* xxxi, pp 112–23 (1973). This relatively minor source contains letters addressed to the secretary of state by private individuals: its limiting dates are 1578 and 1803.

Irish archives have yielded 'Bishop Wadding's notebook', ed. Patrick J. Corish in *Archiv. Hib.,* xxix, pp 49–114 (1970). This manuscript, preserved in the Franciscan library, Killiney, affords detailed insights into the life of this catholic bishop in restoration Ireland. The list of books in his extensive library may be compared with interest with 'The library of Bishop William Daton of Ossory, 1698', ed. Hugh Fenning in *Collect. Hib.,* xx, pp 30–57 (1978). The papers of Sir Nathaniel Rich in N.L.I. have preserved very interesting detail on 'Catholicism in Meath, c. 1622', ed. Robert J. Hunter in *Collect. Hib.,* xiv, pp 7–12 (1971). For the church of Ireland, the following might be noted: P. B. Phair's handlist of the MSS of the royal visitations under James I and Charles I ('Seventeenth-century royal visitations', in *Anal. Hib.,* xviii, pp 79–102 (1978)) and C. C. Ellison, 'Bishop Dopping's visitation book, 1682–1685' in *Ríocht na Midhe,* v and vi (1971–5).

John Bossy's stimulating approach to catholicism in early Stuart Ireland in *Historical Studies VIII* has already been noted. The following studies might be added, as far as possible in chronological order of subject: Conor Ryan, 'Religion and the state in seventeenth-century Ireland', a survey of the problems facing the catholic church, in *Archiv.*

Hib., xxxiii, pp 122–32 (1975); Aidan Clarke, 'Colonial identity in early seventeenth-century Ireland' in T. W. Moody (ed.), *Historical Studies XI: Nationality and the pursuit of national independence* (Belfast, 1978); Michael Ward, 'The Dowdall crosses in County Meath', in *Annála Dhamhliag*, i, 9–14 (1971), a note on the wayside crosses, still standing, erected by Janet Dowdall (ob. 1619); Philomena Kilroy, 'Sermon and pamphlet literature in the Irish reformed church, 1613–34' in *Archiv. Hib.*, xxxiii, pp 110–21 (1975), deriving from a U.C.D. M.A. thesis, 'Puritanism in Ireland in the seventeenth century'; Gerard Rice, 'Attitudes to the counter-reformation in Meath, 1600–30', in *Ríocht na Midhe*, v, pp 54–69 (1972) and 'Thomas Dease, bishop of Meath and some questions concerned with the rights to ecclesiastical property alienated at the reformation', ibid., vi, pp 69–89 (1975); Noel Ó Gallchóir 'Aodh Mac Aingil, Gael san Eoraip, 1571–1626' in *Seanchas Ardmhacha*, viii, pp 81–96 (1976); Augustine Valkenburg, 'The ven. Peter Higgins, Dominican, 1601? – 1642' in *Kildare Arch. Soc. Jn.*, xv, pp 284–309 (1973); Donal F. Cregan, 'The social and cultural background of a counter reformation episcopate' in Art Cosgrove and Donal McCartney (eds.), *Studies in Irish history presented to R. Dudley Edwards* (Dublin, 1979), pp 85–117; Seamus P. Ó Mórdha, 'Hugh O'Reilly (1581 ? – 1653): a reforming primate' in *Breifne*, iv, pp 1–42 (1970), pp 345–69 (1972) and 'Heber MacMahon, soldier bishop of the confederation of Kilkenny' in Joseph Duffy (ed.), *Clogher Record album* ([Monaghan], 1975), pp 41–62; Kieran O'Shea, 'Rickard O'Connell (bishop of Kerry, 1572–1652' in *Kerry Arch. Soc. Jn.*, xi, pp 5–14 (1978); Anselm Faulkner, 'Anthony Gernon, O.F.M. (c. 1610–1680) and the Irish remonstrance' in *Louth Arch. Soc. Jn.*, xvii, pp 141–9 (1971) and 'Philip O'Reilly, O.F.M. (c. 1600–1660)' in *Breifne*, v, pp 320–34 (1979); Seamus Anthony O'Mahony, 'The Irish discalced Carmelites, 1625–53' (unpublished Ph. D. thesis, T.C.D. 1978); Leonard Howard, 'The penal laws in Limerick, 1670–84' in *N. Munster Antiq. Jn.*, xii, pp 41–52 (1969), 'The penal laws in County Clare, 1677–1685', ibid., xiii, pp 30–36 (1970), 'The penal laws in north Kerry, 1677–1685', ibid., xiv, pp 49–52 (1971); J. I. McGuire, 'The church of Ireland and the "glorious revolution" of 1688' in Art Cosgrove and Donal McCartney (eds.), *Studies in Irish history presented to R. Dudley Edwards* (Dublin, 1979), pp 137–49. The canonisation of Oliver Plunkett produced the definitive edition of his letters, edited by John Hanly, with a translation when, as in almost all cases, the original is in Latin or Italian *(The letters of Saint Oliver Plunkett* (Dublin, 1979)); it also produced a few brief but useful studies: Desmond Forristal, *Oliver Plunkett in his own words* (Dublin, 1975), and Tomás Ó Fiaich, *Oliver Plunkett, Ireland's new saint* (Dublin, 1975), *Oilibhéar Pluincéid* (Dublin, 1976) and 'Saint Oliver Plunkett and the diocese of Raphoe' in *Donegal Annual,* xii, pp 99–107 (1976). Finally, if only because the entries span several centuries, there might be mentioned P. O Gallachair, 'Clogherici: Clogher clergy 1535–1835', a dictionary begun in *Clogher Rec.* in 1955 and still in progress and Pilip O Mórdha, 'Some priests and parsons of the Clones area, 1620–1840', ibid., ix, pp 232–60 (1977), drawing on the Clones estate papers for material rich in human interest.

In the eighteenth century we return to less explored territory. The only fascicules of *A history of Irish catholicism* to see publication were John Brady and Patrick J. Corish, *The church under the penal code* and Cathaldus Giblin, *Irish exiles in catholic Europe* (Dublin, 1971). Nevertheless, there has been marked progress. The principal worker in the history of the catholic church in the eighteenth century has been Hugh Fenning. In the Roman periodical *Archivum fratrum praedicatorum* he has published an extensive study of 'Ambrose McDermott, O.P., bishop of Elphin 1707–17' (xl, pp 231–75 (1970)), and, spread over three numbers, a history of the Irish dominican province between 1698 and 1761 (xxxviii, pp 259–357 (1968), xlii, pp 251–368 (1972) and xlv, pp 399–502 (1975)). A closely related work is his *The undoing of the friars of Ireland: a study of the novitiate question in the eighteenth century* (Louvain, 1972), a book which ranges more widely than its title might suggest. His *Publications of Irish catholic interest 1700-1800: an experimental checklist* (Rome, 1973), is based on the holdings of the Irish, English and Scots institutions in Rome, but valuable nonetheless, listing 166 items. He has published the following source-material: 'Letters from a Jesuit in Dublin on the confraternity of the holy name 1747–1748' in *Archiv, Hib.,* xxix, pp 133–54 (1970); 'Clerical recruitment, 1735–1783' and 'Two diocesan reports: Elphin (1753) and Killaloe (1792)', ibid., xx, pp 1–20, 21–8 (1972); 'The book of [dominican] receptions and professions of SS Sixtus and Clement in Rome, 1676–1792' in *Collect. Hib.,* xiv, pp 13–35 (1971), 'The library of a preacher of Drogheda: John Donnelly, O.P. (d. 1748)', ibid., xviii–xix, pp 72–104 (1976–7); and 'Documents of Irish interest in the *Fondo missioni* of the Vatican archives' in *Miscellanea in onore di Monsignor Martino Giusti,* i (Città del Vaticano, 1978), pp 191–254.

The Fondo Albani in the Vatican archives provides the material for Cathaldus Giblin, 'The nomination of Denis Moriarty for the see of Ardfert, 1697–1707' in *Archiv. Hib.,* xxix, pp 115–32 (1970), while he draws on P.R.O.I. and Killiney for 'Papers relating to Meelick friary 1644–1731' in *Collect. Hib.*, xvi, pp 48–88 (1973) and again on Killiney for 'Ten documents relating to Irish diocesan affairs 1740–84, from franciscan library, Killiney', ibid., xx, pp 58–88 (1978). A manuscript in the Nationalbibliothek, Vienna is edited by F. X. Martin, 'Provincial rivalries in eighteenth-century Ireland' [disputes among the Augustinian friars] in *Archiv. Hib.*, xxx, pp 117–35 (1972). The Propaganda archives provide the material for Patrick J. Corish, 'Documents relating to the appointment of John Stafford as coadjutor to the bishop of Ferns, 1772' in *Past*, ix, pp 73–9 (1972). The M. A. thesis of Liam Swords ('A catalogue of the archives of the Irish college Paris (to 1793)', Maynooth, 1979) has been printed in *Archiv. Hib.*, xxxv, pp 3–231 (1980). By the eighteenth century the archives of the catholic bishops are beginning to make their contribution, especially in Cashel, where the Butler archbishops, who came of gentry stock, had a relatively settled existence. Mark Tierney has presented 'A short-title catalogue of the papers of Archbishop James Butler II in Archbishop's House, Thurles: part i, 1773–86 . . . part ii, 1787–91' in *Collect. Hib.*, xviii–xix, pp 105–31 (1976–7) xx, pp 89–103 (1978) (cf. the unpublished M.A. thesis (U.C.C., 1970) by Imelda Donovan, 'Calendar of the letters of the Butler archbishops of Cashel'), while Christopher O'Dwyer has published in full the unique and very rewarding mid-century accounts in 'Archbishop Butler's visitation book' in *Archiv. Hib.*, xxxiii, pp 1–90 (1975), xxxiv, pp 1–49 (1976–7). The Kerry archives have yielded 'The Moylan correspondence in Bishop's House, Killarney', ed. Evelyn Bolster in *Collect. Hib.*, xiv, pp 82–142 (1971), xv, pp 56–110 (1972), Kieran O'Shea, 'Bishop Moylan's *Relatio status*, 1785' in *Kerry Arch. Soc. Jn.*, vii, pp 21–36 (1974) and Michael Manning, 'Dr Nicholas Madgett's *Constitutio ecclesiastica*', ibid., ix, pp 68–91 (1976), a treatise on moral theology composed by the bishop and of considerable interest because it was written for his priests and with an eye on local conditions. From the same journal there might also be noted Gerard J. Lyne, 'Dr Dermot Lyne: an Irish catholic landholder in Cork and Kerry under the penal laws' (vii, pp 45–72 (1975)). It might be noted too that Bishop Francis Moylan noted above has been the subject of an unpublished M. A. thesis (U.C.C., 1974) by Josephine O'Farrell. Finally, there are the two lengthy studies by James S. Donnelly Jr. that assemble material opening up wide new perspectives on the aspirations of the Catholic poor: 'The Whiteboy movement, 1761–5' in *I.H.S.*, xxi, pp 20–54 (1978) and 'The Rightboy movement' in *Studia Hib.*, xvii–xviii, pp 120–202 (1977–8).

For the established church there is the unpublished M. Litt. thesis (T.C.D., 1970) by Raymond Thomas Kennedy, 'The administration of the diocese of Dublin in the eighteenth century'. T. S. Powell contributes a brief survey of 'The huguenots of Portarlington' in *Studies*, lxi, pp 343–53 (1972). Nuala Burke describes catholic Dublin at mid-century: 'A hidden church?' in *Archiv. Hib.*, xxxii, pp 81–92 (1974), drawing principally on Rocque's maps (1756) and the anonymous but detailed account of 'the popish chapels in Dublin' (1749). The catholic archbishops of Dublin begin to have something approaching continuous administrative records with Archbishop Carpenter (1770–86). There have been brief studies of him and his successor, John Thomas Troy (1786–1823): Brian Mac Giolla Phádraig, 'Dr John Carpenter, archbishop of Dublin, 1760–86' in *Dublin Hist. Rec.*, xxx, pp 2–17 (1976) and Henry E. Peel, 'The appointment of Dr Troy to the see of Dublin' in *Reportorium Novum*, iv, pp 5–16 (1971). Troy is also central to Patrick O'Donoghue, 'The holy see and Ireland, 1780–1803' in *Archiv. Hib.*, xxxiv, pp 99–108 (1976–7), a distillation from his Ph. D. thesis (U.C.D., 1975).

Seanchas Ardmhacha contains a number of extensive eighteenth-century studies: Christopher Mohan, 'Archbishop Richard Robinson: builder of Armagh' (vi, pp 94–130 (1971)); T. Ó Fiaich, 'The registration of the clergy in 1704' (ibid., pp 46–69); Brendan Hoban, 'Dominick Bellew, 1745–1812: parish priest of Dundalk and bishop of Killala' (ibid., pp 333–71 (1972)); Laurence J. Flynn' 'Hugh McMahon, bishop of Clogher 1707–15 and archbishop of Armagh 1715–37' (vii, pp 108–75 (1973)) and Patrick J. Larkin, ' "Popish riot" in south Co. Derry, 1725' (viii, pp 97–110 (1976)).

Nora F. O'Callaghan's unpublished M. A. thesis, 'The growth of sectarianism in Ireland in the later eighteenth century' (U.C.C., 1975) might serve as an introduction to the nineteenth century, for it raises an issue that by some near miracle seems not to have been explicitly present until this date, but which was to have an unhappy influence for the future. The theme of 'church and state' dominates modern ecclesiastical historiography: it is set against a background of sectarian dispute, perhaps inevitably, as the political position of the established church was challenged, by the new industrial wealth of the north-east that brought the dissenters into the 'political nation', and by the slowly-rising tide of democracy that brought in the catholic masses, leading with a certain inevitability to the Irish Church Act of 1869.

That religion and politics had now become closely intertwined appears from the title of Jacqueline Hill's study, 'The protestant response to repeal: the case of the Dublin working class' in F.S.L. Lyons and R.A.J. Hawkins (eds) *Ireland under the union . . . essays in honour of T. W. Moody* (Oxford, 1980), pp 35–68. However, writing on the established church has concentrated on the theme of its disestablishment. Donald H. Akenson, *The church of Ireland: ecclesiastical reform and revolution 1800-1885* (Yale, 1971) is essentially a study of church structures. Hugh Shearman, *How the church of Ireland was disestablished* (Dublin, 1970) and John D. Fair, 'The Irish disestablishment conference of 1869' in *Jn. Ecc. Hist.*, xxvi, pp 379–94 (1975) concentrate on the act of disestablishment, while P. M. H. Bell, *Disestablishment in Ireland and Wales* (London, 1969), and more specifically R. B. McDowell, *The church of Ireland 1869-1969* (London, 1975) and M. Hurley (ed.), *Irish anglicanism 1869–1969* (Dublin 1970) explore its consequences

Presbyterianism is represented by J. M. Barkley: an essay on 'Anglican-presbyterian relations' in the work edited by Michael Hurley cited above; *St Enoch's congregation, 1872-1972: an account of presbyterianism in Belfast through the eyes of a congregation* (Belfast, 1972); and 'The presbyterian church in Ireland and the Government of Ireland Act (1920)' in *Studies in church history*, xii, pp 393–403 (1975). There is also an unpublished thesis by Robery Finlay Holmes (T.C.D. M. Litt., 1970) on an important individual figure, 'Henry Cooke (1788–1868)'. For the methodists there is David M. Weir, *Rathgar methodist church, Brighton Road, Dublin, 1874-1974* (Dublin, 1974), while for the baptists a number of contributors in the *Ir. Baptist Hist. Soc. Jn.* provide studies and guides to records.

For the catholic church, John J. Silke's survey article, 'The Roman catholic church in Ireland 1800–1922: a survey of recent historiography' in *Studia Hib.*, xv, pp 61–104 (1975) is detailed and comprehensive. 'Church and state' has been a dominant theme here also. From *A history of Irish catholicism* there are John H. Whyte, *Political problems 1850-1860* and Patrick J. Corish, *Political problems 1860–1878* (Dublin, 1967). The theme surfaces in K. B. Nowlan, 'The catholic clergy and Irish politics in the eighteen thirties and eighteen forties' in J. G. Barry (ed.), *Historical Studies IX* (Belfast, 1974), pp 119–35; Donal McCartney, 'The churches and secret societies' in T. D. Williams (ed.), *Secret societies in Ireland* (Dublin, 1973), pp 68–78; J. R. Hill, 'Nationalism and the catholic church in the 1840s: views of Dublin repealers' in *I.H.S.*, xix, pp 371–95 (1975); Maura Murphy, 'Repeal, popular politics and the catholic clergy of Cork, 1840–50' in *Cork Hist. Soc. Jn.*, lxxxii, pp 39–48 (1977); K. T. Hoppen, 'Tories, catholics and the general election of 1859' in *Hist.*

Jn., xiii, pp 48–67 (1970); and Oliver McDonagh, 'The politicisation of the Irish catholic bishops 1800–1850', ibid., xviii, pp 37–53 (1975). For later years there are a number of substantial studies. Emmet Larkin, *The Roman catholic church and the creation of the modern Irish state 1878–86* (Dublin, 1975), *The Roman catholic church and the plan of campaign 1886-1888* (Cork, 1978) and *The Roman Catholic church in Ireland and the fall of Parnell 1888-91* (University of North Carolina Press, 1980) are closely argued and thought-provoking, though perhaps narrowed in their view by a concentration on a very limited range of sources (his 'Church, state and nation in modern Ireland' in *A.H.R.*, lxxx, pp 1244–76 (1975) does not suffer by attempting a wider survey in a narrower compass); D. W. Miller, *Church, state and nation in Ireland 1898-1921* (Dublin, 1973) and John H. Whyte's meticulously dispassionate study in the difficult field of contemporary history, *Church and state in modern Ireland 1923–1970* (Dublin, 1971). To these might be added the shorter surveys by C. J. Woods, 'Ireland and anglo-papal relations, 1880–85' in *I.H.S.*, xviii, pp 29–60 (1972), 'The politics of Cardinal McCabe, archbishop of Dublin 1879-85' in *Dublin Hist. Rec.* xxvi, pp 101–10 (1973) and 'The general election of 1892: the catholic clergy and the defeat of the Parnellites' in F.S.L. Lyons and R.A.J. Hawkins (eds), *Ireland under the union . . . essays in honour of T. W. Moody* (Oxford, 1980), pp 289–320.

A very striking development is the continuing reassessment of Paul Cardinal Cullen (d. 1878), with emphasis on his nationalist views but also with a growing appreciation of his stature as a pastoral bishop. For all its defects in presentation, pride of place must be given to the now completed work by Peadar MacSuibhne, *Paul Cullen and his contemporaries, with their letters from 1820 to 1902* (5 vols, Naas, 1961–77). Much light is thrown on Cullen in particular in the guide to the letters of the influential rector of the Irish college, Rome, Tobias Kirby, published by Patrick J. Corish, 'Irish college, Rome: Kirby papers' in *Archiv. Hib.*, xxx, pp 29–115 (1972), xxxi, pp 1–94 (1973) and xxxii, pp 1–62 (1974). He has also written on 'Gallicanism at Maynooth: Archbishop Cullen and the royal visitation of 1853' in Art Cosgrove and Donal McCartney (eds), *Studies in Irish history presented to R. Dudley Edwards* (Dublin, 1979), pp 176–89, while E. D. Steele has contributed 'Cardinal Cullen and Irish nationality' in *I.H.S.*, xix, pp 239–60 (1975). Emmet Larkin has just published a major survey, *The making of the Roman catholic church in Ireland 1850-1860* (University of North Carolina Press, 1980). In this his 'mosaic' technique would appear to be working better, coupled with the fact that he is taking more account of previous writing on the question. However, he is still inclined to find 'makings' and creations' precisely at the point where he himself begins to explore the evidence. One might think of a number of other dates equally appropriate to the 'making' of the Roman catholic church in Ireland, and one would hope to be able to resist using the word.

How fortuitously Irish catholic episcopal archives have survived even from the early nineteenth century appears from P. J. Murphy, 'The papers of Nicholas Archdeacon, bishop of Kilmacduagh and Kilfenora 1800–1823' in *Archiv. Hib.*, xxxi, pp 124–31 (1973) – the papers were found in a locked cupboard bought at a Galway auction in 1965 – and in Raymond Murray's brief guide to 'The Armagh diocesan archives' (ibid., xxxii, pp 93–7 (1974)), which indicates how slender they are before Archbishop Dixon (1852–66). This fact may go some distance in explaining the 'political' bias in the welcome biographical studies which have appeared: Martin Coen, 'The choosing of Oliver Kelly for the see of Tuam, 1809–15' in *Galway Arch. Soc. Jn.* xxxvi, pp 14–29 (1977–78); Moira Lysaght, 'Daniel Murray, archbishop of Dublin 1823–52' in *Dublin Hist. Rec.*, xxvii, pp 101–108 (1974), a figure for whom a full study is badly needed; Kieran O'Shea, 'David Moriarty, 1814–77' in *Kerry Arch. Soc. Jn.*, iii, pp 84–98 (1970), iv, pp 107–26 (1971), v, pp 86–102 (1972) and vi, pp 131–42 (1973), and, most substantial, but still essentially a 'political' biography, Mark Tierney, *Croke of Cashel: the life of Archbishop Thomas Croke, 1823-1902* (Dublin, 1976), with 'A short-title catalogue of the papers of Archbishop Thomas William Croke in Archbishop's House, Thurles' in *Collect Hib.*, xv, pp 100–138 (1972), xvi, pp 97–124 (1973) and xvii, pp 110–44 (1974–5). From Maynooth come two unpublished M.A. theses, C. O'Dwyer, 'Archbishop Leahy of Cashel 1806–75' (1971) and John P. Gallagher, 'A life of Patrick Cardinal O'Donnell' (1975), and from Galway (M.A., 1976) 'Bishop Edward Thomas O'Dwyer and the course of Irish politics 1870-1917', a fresh interpretation of this controversial figure (a taste is provided in print in 'Correspondence between Bishop O'Dwyer and Bishop Foley on the Dublin rising, 1916–17', ed. O'Callaghan in *Collect. Hib.*, xviii–xix, pp 184–212 (1976–7) and 'Bishop Edward Thomas O'Dwyer and the fall of Parnell: a reassessment' in *Galway Arch. Soc. Jn.*, xxxvi, pp 5–13 (1977–78).

Among non-episcopal figures there might be singled out the study of a theologian decidely worthy of further attention, Edward J. Quigley, 'Dr Murray of Maynooth' in Joseph Duffy (ed.), *Clogher Record album* ([Monaghan], 1975), pp 78–108, and on the general history of Maynooth

Karl Wöste, *Englands Staat – und Kirchenpolitik in Irland 1795-1869: dargestellt an der Entwicklung des irischen Nationalseminars Maynooth College* (Bonn, 1976), a doctoral dissertation that without providing anything startlingly new is thorough and worth having for its bibliography alone. Finally, it might be noted that the monumental *The letters and diaries of John Henry Newman*, ed. C. S. Dessain and others, has now been carried down to Newman's death. The volumes published (from Oxford) in the 1970s cover the years from 1861 to 1890, when Newman no longer had personal commitments in Ireland, but they continue to provide material of Irish interest.

Education was decidedly a 'political' issue in the nineteenth century. Here the major work, Donald H. Akenson, *the Irish education experiment: the national system of education in the nineteenth century* (London, 1970) has met some criticism, justifiable it would seem, to the the effect that it is written from the point of view of the education commissioners, that it fails to take into account the real and reasonable mistrust of 'undenominational' education in all the churches, and that in particular it seriously misjudges the attitude taken by Cardinal Cullen. The shorter survey in *A history of Irish catholicism* by I. Murphy, *Primary education* (Dublin, 1971), is perhaps more comprehensive in its approach. With the latter work were published S. V. Ó Súilleabháin, *Secondary education* and Fergal McGrath, *The university question*. On a local level there is Mary T. Meagher's unpublished Ph. D. thesis, 'Catholic education in the archdiocese of Cashel, 1780–1880' (U.C.C., 1970). Here too might be noted Liam Kennedy, 'The early response of the Irish catholic clergy to the co-operative movement' in *I.H.S.*, xxi, pp 55–74 (1978), if only because there seems no other obvious place to note it – and this in itself would seem to suggest a wide general area where much work remains to be done.

Interconfessional differences are not perhaps the ideal approach to the inner life of the churches, but the facts of Irish nineteenth-century history go some way to dictate it. There have been two major studies by Desmond Bowen: *Souperism, myth or reality ? a study of Irish catholics and protestants during the great famine* (Cork, 1970) and *The protestant crusade in Ireland 1800-70* (Dublin, 1978). This 'crusade', prompted by the evangelical revival, led to the first sustained effort to induce the Irish catholics to change their religious allegiance since the restoration in 1660. It is tricky ground for the historian, and for all Professor Bowen's achievement it is perhaps not unfair to comment that he has not quite risen above writing in 'the anglican tradition'. Four unpublished theses might be noted: Robert J. Rodgers, 'Presbyterian activity among Irish Roman catholics in the nineteenth century' (M.A., Q.U.B., 1970) and 'The career of Rev. James Carlile (1984-1854)' (Ph.D., Q.U.B., 1973); J. R. Gallagher, 'The presbyterian synod and catholic emancipation' (M.A., U.C.D., 1970) and John P. Day, 'The protestants and catholic emancipation' (M.A., U.C.D., 1973), and a local study, John Logan, 'Oughteragh in 1826: a case study in rural sectarianism' in *Breifne*, v, pp 74–120 (1976). Partick O'Donoghue has discussed another cause of friction, economic rather than sectarian, in 'Opposition to tithe-payment in 1822–3' in *Studia Hib.*, xii, pp 77–108 (1972).

There have been some contributions on the inner life of the churches, but they are relatively few and there is no suggestion of an overall framework in the approach to the subject. Four short 'survey' contributions to *A history of Irish catholicism* (Dublin, 1970) manifestly suffered by reason of the need to pioneer because of a lack of previous studies to survey: *Church reorganisation* by Terence P. Cunningham, *Church building* by Thomas P. Kennedy, *Ecclesiastical learning* by John Corkery and *Epilogue: modern Ireland* by Peter McKevitt. Timothy P. O'Neill has written on 'The catholic church and the relief of the poor, 1815–45' in *Archiv. Hib.*, xxxi, pp 132–45 (1973), and concludes that despite notable efforts by the institutional church by and large it was the poor who helped the poor. Kieran O'Shea has published some of the unfortunately too rare examples of a valuable if of its nature limited appraisal of the state of christian life in a diocese: 'Three early nineteenth-century diocesan reports' – dated 1804, 1815 and 1822 – in *Kerry Arch. Soc. Jn.*, x, pp 55–76 (1977). An unpublished thesis by Brid Cahill (M.A., U.C.G., 1975) studies 'The catholic clergy of Ireland, 1820–45.

Emmet Larkin's article, 'The devotional revolution in Ireland, 1850–75' in *A.H.R.*, lxvii, pp 625–52 (1972) seems to have overstated its case for 'revolution' by not adverting in sufficient depth to what was there before 1850. For the earlier period this topic has received some attention in D. W. Miller, 'Irish catholicism and the great famine' in *Jn. Soc. Hist.*, ix, pp 81–98 (1975) and Seán J. Connolly's unpublished thesis, 'Catholicism and social discipline in pre-famine Ireland' (D. Phil., N.U.U., 1977). We may now be at the interesting stage where Paul Cullen's achievements may be in danger of over-estimation. By any standards, his real achievements were formidable. The routine entries in the franciscan chapter – acts almost manage to conceal his activities as visitor of the Irish religious orders after 1850 *(Liber Dubliniensis,* ed. Anselm Faulkner, Killiney, 1978) but they emerge more clearly from the archives of the franciscan generalate (Patrick Conlan, 'A short-title catalogue of *Hibernia*, vol. i (1706–1869) in the general archives of the friars minor, Rome' in *Collect. Hib.*, xviii–xix, pp 132–83 (1976–7) – all the documents except the first date between 1815 and 1869 – and 'A short-title catalogue of material of Irish interest in five volumes in the general archives of the friars minor, Rome', ibid., xx, pp 104–46 (1978). It was to the 'newer' religious orders and congregations that Cullen turned, especially for the work of parish missions. Here Mary Purcell's *The story of the Vincentians* (Dublin, 1973) is useful, as is Francis Finegan, 'Pages from a Jesuit missioner's diary' [Robert Healy, 1796–1882] in *Clogher Rec.*, viii, pp 135–46 (1974), and the late Eoin MacWhite's fascinating study of the Russian ex-revolutionary who worked as a missionary with the Irish redemptorists and ended as chaplain to Cullen's Mater Hospital, 'Vladimir Pecherin, 1807-1885' in *Studies*, 1x, pp 295–310 (1971), 1xi, pp 22–39 (1972). Two studies of clerical social workers might be mentioned: H. F. Kearney, 'Fr. Mathew, apostle of modernisation' in Art Cosgrove and Donal McCartney (eds.), *Studies in Irish history presented to R. Dudley Edwards* (Dublin, 1979), pp 164–75, and Peter O'Dwyer, *Father John Spratt* (Dublin, 1972), a carmelite friar (d. 1871), less remembered than Father Mathew, but an influential figure in Dublin during his lifetime.

This survey is beginning to spill over the limits of its allotted space. Within these limits, little more has been possible than a listing with some attempt at classification and even so quite an amount has simply had to be omitted. It will be clear that the last ten years have produced an impressive quantity of worthwhile work on ecclesiastical history. Yet this writing has only begun to address itself to the question that I have already suggested is the 'core-question', what must be the 'growth-area' for the future, not what the clergy were doing among themselves, not the relations between the churches and the state, but rather an attempt to evaluate what was being achieved by the churches – and not solely by the clergy – in the development of a christian life, thus surely giving a content Ranke could not have dreamt of to *wie es eigentlich gewesen*.

Everything is urging in this direction: the developments of the christian consciousness within the churches, the developments in historical studies in general, and the developments within ecclesiastical history itself, on the continent and more recently in England. What may be the most encouraging factor at the present time is the strength of local historical societies, for detailed local studies are the indispensable first step. In the past, these societies were markedly 'antiquarian' and 'clerical'. They nevertheless produced much work useful for what should be our current enquiries, but it needs reinterpretation. The local societies have now broadened their interests to include social and economic history as well as ecclesiastical. It must be only a question of time before social history in particular establishes a more organic link with ecclesiastical history.

Irish Economic History since 1500

Joseph Lee

Dr Clarkson suggests, in his recent admirable survey,[1] that 'over 1,000'[2] items may have been published since 1968 on Irish economic and social history. That daunting total would probably be exceeded for economic history alone when we add publications 'dealing with the economic performance of the two Irelands since 1945', which Dr Clarkson excluded from his bibliography.[3] The present survey does not discuss the period before 1500, where it would have to be more an agenda for research than a record of achievement, and it further excludes the economic history of the Irish abroad, now so flourishing a field that it deserves separate treatment. It must still adopt, even with these restrictions, a severely selective approach, and provides no substitute for the detailed perusal of the regular specialised bibliographies now serving scholars in this field.[4]

Strange though it may seem in retrospect, George O'Brien's three volume economic history of Ireland from the seventeenth century to the Famine remained the standard work on that period for more than fifty years.[5] It soon became clear to qualified observers that O'Brien's political determinism, which dramatised Ireland and England 'almost as human beings, instead of complex, articulated societies'[6] could only suffocate serious historical enquiry. As early as 1932 an American scholar, W. F. Adams, referring to the nineteenth century volume, bluntly observed that 'My principal objection to this work, aside from its obviously propagandist nature, is to the indiscriminate use of unreliable sources'.[7] These reservations about O'Brien's 'massive but tendentious'[8] work, which was apparently composed at some speed,[9] would now be widely shared.[10] Yet the fact remains that O'Brien's achievement was a notable one at the time, and that his volumes at least got written. Had all his later critics put their pens where their mouths were, Irish economic history might now be in a more flourishing state. However, the inadequacy of the standard work on the 1600–1845 period, coupled with the absence of even inadequate general works on earlier and later periods, proved a serious obstacle to systematic advance. There was simply no coherent framework into which researchers could integrate their findings, with the result that Irish economic history, despite the occasional impressive monograph, remained very much a patch-work quilt throughout the 1950s and 1960s.

Not until L. M. Cullen ventured into the morass to chart a new path in his *Economic history of Ireland since 1660*[11] was O'Brien superseded as a general text. Cullen's short but powerful work, which consolidates the conclusions of his numerous other studies,[12] has not, curiously, quite received the recognition it deserves, partly because it concentrates on the period before 1800, whereas many readers at the time were more interested in a later period, and partly because Cullen's insistent demand for the improvement of professional standards makes few concessions to readers reared on a more relaxed approach to the subject. The book repays frequent re-reading, and sets the standards by which future general studies of modern Irish economic history must be measured.

The core of Cullen's work concentrates on a long eighteenth century, which might now be christened, with appropriate acknowledgements to Trevor-Roper,[13] 'Cullen's century', to acknowledge the transformation he has wrought in our understanding. Discussion for this generation, however much it may modify his conclusions in detail, must take place within his terms of reference, terms which relentlessly rivet attention on the economic component of economic history, on the primacy of factor proportions and market influences rather than of government policy, on the role of impersonal processes in the form of wider economic movements, and on the role of the personal factor in the reactions of individuals to these processes. This permits, or compels, historians to escape from the strait-jacket of nationalist/imperialist polemic, and to substitute for their obsession with the motives of public men a concern for consequences, whether of policy or of process, as reflected in the responses of private men.

While Cullen has singlemindedly excavated the economic foundations of economic history, his approach shows increasing sensitivity to the variety of 'non-economic' influences affecting the more specifically economic process. Much of his more recent work seeks to systematically relate economic change to wider socio-cultural patterns. In a stimulating comparative survey of Irish and Scottish growth between 1600 and 1900, he combines with Christopher Smout to attribute the decisive divergence, which they locate in the period 1780–1820, to the superiority of Scottish riculture, which in turn they attribute more to broad cultural differences between the societies than to narrow technical differences between the economies.[14] Cullen's study of 'The social and cultural modernization of rural Ireland, 1600–1900' probes further the mutual interactions of economic and non-economic factors.[15]

James Meenan's massive study of the southern Irish economy since independence distils the essence of forty years of observation of, participation in, and reflection on the Irish economy.[16] Though one must agree with criticism of the awkward organisation of the book,[17] the individual sections are exceptionally valuable, and the long introduction, pondering the implications for economic policy of the Irish nationalist *Weltanschauung*, fuses political, intellectual and economic history in a masterly manner. Meenan's contributions to Irish economic history, which blend an unobtrusive command of economic theory with a refined historical sense, and which stretch from his brilliant early paper to the Statistical and Social Enquiry Society through several perceptive occasional pieces down to his *Irish Economy,* and indeed beyond, could perhaps be more fully integrated into the consciousness of Irish economic historians.[18]

The expansion of the economics profession in the past decade has generated a rapid increase in studies of the contemporary economy. Ironically enough, the past thirty years are now covered, and virtually at a stroke, in greater detail than any earlier period. Economic historians have not as yet, however, begun to digest systematically the lessons of the growth era since 1960 for their interpretation of earlier epochs, or to explore the implications for longer term interpretations of the relative roles played by personality and process, accident and design, international and domestic circumstances, in this experience. Almost all the publications of the E.S.R.I., the N.I.E.C. and N.E.S.C. are worth pondering by the economic historian. Kennedy and Dowling has become an immediate standard work,[19] and much may be learned from other general work by Dowling and Durkan, Kennedy and Bruton, Walsh and Whitaker.[20]

The *Atlas of Ireland* produced under the auspices of the Royal Irish Academy[21] contains much relevant information, though it does not supersede Ruth Dudley Edwards, *An Atlas of Irish History,*[22] which condenses an impressive amount of economic information into small compass.

General works have devoted more attention to economic history in the past decade than tended to be the custom previously. The standard history of Ireland since the Famine, by F.S.L. Lyons, provides intelligent guidance on economic matters.[23] The relevant chapters in Vol. III of the *New History of Ireland* lay the foundation for significant progress in the study of the economy of the early modern period.[24] Several shorter general works devote specific, often stimulating, and occasionally original chapters to economic history.[25]

Crawford greeted Cullen's *Economic history* as marking 'the beginning of a new era in the study of the economic and social history of Ireland because the book provides a perspective of the whole country against which we can examine the characteristics of regional economies with their societies'.[26] Crawford himself has made notable contributions to general regional history,[27] and the quality of Dickson's and Almqvist's work points further to the potential of this approach.[28] The most strikingly neglected region is Leinster, a province which tends to be curiously taken for granted by economic historians, and which would surely repay detailed investigation. Both the techniques and the conclusions of recent work on current regional development, north and south, should be closely considered by historians of earlier periods.[29]

Bew, Brody, Crotty, Curtin, Hannan, Hechter, Gibbon, Higgins, Jacobsen, Jones, L. Kennedy, Leyton, MacBride, MacCurtain, O'Connor Lysaght, Patterson, Reaney and Wickham, among others, have grappled courageously with concepts of capitalism ('uneven development of'), centre and periphery, class, colonialism (including 'internal'), core, semi-periphery, periphery, and beyond the periphery ('back of the beyond'?), dependency, family (stem and other), kinship, patronage, pesants, populism (not to be confused with populism), and other constructs fashionable among divers schools in the wider world[30] Even the idea (or perhaps only the vocabulary?) of modernization has made a modest entry into the field, though one suspects that most Irish historians would be surprised, not to say alarmed, to learn that they are 'dominated' by 'modernization theory'.[31] (One shudders to think how modernization theorists may feel about that allegation!).

Few of the original models mentioned here owe their inspiration to professional economic historians, and some may be tempted to dismiss them as seductive subsitutes for scholarship, luring impressionable minds from the stony path of austere archival endeavour along the primrose path of models, not to mention theory, But economic historians can only gain from the challenge posed by these ambitious approaches if they respond positively by clarifying their own concepts and becoming more conscious of the implicit ideological assumptions lurking beneath the smooth (or not so smooth) surface of their prose. Nor should they ignore the warnings of Flanagan and O'Dowd about the implications of research approaches towards the Irish past, which may save them from sinking into a trackless neo-positivistic swamp.[32] However unconvincing one may find the occasionally strident invocation of revealed truth in some of these contributions, one need only turn, at the opposite extreme, to a work like Beckett's elegy to the Anglo-Irish,[33] which instructively neglects the economic dimension, in order to appreciate the importance of the issues they raise. It would be true to say, however, that sustained debate, as distinct from axiomatic assertion, has hardly begun on the numerous issues involved, though Gibbon in particular seems to have a knack of rousing response, whether in his enquiries into Ulster unionism,[34] into gombeenism,[35] or, above all, into the nature of Irish peasant society, where Hannan does not find all his propositions convincing.[36] If the '80s can mount detailed discussions of the validity of the fresh approaches adopted in the '70s it will be a fruitful decade indeed.

Few Irish economic historians would share at this stage Reaney's conviction that 'The lack of a significant Marxist intervention in Irish historiography has most of all meant that there is no coherent model of Irish economic society — a comprehensive knowledge of the forces and relations of production and of the social structure to which they correspond'.[37] It cannot indeed be denied that there is no coherent model. But the lack of such a model, at least in the first instance, is due to something much more elementary than lack of 'a Marxist intervention', and that is the simple fact that economic historians have not done their homework in establishing the growth pattern of the Irish economy. Quantitative, much less econometric, techniques have not yet adequately influenced approaches to the economic past. The historiographical significance of Larkin's pioneering estimates of nineteenth century national income[38] has not remotely received the recognition it deserves. Although his estimates are widely assumed to be too low,[39] no detailed alternatives have yet been proposed. Ó Gráda, Solow, and Vaughan have approached aspects of the problem more systematically for a limited time span,[40] but the overall pattern of growth has not yet been established sufficiently precisely to permit confident conclusions about growth possibilities, sectoral linkages, missed opportunities, etc. Until this basic work is done most hypotheses about the potential of the economy must remain unduly speculative. It is not clear how a Marxist approach in itself, however illuminating the individual insights it may inspire, would necessarily remedy this fundamental deficiency.

Calculations of national aggregates will have to be built up from sectoral estimates. But just as the lack of a satisfactory general text made it difficult to tackle regional history, so it hindered the writing of sectoral surveys. It is, after all, exceptionally difficult to write a satisfactory study of a sector of the economy if one has no firm idea of the overall parameters within which to locate one's chosen sector. We have still no detailed general history of any major economic sector, whether agriculture, services, or industry.

The most promising beginning has been made with agriculture, where Crotty's *tour de force* of 1966 exposed by its brilliance the bleakness of the general landscape.[41] Crotty devotes close attention to policy – his work counts among the few significant recent contributions to Irish intellectual history – but he does not fall into the trap of confusing the history of economic policy with economic history. Indeed, he is particularly illuminating on how policy-makers frequently achieved results not only different from, but directly contrary to, their intentions, insofar as they achieved results at all. Virtually all Crotty's theses with regard to the nineteenth and twentieth centuries deserve more detailed presentation and debate. Donnelly's excellent general account of landlord-tenant relations has not received due recognition, perhaps because of its unpretentious format, as an authorative yet succinct survey.[42] Solow's sparkling study of the post-Famine decades,[43] which insists that landlordism was not the rapacious beast prowling among a defenceless tenantry so lovingly drawn in nationalist portraiture, adds a fresh dimension to the agricultural history of the period by the simple device of submitting economic data to economic analysis. Nevertheless, her conclusion that 'the Irish sacrificed economic progress on the altar of Irish nationalism'[44] does not seem to necessarily follow from her evidence. Ó Gráda has queried some of Solow's assumptions concerning landlord investment propensities before 1870, and accordingly cast doubt on the alleged economic irrationality of tenants, but there remains ample scope for further invigorating discussion of a work distinguished, like Crotty's, not only by technical skill, by by sheer luminous intelligence.

Crotty argues strongly that the land legislation paralysed Irish agriculture. This seems to be based on the assumption that trends in the decades before the land legislation portended a dynamic future, whose promise was suddenly blighted by ill-considered legislation. Crotty tended to assert rather than demonstrate this proposition. Until the pre-legislation trends, as well as the post-legislation ones, are established satisfactorily, it is difficult to generalise confidently about the impact of land legislation per se.[46] Despite the valuable material it contains, Huttman, 'The impact of land reform on agricultural production in Ireland',[47] does not quite fulfil the promise of the title. When the task of establishing the impact of land legislation is finally tackled, the estimates of Ó Gráda, Solow and Vaughan on the trend and structure of output between 1850 and 1880 will inevitably be the foundation on which all else must be built. The only other variable that is reasonably clear at the moment is that contemporary economists seem convinced that the present structure of proprietorship constitutes a serious obstacle to maximising agricultural output.[48]

Important work has been done at the county and estate level, though many achievements tend to make the remaining gaps appear more glaring, in the sense that there are still thirty one counties to be tackled after Donnelly's conquest of nineteenth century Cork,[49] to say nothing of Cork itself at earlier or later periods, 273 baronies after Nolan's formidable Fassadinin,[50] and goodness knows how many estates after Maguire's Downshire and Roebuck's Chichester.[51] Of course, for purposes of a general picture, a limited number will often add up to a reasonably satisfactory sample.

The tendency of much valuable research on landlord-tenant relations has been to rescue the landlord from the demonology of partisan nationalist polemic, a perspective which, in the muted shades more appropriate to the study than to the arena, continued to effectively pervade 'objective' positivistic historiography blissfully innocent of any idea of the use of economic evidence.[52] Even the revisionist approach to landlord-tenant relations has not always fully succeeded in transcending the limitations of institutional history, inadequately related to agricultural reality. Vaughan's work leaves little excuse for failure to consider economic criteria, at least for the third quarter of the nineteenth century.[53]

The pre-occupation with landlord-tenant relations tended for long to obscure both tenant-labourer relations and the internal dynamics of the rural classes themselves, who have too often been marched into battle as solid phalanxes. The 1970s have seen the recovery from historical oblivion of the agricultural labourer, partly through work on agrarian unrest,[54] though the economics of labour in agriculture, as everywhere else, have scarcely begun to be examined. The internal composition and combustion of the landlord, tenant and labourer classes require further investigation. Recent significant advances, consolidated in Clark's fine work, have fortunately cleared the ground for rapid progress in the '80s.[55] Nevertheless, as Solow delicately reminds us,[56] we lack studies comparable to those contained in Spring's compendium on European landlords,[57] though Crawford's survey of landlord-tenant relations in seventeenth and eighteenth century Ulster and Nicholls's O'Donnell lecture on the sixteenth century, must surely count among the major contributions of the decade.[58]

We need many more enquiries like Bell's 'Hiring fairs in Ulster',[59] which casts much light on farmer-servant relations, or like his 'Relations of mutual help between Ulster farmers'[60] which, informed by insights derived from anthropology, illuminates the mental as well as the material world of this neglected group. 'Hidden Irelands' are now surfacing with growing frequency, as scholars set out to rescue for history the plain people of Ireland, who have been so long condemned to serve as cannon fodder for conflicting ideologies. Lyne, in the course of several scholarly studies of landholding in the south west,[61] where he traces, inter alia, the chequered relations of Sir William Petty and his successors with their tenants, observes that 'The social composition of Gaelic Ireland in the eighteenth century was rather more complex than is sometimes suspected and included numerous groups living at a considerable remove from the abject poverty believed by older writers such as Daniel Corkery to be almost universally characteristic of the contemporary Gaelic world'.[62] Lyne concludes from his richly documented recreation of a vanished world that 'There is a sense in which one may venture to say that the social and economic history of many parts of rural Ireland in the eighteenth century can best be reconstructed through a study of the local leaseholding families'.[63] While Margaret MacCurtain concentrates on proprietorship in 'Rural society in post-Cromwellian Ireland',[64] she stresses that 'the unnoticed class in seventeenth century Ireland were the tenant farmers'.[65] MacNiocaill's short but significant note on 'Land transfer in sixteenth century Thomond: the case of Domhnall Óg Ó Cearnaigh' provides a tantalising glimpse of strong-farmer property relations in the 1540s and '50s.[66] Other figures once prominent in the rural portrait gallery can now be glimpsed only dimly through the historical mists. Dickson has, however, made an important contribution to our understanding of middle men.[67] Land agents remain an elusive breed, but Donnelly's Cork has pioneered the study of agents, as of so much else, at the county level,[68] and connoisseurs will cherish Vaughan's delectable description of the typical mid-nineteenth century agent as 'more a rustic statesman with pro-consular functions than the manager of a vast agricultural enterprise'.[69]

The historian of agriculture will be grateful for the growing number of settlement studies, even if many confine themselves to purely topographical questions. Several impressive contributions demonstrate both how much more material survives on the early modern period than was once conceded, and how much more can be done with it when appropriate analytical techniques are applied.[70] Due heed must be paid to MacCurtain's timely warning that 'one of the tasks that lies ahead for

Irish scholars is to define a clearly theoretical framework for a methodology of rural history',[71] so essential if the best use is to be made of the evidence. Place name and family name studies have also begun to prove themselves helpful in parts of this field.[72]

Valuable source material has been published on agriculture, mostly in the local journals. This material includes specially commissioned reports, whether for estate owners or for public bodies, diaries, more numerous than might have been suspected, and travellers' accounts. In the editing of this material, pride of place must go to Thompson's magesterial introduction to William Greig's survey of the Gosford estates in Armagh, which shows just what can be done when a superior mind, familiar with wider perspectives, begins to play on Irish material.[73] Reports on the state of late eighteenth century agriculture in Kerry and Louth count among the most useful documents made available.[74] If few diaries can be expected to compare with *Chin Lae Amhlaibh* or with Elizabeth Smith's Irish journals, nevertheless useful snippets can be gleaned from less capacious chronicles.[75] Síle Ní Chinnéide edited extracts from the diary of Coquebert de Montbert, which provide an interesting perspective on, inter alia, the economic scene in 1790–91 through the eyes of the French Consul in Ireland.[76] Among many travellers' observations are those of Lord Orrery in Kerry in 1735, edited by the Knight of Glin.[77] Readers will, no doubt, feel baffled by the compulsion his Lordship felt to designate, for some obscure reason, those among whom he sojourned as 'the Yahoes of Kerry'.[78]

If it proves difficult to construct adequate sectoral histories in the absence of a general framework, sub-sectoral studies pose, almost by definition, even more refractory problems, except in very special cases. One such case is forestry, with which Eileen MacCracken has dealt so instructively in her various studies of the Irish woods since Tudor times.[79] Another case is hunting, whose fortunes Lewis has examined, particularly in the late nineteenth and early twentieth century.[80] The range of work on sub-sectors in post-war agriculture can only serve to remind us how much remains to be done for earlier periods.[81]

Post-war statistics are superior in certain respects to those of an earlier vintage. But the fact remains that Ireland has unusually detailed agricultural statistics since 1847, and that their wealth remains largely unexploited. They provide the essential basis for the study of agricultural fluctuations, which have been sadly neglected. Donnelly's detailed description of the agricultural depression of 1859–64, and Solow's chapter on the slump of the late 1870s show how a systematic approach can extract important conclusions from the available data.[82] Astonishingly, only Bourke has approached the Great Famine from this perspective.[83] When the economic history of the Famine finally comes to be written, it will certainly draw in the first instance on Bourke, then on Donnelly, Nolan, some parish histories, whose value tends to be neglected, and on a few special studies, including accounts of workhouses during the Famine, even if these tend to concentrate more on the social than on the economic consequences.[84] Discussion about whether the Famine constituted a watershed often seems to take for granted that we know what happened during the Famine. We don't.

We don't even know how many people died from the Famine, as Mokyr rightly insists.[85] He concludes in his exciting inquiry that excess mortality must have exceeded one million, and may have reached one and a half million.[86] If this represents a particularly striking contribution, the decade recorded notable advances across nearly the whole range of demographic history. Realisation began to sink in that the survival of the complete manuscript returns for the censuses of 1901 and 1911 provided immensely rich and virtually untapped sources for the population historian. Unfortunately, the inadequate training in demographic techniques given by the history departments of Irish universities meant that it was mostly left to either foreign historians, or to sociologists and economists, to make the best use of the material.[87] Scholars also began to scrutinise more closely the surviving returns for the 1821, 1841 and 1851 censuses, which, however limited their coverage, are still capable of yielding important results. It now transpires that copies of some material destroyed in 1922 have survived. This material, which has been unearthed mainly by the devoted labours of genealogists and local historians, promises to repay close attention.[88] Further insights can be gleaned from estate census material, as well as from Catholic parish censuses.[89] The American, or American trained, scholars who have grasped the potential of the census manuscripts have already made valuable contributions. Kevin O'Neill, in a recent Ph.D. thesis, subjects the Killeshandra returns for 1841 to sophisticated analysis.[90] Carney has extracted intriguing conclusions from the 1821 material concerning several key demographic variables.[91] This work has the signal merit of substituting precision – precision concerning household size, precision concerning age at marriage – for the plethora of prevailing assumptions, estimates/guesstimates, and hypotheses which, however beguiling, can carry no ultimate conviction until supported by satisfactory evidence. The great advantage of the new work is that those who wish to query conclusions based on census manuscript material can now do so only by advancing the discussion further, not by going round in yet more circles.

The published censuses contain a mine of information, almost ignored before the '70s, as the impressive body of recent work by Fitzpatrick, Hannan, R. E. Kennedy, McKenna, Tucker, and Brendan Walsh, a virtual one-man industry in himself, has made abundantly clear.[92] Workers in this field will find their labours lightened by the reference volume published under the auspices of the *New History of Ireland*.[93] Ó Gráda, whose contributions are as fundamental to demographic as to agricultural history, and marked by the same flair for fusing literary and quantitative evidence, has conducted probing enquiries into emigration statistics, concluding that post-Famine emigration from Connacht was significantly higher than hitherto assumed, a conclusion which, if confirmed, has interesting implications for models of post-Famine society.[94]

Students of the pre-censal centuries must plough stonier ground. Dickson has suggested, in a highly original if cryptic contribution, that hearth tax returns were probably more reliable for the first half of the eighteenth century than for the second half, and has stressed the necessity of examining the regional variations in the incidence of eighteenth century demographic crises, arguing that the potato may have helped to reduce the ravages of famine in the first half of the century, but that 'an expanding economy and an end to subsistence crises seem more relevant than the potato and immiseration as catalysts of population increase' in the third quarter of the century.[95] The results of the further research which Dickson is pursuing with Cormac Ó Gráda are eagerly awaited. They should, together with Clarkson's revisionist reflections on possible eighteenth century population trends,[96] provoke fruitful discussion. Parish registers have at last begun to be systematically analysed, by Valerie Morgan, more than thirty years after the pioneering but neglected work of the late M. D. McCarthy failed to stimulate interest among his uncomprehending colleagues.[97] If it is still premature to base generalisations on the early results, another decade should at least enable the parameters of plausibility to be drawn more confidently with regard to eighteenth century population. How the conflicting estimates proposed for the seventeenth century are to be reconciled remains as conjectural as the estimates themselves. Contributors to the *New History of Ireland* offered tentative estimates of the population in 1600 ranging from Butlin's 'less than one million' to Cullen's 1.4 million, while Canny has marshalled the evidence against Cullen in favour of some lower figure.[98] No one has yet ventured to suggest that Cullen's estimate may be too low! However instinctively implausible this may sound, one would have to observe that in the present state of knowledge the evidence for this view would be no more conjectural than the evidence for the contrary. The question remains open.

Research on population has made encouraging progress in the past decade. But the relationships between demographic and economic history, between population and economic growth, between population and poverty – about which Mokyr has posed basic questions[99] – often remain obscure. One of the few assumptions which still seem safe is that excess Famine mortality was higher in the west than in the east. It was this observation that prompted Lynch and Vaizey to apply a dual economy model to pre-Famine Ireland, claiming that the east was essentially a market economy, the west a non-market economy, and that there were few contacts between them.[100] This stimulating hypothesis has provoked a lively discussion, with the balance of opinion tending to resist, or at least modify, the model.[101] Crawford's conclusion that the eighteenth century case of John McNeelans, a thirteen acre farmer in Shanoney, six miles south-east of Strabane, 'reveals the complex nature of the economic network among even the poorer farmers . . . It challenges the assumptions of historians that the character of farming was essentially subsistence and compels them to recognise that markets and money were the predominant factors even in eighteenth century Ulster agriculture'[102] perhaps best captures the general consensus concerning the dual economy model. Critics claim that not only did the 'non-market economy' have markets, but that the 'market economy', contrary to Lynch and Vaizey, suffered severely from the Famine. The extent to which the undoubted depression in the 'market economy' can be directly attributed to the Famine, as distinct from a cyclical downswing imported independently of the Famine, may however require further investigation.

Cullen has stressed the decisive influence frequently exerted by foreign markets on Irish economic fortunes. Clarkson concludes, somewhat to the contrary, in the course of a series of basic papers[103] which promise to make Armagh one of the best known towns of eighteenth century Europe, that as less than fifteen percent of the working population in Armagh in 1770 was directly dependent on foreign trade 'purely local urban and rural markets were clearly more important than distant connections'.[104] Having uncovered another hidden Ireland, Clarkson feels that 'the "inland trading economy" has been hidden by the long-standing assumption in Irish historical writing, from George O'Brien to Lynch and Vaizey, that Ireland was an economy without a market; and obscured more recently by the strong emphasis in revisionist literature on the overseas trade sector of the Irish economy'.[105]

Before attempting to resolve these differences, we must note that concern with trading economies, whether inland or overseas, directs attention, in the first instance, to the role of towns. Unfortunately, urban history has gained only a precarious foothold in Irish historical studies.[105a] The Irish Committee of Historical Sciences hoped that the subject would acquire impetus from its decision to devote the Irish Conference of Historians, held in Belfast in 1979, to 'The Town in Irish History'. The proceedings of that conference, edited by David Harkness, should be published shortly. Enough has been done on Belfast and Cork to whet the appetite for more.[106] Students of Dublin history will be grateful for the index to the first thirty volumes of the *Dublin Historical Record, 1938 – 77,* compiled by G. L. Barrow.[107] But Dublin remains, despite recent advances,[108] the most conspicuously neglected city in proportion to the potential return on the intellectual investment. Mary Daly's forthcoming study should fill part of this most glaring of all gaps in Irish urban history.

Inland towns offer rich possibilities, even if few can be expected to yield such choice fruit as Clarkson's Armagh. Nevertheless, the 1821 census returns, for instance, not to mention those for 1901 and 1911, hold immense possibilities for the alert urban historian. Indeed, this material is probably more manageable, at least in the short term, for smaller towns than for bigger ones. Peter Connell's study of urban estate management in nineteenth century Navan points to the opportunities waiting to be seized.[109] Connell stresses the fluidity of the urban population at all social levels, and advances the interesting thesis that the high mobility he detects among the lower urban classes suggests that much pre-Famine emigration took place from towns.[110]

The study of rural communities, including small towns and villages, is just beginning to be systematically tackled. Economic historians may count themselves fortunate that this topic has stimulated particularly impressive investigations by geographers and sociologists, whose work is crammed with relevant material and ideas. Smyth's exploration of continuity and change in the territorial organisation of a Tipperary community and Hannan's exploration of the network of relationships in a Roscommon community rank among the seminal studies of the seventies.[111]

Once we turn from the internal economic history of towns to their role in the wider economy, we find abundant scope for rewarding research. Kearney adopts this approach in his illuminating study of the temperance movement, where he depicts towns as diffusers of 'improvement', a variation on the 'spread of the market' idea.[112] His conclusion that 'the urban thrust of the crusade, its emphasis upon such values as literacy, thrift, and insurance against illness and its involvement in politcs in some areas link it with other movements which were attempting to cope with the new problems of a changing world'[113] helps locate Irish experience in a more universal perspective. 'Diffusion' seems likely to become a central theme in the economic, as indeed in the social, political and cultural historiography of the '80s. It has the advantage of combining supply with demand analysis, production with consumption, whether of goods, services, ideas, or institutions, of neglecting neither the hand that knocks on the door nor the hand that opens it.[114] It may do something to broaden perspectives too often confined to a world inhabited only by Celt and Saxon, and may serve the further worthy purpose of linking economic with social, political and intellectual history, reminding the votaries of cognate creeds of the benefits of scholarly ecumenicism.

Promising though the theme of 'diffusion' may be, it must be stressed that most of the work remains to be done. Transport, by definition, plays a crucial role in the diffusion of both material and mental products from town to town, from town to country, and indeed from country to country, a relation which should not be overlooked, as the work of Danaher, Jenkins, and McCourt makes clear.[115] Transport history has attracted a few useful contributions, but there cannot be said to be any comprehensive history of transport in Ireland. Nowlan's volume of Thomas Davis lectures contains useful chapters, including original contributions by MacDonagh on shipping and Miriam Daly on the mechanisation of road transport.[116] Horner has pioneered the investigation of transport linkages between Dublin and its hinterland, comparing the situation recorded by the Drummond Report in the 1830s with more recent developments.[117] Towns were crucial links in the chain of credit, but there is still no satisfactory study of any big commercial bank, though Ollerenshaw's work on Belfast banks promises to fill a serious gap.[118]

Transport and credit were central to both 'the inland trading economy' and 'the overseas trade sector'. The relationship between domestic and foreign markets demands detailed exploration.[118a] The stimulating difference of emphasis that Clarkson detects between himself and Cullen on the relative roles of the two markets may not be impossible to reconcile. Inland towns, like Armagh, were less likely to be directly involved than ports with overseas trade, but it would be strange if there were not important interconnections between the two sectors. How much, for instance, of the purchasing power of the domestic market depended on export earnings? The inland market must be disaggregated into its component parts. As a first step, estimates of the size of the market, over as long a period as possible, for food and drink, clothing, housing, fuel and furniture should be constructed. The study of inventories can be particularly illuminating in this respect, especially for the pre-statistical centuries, as a glance at Gailey's Ballyhagen will confirm.[119] Students of earlier periods do not have at their disposal the data available to researchers into the more recent past, but they must take cognisance of their findings and, where relevant, of their techniques.[120] More can certainly be gleaned from the available data, frustratingly fragmentary though it may be, once the question begins to be approached systematically.

Emphasis on the domestic market compels consideration of the distribution of income, whose implications for economic growth have been widely neglected. It has been argued that the grossly unequal distribution of income imposed by the landlord system in the eighteenth and nineteenth centuries, when reinforced by the high marginal propensity to import of landlords, may have proved a serious obstacle to growth.[121] While this argument may not command universal assent, it does at least draw attention to the role of consumption in the economy. The understandable pre-occupation with how landlords got their money has diverted attention from what they did with it.[122]

Concern for the domestic market, particularly in consumer goods, also draws attention to the role of the family as a unit of consumption, and to the role of women, whose influence as economic decision-makers was probably more important in the area of consumption than of production. One must bleakly record here that we know singularly little about either of these intrinsically interesting topics for either town or country.[123]

Assessment of the potential size of the domestic market also constitutes a pre-requisite for any but the most impressionistic appraisals of the quality of entrepreneurship. Even economic historians can hardly reprove businessmen for failing to seize opportunities if they themselves are unable to specify the opportunities the businessmen failed to seize. The literature as yet contains little explicit analysis of entrepreneurial performance, though the context of decision-making, particularly mercantile decision-making, is gradually assuming shape.[124] Much instructive business history must lurk behind the differences economists detect between the economic efficiency, and particularly the export orientation, of foreign industry established in Ireland since about 1960, and the apparent economic inefficiency of native industry oriented towards the home market, differences sufficiently striking to prompt some scholars to invoke the term 'dual economy' to emphasise the distinction.[125] One suspects that business historians are unlikely to be invited to probe these differences too closely, at least in the immediate future! Business history has not developed as much as might have been expected following the success of Lynch and Vaizey, which remains in a class of its own in this field. The response to John O'Brien's call for more business history has been muted.[126] Nevertheless, a number of useful studies have appeared,[127] the sources situation has improved,[128] and the '80s may yet achieve a solid record in this sphere.

Labour history, on the other hand, is simultaneously in both a flourishing and a frustrating condition, at least from the economic historian's viewpoint. The impetus given by the success of a specialist journal, *Saothar, Journal of the Irish Labour History Society* since 1975 has stimulated much interesting work. But relatively little of this deals, as yet, with the economics of labour, either in the sense of reconstructing the record of wages and working conditions, or of assessing the role of labour as a factor of production.[129] Labour history remains overwhelmingly institutional history at this stage. That is not to decry the importance of the history of organisations and movements,[130] which indeed often have direct economic consequences. But it is to note that the economic history of labour has to be still written in a vacuum. Perhaps in no other field has the lack of a satisfactory standard economic history, or indeed of a standard social history, been so seriously felt. The strides made in recent issues of *Saothar,* as well as the growing alertness to the approach adopted by economists toward labour in the post-war economy raise hopes of marked progress in this field in the next decade.[131]

The market is likely to retain its prime position for the immediate future as the fulcrum around which economic historiography revolves. But how efficient was the market, whether overseas or domestic, as an allocator of scarce resources? Did its efficiency change over time? What if the market failed to optimise either growth or welfare, as Liam Kennedy's discerning appraisal of 'Retail markets in rural Ireland at the end of the nineteenth century'[132] concludes that it did in certain respects? Kennedy found that the market was not enough, because 'the solution to many of the problems lay at societal rather than shop level'.[133] If one accepts this argument, the only realistic alternative was state intervention. Appraisal of the role of the state has been inhibited not only by the lack of a good general text on the economy before Cullen, but by the lack of sustained analysis of the role of the state in Irish history.[134] It may be tentatively suggested that analysis of economic policy must consider at least four inter-related aspects, the ideology of the decision-makers, the information available to them, the intelligence with which they diagnosed problems and prescribed solutions, and the efficiency with which the decisions were implemented.

The question of the ideological inspiration of economic policies raises a host of familiar but contentious issues. The role of ideology in any age rightly remains a perennial topic of historical discourse, whether we are dealing, in the Irish context, with questions of plantation, colonisation, mercantilism, laissez faire, utilitarianism, romanticism, free trade, protectionism, individualism, collectivism, or corporatism. Numerous scholars have tackled various aspects of the question.[135] Only Oliver MacDonagh, however, has proposed a general model of administrative action which consistently subsumes ideology to his concept of 'necessity'.[136] It would be interesting to see this model, formulated originally in reaction to the alleged influence of the ideology of 'Benthamism' in Britain, tested systematically in the context of Irish history.

The nature of the information available varied over time. Cartographical and topographical information remained a basic problem until well into the nineteenth century. J. H. Andrews has been particularly productive in reconstructing the sources of information available in this area from Tudor to Victorian times, culminating in his masterpiece, *A paper landscape: the ordnance survey in nineteenth century Ireland.*[137] The whole question of the nature of economic information, and the manner in which ideology influenced 'information' in the pre-statistical age requires closer attention. So, of course, does the collection and presentation of statistical material. The demand for statistical information began to become more pressing as the idea of widespread government intervention became both more plausible and more possible as scientific progress suggested new ways of using statistics. The development of statistical services in Ireland would repay systematic investigation.[138]

Even when scholars have sorted out to their satisfaction the relative roles of ideology and 'necessity', of long term and short term considerations, of conviction and opportunism, of selfishness and selflessness, of Keynes's 'ideas' and 'vested interests' (could an observer of Irish government have ventured that famous generalisation?), this simply brings them to the stage of deciding how intelligently, within their own terms of reference, policy-makers reached their decisions. Crotty provides many examples of the incapacity of policy-makers to grasp the implications of their own policies and to relate means to ends in the field of agriculture.

There is little reason to suppose that agricultural policy-makers have a monopoly of this quality. If this turns out to be frequently the case in the twentieth century, where government has so much more information at its disposal, it was all the more likely – even if the objectives to be achieved appear superficially simpler – in earlier centuries.

The efficiency of implementation has presumably increased over time, at least on trend, as central government has found itself able to exercise growing control over local administration, however striking a role corruption and incompetence no doubt still play. For an earlier period, however, efficiency of implementation constitutes a major subject of enquiry in its own right.[139]

In an ideal historiographical world, studies of government departments and other major public institutions would capture the complexity of relationships between these four variables as well as revealing others that require consideration. The experience with this genre of historical writing has, however, been mixed. Hoctor's account of the Department of Agriculture must rank as a missed opportunity.[140] Moynihan's history of the Central Bank achieves a far higher standard but, as befits a master of discretion, is at its most revealing between the lines.[141] Oliver's recollections of his Northern Ireland experience leave many questions unanswered.[142] Buckland effectively summarises the viewpoints of various departments concerned with the formulation of economic policy in Northern Ireland in the inter-war period.[143] The outstanding example of this genre is Ronan Fanning's authorised history of the Department of Finance, a beautifully clear study, whose value is further enhanced by the extensive extracts from the documents which the author generously weaves into the narrative.[144]

Assessing the role of the state in the economy is no simple matter, even when the causes and consequences of state action can be analysed in a relatively narrow economic context. The problems become even more complicated when allowance is made for the fact that the economy cannot be isolated from the society or from the polity, and that its condition at any time reflects the role not only of land, labour and capital but of what some economists call the residual, with the disarming rider that 'There are times when the residual contribution to the growth of output is very large'.[145] The influence of everything from religious belief, through the legal system and the educational system, to weaning habits may effect economic performance. The influence of policy may well be affected by the attitudes of its subjects/citizens towards the legitimacy of the state itself.[146] The economic historian finds mentalitè all about him.[147] Opinions vary on the importance to be attached to any of the potentially innumerable variables. If, for instance, Hutchinson's view that the Irish failed to achieve economic growth because they didn't want it in the first place (such growth as inadvertently occurred from time to time being the result of minunderstanding their own objectives!) were to carry general conviction, it would greatly lighten the labours of economic historians trying to explain Ireland's relative stagnation.[148] However unconvincing some, like the present writer, may find this particular contention, it would be unhistorical to claim that value systems do not influence behaviour in the economic as in other spheres, though opinions may again vary on whether the values may not flow from, as well as to, the material sphere.[149]

Once economic historians systematically incorporate 'the residual' into their framework they must adopt a comparative perspective to make the best use of their material. Only by placing Irish experince in a wider perspective can the specifically Irish element in that experience be distinguished. Comparison demands discriminating choice of the units to be compared. The instinctive comparison – with England – may be often less relevant than comparison with particular regions of Britain, as Cullen and Smout have shown with respect to Scotland, or with other areas entirely. The potential of a properly disciplined comparative approach has been well shown by the fruitful manner in which Canny and Smyth have developed comparisons between English settlement in Ireland and in America.[150] Students of economic policy have been slow to take advantage of the quasi-laboratory type situation afforded by partition, which offers opportunities for a comparative approach to policy between North and South. It is only recently that these possibilities have begun to be seized, particularly by Dermot McAleese and David Johnson[151] Fortunately, the explicitly comparative interests of several foreign scholars now working on Ireland ensure that comparative perspectives will remain prominent in further work[152]

The past decade has therefore seen a fair harvest reaped, and good seed sown on fertile ground. It has seen the emergence of a cadre of young, able and productive scholars, the best guarantee for the future vitality of the subject. The profession has acquired an increasing sense of identity with the creation of a secure institutional base, the Irish Economic and Social History Society, founded in 1970, thanks mainly to the drive and dedication of Cullen.[153] The Society has published annually since 1974 *Irish Economic and Social History* which, under the editorship of David Dickson and Peter Roebuck, has given a marked impetus to professional publication in the field. If it is still premature to pass a definitive verdict on the journal's achievement, its early years augur well for the future.[154]

The Irish Labour History Society has also begun to flourish. Its annual journal, *Saothar,* which began publication in 1975, is achieving, under the editorship of Francis Devine and John Horne, an impressive level of performance. *The Economic and Social Review* began publication in 1969. It tends to concentrate on the contemporary, but has opened its pages from time to time to interesting historical articles, or articles with important historical implications.[155] Among the other most relevant journals, *Ulster Folklife,* surely one of the most remarkable periodicals of its type in the world, and a jewel in the already glittering crown of the Ulster Folk Museum, has gone from strength to strength. *The Irish Ancestor,* founded in 1969, though not geared exclusively for an academic market, is a treasure trove for the economic historian. Its indefatigable editor, Miss Rosemary ffolliott, noted with pardonable pride on 'Our tenth birthday' that 'The journal has managed without grant or subsidy from anybody, and paid its way every year with only one modest price rise ... Issues have appeared unfailingly each spring and autumn.[156] Other journals, please copy! The *Proceedings* of the Annual Conference of the Sociological Association of Ireland, which began in 1974, contain some stimulating contributions, as does *Anglo-Irish Studies* founded in 1975 by P. J. Drudy. Among longer established journals, *Irish Geography, Irish Historical Studies* and *Studia Hibernica* continued to publish relevant work.

The rise of new societies and the changing publication prospects have influenced developments in a number of ways, mostly salutary. Both the Economic and Social History Society and the Labour History Society have shown admirable anxiety to place Irish experience in a comparative framework. The early conferences of the Economic and Social History Society devoted particular attention to methodological issues, seeking to alert Irish students to best international practice.[157] Cullen was again particularly active in pioneering the systematic widening of contacts and perspectives. The ambitious and successful conferences which he was mainly instrumental in organising, on the Irish side, with Scottish scholars in 1976,[158] and with French colleagues in 1977 and 1978,[159] have subtly influenced the perspectives of the Irish participants. The Labour History Society mounted a major international conference in Dublin in 1980, whose numerous sessions included contributions by Francois Bedaraida and Maurice Goldring, as well as a memorable paper by Eric Hobsbawn.

IRISH ECONOMIC HISTORY SINCE 1500   193

The Dublin History Workshop has attracted lively public support.[160]

Not the least of the advances associated with the new journals is the guarantee of professionally qualified reviewing for work in economic history. Standards have undoubtedly improved during the '70s in this previously somewhat erratic area. Though sustained debate remains rare, the past decade has seen some notable review articles, as well as several impressive reviews, not all confined to the journals already mentioned.[161]

A further encouraging development has been the systematic collection of source material in economic history, strongly supported by the Irish Association for Archives and reported generously in *Irish Archives Bulletin*.[162] The Labour History Society too has been particularly active in this direction.[163] While the sources situation in economic history may be frequently unsatisfactory in absolute terms, it should be clear by now that a vast amount of unexploited material does exist.

Irish economic historians no longer concentrate disproportionately on the nineteenth century, as seemed to be at one time the case. The most relatively neglected periods since 1500 are probably the sixteenth century in general, and the seventy years from 1880 to 1950. The work of Clarkson, Crawford, Cullen, Dickson and Malcolmson has brought major advances in the study of the eighteenth century. There has been a lesser but still gratifying increase in work on the seventeenth century. Much recent research on the early modern period has not yet reached the synthesis stage, or at least the book stage, and has not therefore received full acknowledgement from the historical profession at large. There could be few more valuable services, for instance, than a collection of Crawford's widely scattered essays, whose cumulative contribution amounts to an historiographical achievement of the first importance.

Our understanding of the nineteenth century has deepened during the past decade, but the most remarkable feature here has been the contribution of non-Irish scholars who have happily been attracted to Irish economic history. Their work, not exclusively confined of course to the nineteenth century, places the domestic achievement in more realistic perspective. Population history, for instance, would rank among the least developed instead of the most developed branches of the subject without the contributions of Carney, Clarkson, Connell, Drake, Fitzpatrick, Hepburn, R. E. Kennedy, Mokyr, Morgan, O'Neill and Tucker. Agrarian history, in its manifold ramifications, would be impoverished indeed without the work of Aalen, Beames, Bottigheimer, Broeker, Clark, Curtis, Donnelly, Fitzpatrick, Huttman, Lowe, Roebuck, Solar, Solow and Woodward. It seems doubtful if any country in western Europe relies so heavily on foreign intellectual investment to reconstruct the basis of its own economic history. One need not fully share the fears of Professor Edwards, while acknowledging his prescience, when he warns that 'Irish historians need expect no mercy if they are not prepared to accept that their quantitative and qualitative productions will have to increase fantastically if they are going to avoid being consigned to lower third level teaching, making way for experts from more affluent nations. however inadequately equipped they may be'.[164] There may indeed be a danger of a new 'dual economy' emerging here, though the native may be permitted to hope at this stage that the domestic product can still prove competitive on export markets. In any case, one can only be grateful for the growth of foreign investment during the '70s.

It is true that Irish scholars, or at least Southern Irish scholars, suffer severely compared with their colleagues abroad in the matter of research funding. This is an area in which the Irish Economic and Social History Society, and the Labour History Society, must surely exert pressure in the coming decade. But that is hardly the whole explanation for the neglect of opportunities which foreign scholars have obviously found appealing.

Clarkson noted that 'If economic history is defined as that which is written by professional economic historians, there is little of it: the combined profession in Irish universities, North and South, would be hard pressed to raise a rugby team. Much recent economic history is the work of general historians, economists, archivists, folklorists, antiquarians, and enthusiastic amateurs. A large part of their writing qualifies as economic or social history only on the most elastic definitions; a good deal is ephemeral and some is trivial'.[165] Only Queen's University Belfast has a Department of Economic History. The New University of Ulster, and Trinity College Dublin have encouraged the subject, though without according departmental status to its practitioners. The National University of Ireland, comprising University Colleges Dublin, Cork and Galway, as well as Maynooth, would not seem to have found itself able to offer comparable encouragement. There is no Department of Economic History in the National University, and of roughly ninety posts in History and Economics Departments only one, established in Cork, thanks to the initiative of Oliver MacDonagh, is statutorily devoted to economic and social history.

There have been, unfortunately, grievous losses to set against the progress of the past decade, through the premature deaths of Kenneth Connell, Maureen Wall, and Miriam Daly. Students of population and of rural society must return again and again to Connell's classic works. A fastidious stylist, Connell's diet of caviar and champagne could cause severe digestive difficulties for constitutions reared on potatoes and water. 'Outside Ireland almost certainly the most widely known living Irish historian',[166] he rendered one posthumous service, in that three distinguished obituaries saluted his stature by dispensing with the cant customary on these occasions, recognising that Ken Connell was too big a man to be buried in blamange.[167]

A second sad loss was the death of Maureen Wall in 1972. Gifted with one of the most acute historical intelligences of her generation in Ireland, but obliged to take her degree as an evening student, and lacking the opportunity to study abroad enjoyed by a more fortunate younger generation, it is doubtful if the loss sustained by her death has been fully appreciated by those more favoured by the roll of fortune's dice. She seemed poised for major work at the time of her death, and her interests were extending increasingly from politico-ecclesiastical to socio-economic history, as reflected in her two crisp Thomas Davis lectures, one published posthumously.[168] Miriam Daly's assassination this year, at the age of 45, is still too recent to allow one to write with detachment about her. Much of her energy in recent years was taken up with the political situation, and her corpus of published work was slender, though some essays which will now appear posthumously may hint at the potential magnitude of the loss sustained by economic history. She obviously remained a gifted teacher, but her case brings home the poignant relevance of the Irish aphorism *Maireann lorg an phinn ach ní mhaireann an béal a chan.*[169]

Sadness at the recent deaths of two other scholars mentioned in this paper, Síle Ní Chinnéide and Gerald Simms, can at least be tempered with relief and gratitude that they had reached retirement age.

It may not be inappropriate to conclude with some reflections on the changing relationship of economic history to history. Hitherto there has been a reasonably easy relationship, but it seems clear that paths are gradually diverging. There is increasingly little overlap in the identity of those contributing in different areas. As economic history grows more technical, and as the flow of publication in both Irish economic and non-economic history increases, there will be less and less opportunity to keep fully abreast of all the potentially relevant literature across the historical spectrum. Econometric history, which can yield enormous dividends on the intellectual investment, will become more fashionable during the '80s, both through foreign and domestic investment. It is reassuring that some of the mellowed 'new economic historians' are becoming disenchanted with the metallic certainty of the more confident cliometricians, and growing increasingly aware of the limitations imposed by the assumptions inherent in neo-classical theory for explanations of historical change.[170] But this is far from bringing them full circle back to 'old economic history', much less to general history, as North correctly observes.[171]

Total economic history, never mind total history, may be a chimera, but it is a chimera worth pursuing if historians, not least economic historians, are not to become mere technicians. This danger arises even if econometric history never achieves in Ireland as dominant a role as it did in the 1970s in America.[172] For history is not only in the nuances. It is, above all, in the linkages. Economic historians enjoy a major opportunity to make the key linkages when economic data is involved. If total history is to be written, or even aspired after, the economic historian may have a vital role to play.[173] There thus rests a heavy responsibility on economic historians to maintain contact with non-economic history. It may be that the supreme challenge confronting the Irish economic historian in the final decades of the twentieth century is how to simultaneously both extend and transcend the boundaries of his subject.

[1] L. A. Clarkson, 'The writing of Irish economic and social history since 1968' *Econ. Hist. Rev.*, 2nd ser. xxxiii, 1 (Feb. 1980), 100–11.

[2] *Ibid.*, 100.

[3] *Ibid.*, 101.

[4] The most comprehensive bibliographies are published annually in *Irish Economic and Social History* (since 1974). *Saothar, Journal of the Irish Labour History Society* has carried excellent bibliographies in v, 1979, and vi, 1980. *The Economic History Review* and *Irish Historical Studies* also carry extremely useful annual bibliographies.

[5] G. O'Brien, *Economic history of Ireland in the seventeenth century* (Dublin, 1919); *Economic history of Ireland in the eighteenth century* (Dublin, 1918); *Economic history of Ireland from the Union to the Famine* (London, 1921).

[6] H. F. Kearney, 'Mercantilism and Ireland', in T. D. Williams (ed.), *Historical Studies*, 1 (London, 1958), 66.

[7] W. F. Adams, *Ireland and Irish emigration to the New World from 1815 to the Famine* (New Haven, 1932), 3, n. 3.

[8] J. Mokyr, 'Malthusian models and Irish history', *Journal of Economic History*, xl, 1 (Mar. 1980), 160.

[9] J. Meenan, *George O'Brien: a biographical memoir* (Dublin, 1980), 71.

[10] Readers may wish to note that Lord Vaizey considers O'Brien's volume on the seventeenth century 'splendidly balanced'. See J. Vaizey, 'First choose your theory', in J. Vaizey (ed.), *Economic sovereignty and regional policy* (Dublin, 1975), 260, n. 5.

[11] London, 1972.

[12] Cullen's publications before his *Economic History* include the following: 'The value of contemporary printed sources for Irish economic history in the eighteenth century', *I.H.S.*, xiv, 54 (Sept. 1964), 142–55; 'Problems in the interpretation and revision of eighteenth century Irish economic history', *T.R.H.S.*, 5th ser., xvii (1967), 1–22; 'The reinterpretation of Irish economic history', *Topic*, 13 (1967), 68–77; 'Irish history without the potato', *Past and Present*, 40 (July 1968), 72–83; *Anglo-Irish Trade* (Manchester, 1968); *Life in Ireland* (London, 1968); 'The Irish economy in the eighteenth century', in L. M. Cullen (ed.), *The formation of the Irish economy* (Cork, 1969), 9–22; 'Irish economic history: fact and myth', *ibid.*, 113–24; 'The smuggling trade in Ireland in the eighteenth century', *P.R.I.A.*, 67, C, 5 (1969), 149–75; 'The hidden Ireland: reassessment of a concept', *Studia Hibernica*, 9 (1969), 7–47; *Six generations: everyday work and life in Ireland from 1790* (Cork, 1970); *Merchants,*

ships and trade, 1660–1830 (Dublin, 1971).

[13] It was Trevor-Roper who coined the phrase 'Tawney's century' in *The Gentry, 1540–1640 (1953), 1.*

[14] L. M. Cullen & T. C. Smout, 'Economic growth in Scotland and Ireland', in L. M. Cullen and T. C. Smout (eds.), *Comparative aspects of Scottish and Irish economic and social history 1600–1900* (Edinburgh, n.d., 1977?), 16.

[15] Paper presented at the conference of Franco-Irish historians in Dublin, 1977.

[16] J. Meenan, *The Irish economy since 1922* (Liverpool, 1970).

[17] D. S. Johnson, 'The economic history of Ireland between the wars', *Ir. Econ. Soc. Hist.*, i (1974), 49.

[18] Meenan's publications on Irish economic history include the following: 'Some causes and consequences of the low Irish marriage rate', *J.S.S.I.S.I.*, xv (1932–3), 19–27; 'Irish industrial policy 1921–43', *Studies*, xxxii, 126 (1943), 209–18; 'From free trade to self sufficiency', in F. MacManus (ed.), *The Years of the Great Test 1926–1939* (Cork, 1967), 69–79; 'Economic life', in M. Hurley (ed.), *Irish Anglicanism 1869–1969* (Dublin, 1970), 133–42. 'Irish agricultural policies in the last 20 years', in I. F. Baillie and S. Sheehy (eds.), *Irish agriculture in a changing world* (Edinburgh, 1971). Perhaps the best single guide to Meenan's mind is his classic minority report in Commission on Emigration and other population problems, 1948–1954: *Reports* (Dublin, n.d., 1955), 367–406.

[19] K. A. Kennedy and B. R. Dowling, *Economic growth in Ireland: the experience since 1947* (Dublin, 1975).

[20] B. R. Dowling & J. Durkan (eds.), *Irish economic policy: a review of major issues* (Dublin, 1978); K. A. Kennedy & R. Bruton, *The Irish economy* (Brussels, 1975); B. M. Walsh, 'Economic growth and development, 1945–70', in J. Lee (ed.), *Ireland 1945–70* (Dublin, 1979), 27–37; T. K. Whitaker, 'The Irish economy since the Treaty', *Central Bank of Ireland Annual Report 1976*, 91–103.

[21] Dublin, 1980.

[22] London, 1973.

[23] London, 1970.

[24] D. B. Quinn & K. W. Nicholls, 'Ireland in 1534', 33–8; R. A. Butlin, 'Land and people, c. 1600', 142–86; A. Clarke, 'The Irish economy 1600–60', 168–86; L. M. Cullen, 'Economic trends 1660–91', 387–407; J. H. Andrews, 'Land and people, c. 1685', 454–77, in T. W. Moody, F. X. Martin & F. J. Byrne (eds.), *A new history of Ireland, iii: early modern Ireland, 1534–1691* (Oxford, 1976).

²⁵ T. C. Barnard, *Cromwellian Ireland: English government and reform in Ireland, 1649–1660* (Oxford, 1975); N. Canny, *The Elizabethan conquest of Ireland: a pattern established, 1565–76* (Hassocks, Sussex, 1976); F. G. James, *Ireland in the empire, 1688*–1770 (London, 1973); E. M. Johnston, *Ireland in the eighteenth century* (Dublin, 1973); J. Lee, *The modernisation of Irish society 1848–1918* (Dublin, 1973); M. MacCurtain, *Tudor and Stuart Ireland* (Dublin, 1972); O. MacDonagh, *Ireland* (Englewood Cliffs, 1968; rev. ed. London, 1977); K. W. Nicholls, *Gaelic and Gaelicised Ireland in the Middle Ages* (Dublin, 1972); P. O'Farrell, *England and Ireland since 1800* (Oxford, 1975); H. Orel (ed.), *Irish history and culture: aspects of a people's heritage* (Lawrence, Kansas, 1976); M. A. G. Ó Tuathaigh, *Ireland before the Famine* (Dublin, 1972).

²⁶ W. H. Crawford, 'Economy and society in south Ulster in the eighteenth century', *Clogher Record*, viii, 3 (1975), 241.

²⁷ Ibid., 241–58; 'Change in Ulster in the late eighteenth century', in T. J. Bartlett and D. W. Hayton (eds.), *Penal era and golden age: essays in Irish history, 1690–1900* (Belfast, 1979), 186–203.

²⁸ D. Dickson, 'An economic history of the Cork region in the eighteenth century' (Ph.D., T.C.D., 1977); E. L. Almqvist, 'Mayo and beyond: land, domestic industry and rural transformation in the Irish west' (Ph.D., Boston University, 1977); Abstract in *Ir. Econ. Soc. Hist.*, v (1978), 71–2; 'Pre-Famine Ireland and the theory of European proto-industrialisation', *Journal of Economic History*, xxxix, 3 (Sept. 1979) 699–718.

²⁹ T. J. Baker, *Regional employment patterns in the Republic of Ireland*, E.S.R.I., no. 32 (Dublin, 1966); W. Black and C. W. Jefferson, *Regional employment patterns in Northern Ireland*, E.S.R.I., no. 73 (Dublin, 1974); P. N. O'Farrell, 'Regional development in Ireland: problems of goal formulation and objective specification', *Econ. Soc. Rev.*, ii, 1 (Oct. 1970), 71–92; *Regional industrial development trends in Ireland 1960–1973* (Dublin, 1975); N.E.S.C., *Regional policy in Ireland: a review*, report no. 4 (Dublin, 1975); J. P. P. O'Carroll, N. P. Passchier and H. H. van der Wusten, 'Regional aspects of restructuring use and ownership of agricultural land in Ireland', *Econ. Soc. Rev.*, ix, 2, (1978), 79–106.

³⁰ P. Bew, P. Gibbon and H. Patterson, *The state in Northern Ireland* (Manchester, 1979); H. Brodie, *Inishkillane* (London, 1973); R. Crotty, 'Captialism, colonialism and peripheralisation: the Irish case' in D. Seers, D. Schaffer and M. Kiljunin (eds.), *Underdeveloped Europe: studies in core-periphery relations* (Hassocks, 1979), 225–35; D. F. Hannan,

Displacement and development: class, kinship and social change in Irish rural communities, E.S.R.I., paper no. 96, (Dublin, 1979); M. Hechter, *Internal colonialism; the Celtic fringe in British national development 1536–1966* (London, 1975); P. Gibbon, *The origins of Ulster unionism* (Manchester, 1975); 'Arensberg and Kimball revisited', *Economy and society,* ii, 4 (1973), 479–98; 'Colonialism and the great starvation in Ireland, 1845–9', *Race,* xvii, 2 (1975), 131–40; P. Gibbon and C. Curtin, 'The stem family in Ireland', *Comparative studies in society and history,* xx, 3 (1978), 429–53; P. Gibbon and M. D. Higgins, 'Patronage, tradition and modernisation: the case of the Irish "gombeen man" ', *Econ. Soc. Rev.,* vi, 1 (Oct. 1974), 27–44 and 'The Irish "gombeen man": reincarnation or rehabilitation', *ibid.,* viii, 4 (July, 1977), 313–20; K. Jacobsen, 'Changing utterly? Irish development and the problem of dependence', *Studies,* lxvii, (winter 1978), 279–91; D. S. James, 'Agrarian capitalism and rural social development in Ireland' (Ph.D., Q.U.B., 1978); L. Kennedy, 'A sceptical view of the reincarnation of the Irish "gombeen man"'; *Econ. Soc. Rev.,* viii, 3 (April 1977), 213–22; E. Leyton, *The one blood; kinship and class in an Irish village (St Johns, Newfoundland, 1975);* M. MacBride (ed.), *The ripening of time,* no. 6, 'Social classes' (Dublin, 1976), no. 7, 'Capital in Ireland' (Dublin, 1977); M. MacCurtain 'Pre-Famine peasantry in Ireland: definition and theme', *Irish University Review,* iv (1974), 188–98; D. R. O'Connor Lysaght, *The republic of Ireland* (Cork, 1970); H. Patterson, 'Conservative politics and class conflict in Belfast', *Saothar,* ii (1976), 22–32; B. Reaney, 'Historians and nineteenth century Irish working class history', *Ruskin history workship,* 13 (1979), 10–19; J. Wickham, 'Nation, nationalism and dependency: the case of Ireland', Sociological association of Ireland, *Proceedings of the third annual conference* (Belfast, 1977), 46–50; 'The politics of dependent capitalism: International capital and the nation's fate', in A. Morgan and B. Purdie (eds.), *Ireland: divided nation, divided class* (London, 1980), 53–73.

[31] J. Wickham, 'The new Irish working class', *Saothar,* vi (1980), 82.

[32] K. Flanagan, 'Speculations on historical sociology in Irish society', Sociological association of Ireland, *Proceedings of the second annual conference* (Belfast, 1978), 53–74; Liam O'Dowd, 'The construction of Irish social reality: Some implications of social "knowledge" ', *ibid.,* 102–14; 'Toward a structural analysis of Irish urbanisation', Sociological association of Ireland, *Proceedings of the fourth annual conference* (Belfast, 1978), 68–74.

[33] J. C. Beckett, *The Anglo-Irish tradition* (London, 1976). The index

does not descend to that vulgar term, 'rent', without which the Anglo-Irish tradition might have been rather different.

[34] See the reviews of *The Origins of Ulster unionism* by S. Gribbon, 'The social origins of Ulster unionism', *Ir. Econ. Soc. Hist.*, iv (1977), 66–72 and P. Bew, 'The problem of Irish unionism', *Economy and Society*, vi, 1 (1977), 89–109.

[35] L. Kennedy, op. cit.

[36] D. Hannan, op. cit., and very crisply, 'Patterns of inter-generational replacement in traditional Irish agriculture', Sociological Association of Ireland, *Proceedings of the fourth annual conference* (Belfast, 1978), 56–61.

[37] Reaney, op. cit., G. 11.

[38] E. Larkin, 'Economic growth, capital investment, and the Roman Catholic Church in nineteenth century Ireland', *A.H.R.*, lxxii, 3 (April 1967), 880.

[39] L. Kennedy, 'The Roman Catholic Church and economic growth in nineteenth century Ireland', *Econ. Soc. Rev.*, x, 1 (Oct. 1978), 48–9.

[40] C. Ó Gráda, 'Post-Famine adjustment: essays in nineteenth century Irish economic history' (Ph.D., Columbia, 1973), abstracted in *Ir. Econ. Soc. Hist.*, i (1974), 65–6; 'Agricultural head-rents, pre-Famine and post-Famine', *Econ. Soc. Rev.*, v, 3 (1974), 385–92; W. E. Vaughan, 'A study of landlord and tenant relations in Ireland between the Famine and the land war, 1850–78' (Ph.D., T.C.D., 1974), abstracted in *Ir. Econ. Soc. Hist.*, i (1974), 62–3; 'Agricultural output, rents and wages in Ireland 1850–81', paper presented to the Conference of Franco-Irish Historians in Dublin, 1977; B. L. Solow, *The land question and the Irish economy, 1870–1903* (Cambridge, Mass., 1971).

[41] R. Crotty, *Irish agricultural production: its volume and structure* (Cork, 1966).

[42] J. S. Donnelly, Jr., *Landlord and tenant in nineteenth century Ireland* (Dublin, 1973).

[43] B. Solow, op. cit.

[44] *ibid.*, 204.

[45] C. Ó Gráda, 'The investment behaviour of Irish landlords 1850–75: some preliminary findings', *Agricultural History Review*, xxiii, 1 (1975), 129–55.

[46] Reservations about Crotty's contentions on this issue have been expressed by Ó Gráda, *ibid.*, 155, n. 2, and J. Lee, 'Irish Agriculture', *Agricultural History Review*, xvii, 1 (1969), 71.

[47] J. P. Huttman, 'The impact of land reform on agricultural produc-

tion in Ireland', *Agricultural History*, xlvi, (1972).

[48] P. J. Drudy, 'Land use in Britain and Ireland', *Anglo-Irish Studies*, i (1975), 105–16, reflects the current consensus on this question. Among the first to make this point was Meenan, 'Some causes and consequences', *op. cit.*, 26.

[49] J. S. Donnelly, Jr., *The land and the people of nineteenth century Cork: the rural economy and the land question* (London, 1975).

[50] W. Nolan, *Fassadinin: land, settlement and society in south-east Ireland 1600–1850* (Dublin, 1979), abstracted in *Ir. Econ. Soc. Hist.*, iii (1976), 75–7.

[51] W. A. Maguire, *The Downshire estates in Ireland, 1801–45: the management of Irish landed estates in the early nineteenth century* (Oxford, 1972); (ed.), *Letters of a great Irish landlord: a selection from the estate correspondence of the Third Marquess of Downshire, 1809–45* (Belfast, 1974); 'Lord Donegall and the sale of Belfast: a case history from the encumbered estates courts', *Econ. Hist. Rev.*, 2nd ser., xxiv (1976), 570–84; 'The 1822 settlement of the Donegall estates', *Ir. Ec. Soc. Hist.*, iii (1976), 17–32; P. Roebuck, 'The making of an Ulster great estate: the Chichesters, Barons of Belfast and Viscounts of Carrigfergus, 1599–1648', *P.R.I.A.*, 79, C (1979), 1–25.

[52] A selection of serious work on landlordism, estate management, and agricultural practices would include: R. A. Butlin, 'Agriculture in Co. Dublin in the late eighteenth century', *Studia Hibernica*, 9 (1969), 93–108; W. H. Crawford, 'The Murray of Broughton estate, 1730', *Donegal Annual*, xii (1977), 272–85; E. A. Currie, 'Land tenures, enclosures and field patterns in Co. Derry in the eighteenth and nineteenth centuries', *Ir. Geog.*, ix (1976), 50–62; J. S. Donnelly, Jr., 'The journals of Sir John Benn-Walsh relating to the management of his Irish estates 1823–64', *Cork Hist. Arch. Soc. Jnl*, lxxix, 230 (1974), 86–123, lxxx, 231 (1975), 15–42; M. Hurst, *Marie Edgeworth and the public scene: intellect, fine feeling and landlordism in the age of reform* (London, 1969); P. G. Lane, 'The management of estates by financial corporations in Ireland after the Famine', *Studia Hibernica*, 14 (1974), 67–89; W. J. Lowe, 'Landlord and tenant on the estate of Trinity College Dublin, 1851–1903', *Hermathena*, cxx (1976), 5–24; E. McCourt, 'The management of the Farnham estates during the nineteenth century', *Breifne*, iv, 16 (1975), 531–60; A. P. W. Malcomson, 'Absenteeism in eighteenth century Ireland', *Ir. Ec. Soc. Hist.*, i (1974), 15–35; H. T. Masterson, 'Land use patterns and farming practice in Co. Fermanagh 1609–1849', *Clogher Record*, vii (1969), 56–88; O. Robinson, 'The London companies and

tenant right in nineteenth century Ireland', *Agricultural History Review,* xviii (1970), 54–63; J. Sheehan, *South Westmeath: farm and folk* (Dublin, 1978); W. J. Smyth, 'Estate records and the making of the Irish landscape: an example from County Tipperary', *Ir. Geog.,* ix (1976), 29–49; W. E. Vaughan, 'Landlord and tenant relations in Ireland between the famine and the Land War, 1850–78', in Cullen & Smout, *op. cit.,* 216–26.

[53] W. E. Vaughan, 'An assessment of the economic performance of Irish landlords, 1851–81', in F. S. L. Lyons & R. A. J. Hawkins (eds.), *Ireland under the Union* (Oxford, 1980), 173–200. C. Ó Gráda, 'Supply responsiveness in Irish agriculture during the nineteenth century', *Econ. Hist. Rev.,* 2nd ser., xxviii, 2 (1975), 312–17 is basic to a proper understanding of agricultural reality.

[54] M. R. Beames, 'Cottiers and conacre in pre-Famine Ireland', *Journal of Peasant Studies,* ii, 3 (1975), 352–4; 'Peasant movements: Ireland 1785–95', *ibid.,* ii, 4 (1975), 502–6; 'Rural conflict in pre-Famine Ireland', *Past and Present,* 81 (Nov. 1978), 75–91; J. S. Donnelly, Jr., 'The rightboy movement, 1785–8', *Studia Hibernica,* 17–18 (1977–8), 120–202; 'The whiteboy movement, 1761–65', *I.H.S.,* xxi, 81 (March 1978), 20–54; D. Fitzpatrick, 'The disappearance of the Irish agricultural labourer, 1841–1912', *Ir. Econ. Soc. Hist.,* vii (1980), 66–92; P. L. Horn, 'The National Agricultural Labourers Union in Ireland, 1873–9' *I.H.S.,* xvii, 67 (March 1971), 340–52; J. Lee, 'The ribbonmen', in T. D. Williams (ed.), *Secret societies in Ireland* (Dublin, 1973), 26–35; 'Rural unrest in the nineteenth century', paper presented to the conference of Franco-Irish historians in Dublin, 1977; E. O'Connor, 'Agrarian unrest and the labour movement in Co. Waterford, 1917–23', *Saothar,* vi (1980), 40–58; M. Wall, 'The whiteboys', in T. D. Williams (ed.), *op. cit.,* 13–25.

[55] P. Bew, *Land and the national question in Ireland 1858–82* (Dublin, 1978); S. Clark, 'The social composition of the Land League', *I.H.S.,* xvii, 68 (Sept. 1971), 447–69; 'The political mobilisation of Irish farmers', *Canadian Review of Sociology and Anthropology,* xxii, 4, Pt II (Nov. 1975), 483–99; 'The importance of agrarian classes: agrarian class structure and collective action in nineteenth century Ireland', *British Journal of Sociology,* xxix, 1 (March 1978); *Social origins of the Irish land war* (London, 1979); P. Duffy, 'Irish landholding structure and population in the mid-nineteenth century', *Maynooth Review,* iii, 2 (1977), 3–27; D. S. Jones, 'The role of the graziers in agrarian conflict 1870–1910', paper presented to E.S.R.I. Seminar, March 1978; 'Agrarian capitalism and Irish landlordism', in A. E. C. W. Spencer (ed.), *Dependency: social, political and cultural,* (Belfast, 1979).

⁵⁶ B. Solow, *Ir. Econ. Soc. Hist.*, vi (1979), 106.

⁵⁷ D. Spring (ed.), *European landed elites in the nineteenth century* (London, 1977).

⁵⁸ W. H. Crawford, 'Landlord-tenant relations in Ulster 1609–1820', *Ir. Econ. Soc. Hist.*, ii (1975), 5–21; 'The influence of the landlord in eighteenth century Ulster', in L. M. Cullen & T. C. Smout (eds.), *op cit.*, 193–203; K. W. Nicholls, *Land, law and society in sixteenth century Ireland* (Dublin, 1976).

⁵⁹ *Ulster Folklife*, 25 (1979), 67–78.

⁶⁰ *ibid.*, 24 (1978), 48–58.

⁶¹ G. Lyne, 'Dr Dermot Lyne: an Irish Catholic land-holder in Cork and Kerry under the Penal Laws', *Kerry Arch. Soc. Jnl.*, 8 (1975), 45–72; 'The Mac Finín Duibh O'Sullivans of Tuosist and Berehaven', *ibid.*, 9 (1976), 32–67; 'Land tenure in Kenmare and Tuosist, 1696–c. 1716, with notes on the tenants and their holdings', *ibid.*, 10 (1977), 19–54; 'Land tenure in Kenmare, Bonane and Tuosist, 1720–70, with lists of tenants and their holdings', *ibid.*, 11 (1978), 25–55.

⁶² G. Lyne, 'The Mac Finín Duibh O'Sullivans of Tuosist and Berehaven', *op. cit.*, 31.

⁶³ *ibid.*

⁶⁴ In A. Cosgrove & D. McCartney (eds.), *Studies in Irish history presented to R. Dudley Edwards* (Dublin, 1979), 118–136.

⁶⁵ *ibid.*, 128.

⁶⁶ G. MacNiocaill, 'Land transfer in sixteenth century Thomond: the case of Domhnall Óg Ó Cearnaigh', *North Munster Antiquarian Journal*, xvii (1975), 43–5.

⁶⁷ D. Dickson, 'Middlemen', in T. J. Bartlett & D. W. Hayton (eds.), *Penal era and golden age. Essays in Irish history, 1690–1900* (Belfast, 1979).

⁶⁸ J. S. Donnelly, Jr., *The land and the people of nineteenth century Cork op. cit.*, 173–87; see also W. H. Crawford (ed.), *Letters from an Ulster land agent, 1774–85: the letter books of John Moore of Clough, Co. Down* (Belfast, 1976); S. Adams, 'Relations between land agent and tenant on the Hertford estate', *Lisburn Hist. Soc. Jnl*, ii (1979), 3–10.

⁶⁹ W. E. Vaughan, 'An assessment of the economic performance of Irish landlords, 1851–81', *op. cit.*, 196.

⁷⁰ In addition to Butlin and Andrews in *The New History of Ireland*, the following list represents a selection of settlement studies: F. H. A. Aalen, *Man and the landscape in Ireland* (London, 1978); 'The origins of enclosures in eastern Ireland' in N. Stephens and R. E. Glasscock (eds.),

Irish Geographical Studies in honour of E. E. Evans (Belfast, 1970), 209–23; K. S. Bottigheimer, 'The restoration land settlement in Ireland: a structural view', *I.H.S.*, xviii, 69 (March 1972), 1–21; *English money and Irish land: the 'adventurers' in the Cromwellian settlement of Ireland* (Oxford, 1971); R. H. Buchanan, 'Rural settlement in Ireland', in N. Stephens & R. E. Glasscock (eds.), *op. cit.,* 146–61; 'Field systems of Ireland', in A. R. H. Baker & R. A. Butlin (eds.), *Studies of field systems in the British Isles* (Cambridge, 1973), 580–618; 'Common fields and enclosure: an eighteenth century example from Lecale, Co. Down', in *Stephens and Glasscock, op. cit.,* (1970), 99–118; Jean M. Graham, 'Rural society in Connacht, 1600–1640', *ibid.,* 192–208; 'South west Donegal in the seventeenth century', *Ir. Geog.,* vi (1970), 136–52; B. J. Graham, 'The disappearance of Clachans from south Ards, Co. Down, in the nineteenth century', *Ir. Geog.,* vi (1972), 263–9; A Horner, 'Land transactions and the making of Carton demesne', *Kildare Arch. Soc. Jnl.,* xv, 4 (1974–5), 387–96; R. J. Hunter, 'The English undertakers in the Plantation of Ulster, 1610–41', *Breifne,* iv, 16 (1975), 471–500; R. J. Hunter & M. Perceval-Maxwell, 'The muster role of c. 1630: Co. Cavan', *Breifne,* v, 18 (1977–8), 206–22; J. Johnston, 'English settlement in Co. Fermanagh, 1610–1640', *Clogher Record,* x, 1 (1979), 137–43; 'Scotch settlement in Co. Fermanagh', *Clogher Record,* ix, 3 (1978), 367–73; J. Kelly, 'Rural settlement in the neighbourhood of Kells, Co. Meath: a review of the Civil and Down Survey evidence', *Riocht na Midhe,* vi, 2 (1976), 43–57; I. Leister, *Peasant openfield farming and its territorial organisation in County Tipperary* (Marburg, 1976); J. Logan, 'Tadhg O Roddy and two surveys of County Leitrim', *Breifne,* iv, 14 (1971), 318–34; W. MacAfee, 'The colonisation of the Maghera region of south Derry in the seventeenth and eighteenth centuries', *Ulster Folklife,* 23 (1977), 70–91; D. McCourt, 'The dynamic quality of Irish rural settlement', in R. H. Buchanan, E. Jones and D. McCourt (eds.), *Man and his habitat* (London, 1971), 126–64; D. Mac an Ghallóglaigh, 'Leitrim, 1600–1641', *Breifne,* iv, 14 (1971), 225–64; A. R. Orme, *The world's landscapes: Ireland* (London, 1970); M. Perceval-Maxwell, *The Scottish migration to Ulster in the reign of James I* (London, 1973); B. Ó Bric, 'Landholding by Galway townsmen in Connacht 1585–1641' (M.A. N.U.I., 1974), abstracted in *Ir. Econ. Soc. Hist.,* ii (1975), 60–1; C. P. Ó Cnáimhsí, 'A historical geography of south Donegal', *Donegal Annual,* x, 1 (1971), 6–61; H. O'Sullivan, 'The Cromwellian and restoration settlements in the civil parish of Dundalk, 1649–1673', *Louth Arch. Hist. Soc. Jnl,* xix, 1 (1977), 24–58; P. Robinson, 'The spread of hedged enclosure in Ulster', *Ulster Folklife,* 23 (1977), 57–69; 'British settlement in County Tyrone, 1610–1666', *Ir. Econ. Soc. Hist.,* v (1978), 5–26; R. C. Simington, *The transplantation to Connacht* (Dublin, 1970); J. G. Simms, 'Donegal in the Ulster plantation', *Ir. Geog.,* vi (1972), 386–93; 'The Ulster Plantation in Co. Donegal', *Donegal Annual,* x, 1 (1971), 3–14.

Four important papers presented to the conference of Franco-Irish historians in Dublin in 1977 should also be noted: J. H. Andrews, 'The limits of agricultural settlement in pre-Famine Ireland'; W. H. Crawford, 'The structure of rural society in eighteenth century Ulster'; D. J. Dickson, 'The evolution of social structures in eighteenth century south Munster'; W. J. Smyth, 'Settlement and land holding changes in Co. Tipperary 1650–1850'.

[71] M. MacCurtain, 'Rural society in post-Cromwellian Ireland', *op. cit.,* 131.

[72] Examples include B. S. Mac Aodha, 'Placename research in Ireland', *Anglo-Irish Studies,* i (1975), 97–104; P. O'Flanagan, 'Colonisation and Co. Cork's changing cultural landscape: the evidence from placenames', *Cork Hist. Arch. Jnl.* lxxiv, 239 (1979), 1–14; B. S. Turner, 'An observation on settler names in Fermanagh', *Clogher Record,* viii, 3 (1975), 85–89.

[73] *General Report on the Gosford Estates in County Armagh, 1821,* by William Greig, with an introduction by F. M. L. Thompson and D. Tierney (Belfast, 1976).

[74] M. G. Moyles and P. S. De Brún (ed.); 'Charles O'Brien's agricultural survey of Kerry, 1800', *Kerry Arch. Soc. Jnl., 1* (1968), 73–100, 2 (1969), 108–33; C. C. Ellison (ed.), 'Materials for the Dublin Agricultural Society survey of County Louth', *Louth Arch. Soc. Jnl.,* xviii, 2 (1974), 121–31, xviii, 3 (1974), 187–94.

[75] T. de Bhaldraithe (ed.), *Chín lae Amhlaimh* (Dublin, 1970). See also T. de Bhaldraithe (ed.), *Seanchas Thomáis Laighléis,* (Dublin, 1977). D. Thomson with M. McGusty, *The Irish Journals of Elizabeth Smith 1840–1850* (Oxford, 1980); M. Hewson, 'The Diaries of John Singleton of Quinville, County Clare', *North Munster Antiquarian Journal,* xvii (1975), 103–10; P. Mulvaney, 'Extracts from a Ratoath diary, 1804–78', *Ríocht na Mídhe,* vi, 1 (1975), 23–33.

[76] Síle Ní Chinnéide, 'A new view of eighteenth century life in Kerry', *Kerry Arch. Soc. Jnl,* vi (1973), 83–100; 'An eighteenth century French traveller in Kildare', *Kildare Arch. Soc. Jnl.,* xv, 4 (1974–5), 376–86; 'View of Kilkenny, city and county, in 1790', *R.S.A.I. Jnl,* civ (1974), 29–38; 'A Frenchman's tour of Connaught', *Galway Arch. Soc. Jnl.,* xxxv

(1976), 52–66; 'A journey from Mullingar to Loughrea in 1791', *Old Athlone Society Journal*, ii, 5 (1978), 15–23; 'A new view of Cork City in 1790', *Cork Hist. Arch. Soc. Jnl*, lxxviii, 227 (1973), 1–13.

77 Knight of Glin, 'Lord Orrery's travels in Kerry, 1735', *Kerry Arch. Soc. Jnl.*, 5 (1971), 46–59.

78 *Ibid.*, 48.

79 E. McCracken, *The Irish woods since Tudor times: their distribution and exploitation* (London, 1971); D. P. McCracken and E. McCracken, 'A register of trees, Co. Cork, 1790–1860', *Cork Hist. Arch. Soc. Jnl.* lxxxi, 233–4 (1976), 31–60; E. McCracken, 'A register of trees: County Kildare, 1769–1909', *Kildare Arch. Soc. Jnl*, xvi, 1 (1977–78), 41–59.

80 C. A. Lewis, *Hunting in Ireland: a historical and geographical analysis* (London, 1975). See also C. A. Lewis and M. E. McCarthy, 'The horse-breeding industry in Ireland', *Ir. Geog.*, x (1977), 72–89.

81 See, for example, R. O'Connor, *The implications for cattle producers of seasonal price fluctuations*, E.S.R.I., paper no. 46 (Dublin, 1969); T. J. Baker, R. O'Connor and R. Dunne, *A study of the Irish cattle and beef industries*, E.S.R.I., paper no. 72 (Dublin 1973); D. A. Gillmor, 'The spatial structure of agricultural output in the republic of Ireland', *Econ. Soc. Rev.*, viii, 2 (1977); C. J. W. Edwards, 'Farm enterprise systems in East County Londonderry', *Ir. Geog.*, vii (1974), 29–53.

82 J. F. Donnelly, Jr., 'The Irish agricultural depression of 1859–64', *Ir. Econ. Soc. Hist.*, iii (1976), 33–54; B. L. Solow, op. cit.

83 P. M. A. Bourke's work deserves a review article in itself. His most important contributions include 'The potato, blight, weather and the Irish Famine', (Ph.D., N.U.I., 1965); 'Notes on some agricultural units of measurement in use in pre-Famine Ireland', *I.H.S.*, xiv, 55 (Mar. 1965), 236–45; 'The agricultural statistics of the 1841 census of Ireland: a critical review', *Econ. Hist. Rev.*, 2nd ser., xviii, 2 (Aug. 1965), 376–391; 'The average yields of food crops in Ireland on the eve of the Great Famine', *Department of Agriculture Journal*, lxvi (1969); 'The climate of Ireland as a natural resource', *Administration*, xxi, 3 (Autumn 1973), 365–83; 'The Irish grain trade, 1839–48', *I.H.S.*, xx, 78 (Sept. 1976), 156–69.

84 Parish histories with useful accounts of the Famine include M. Tierney, *Murroe and Boher* (Dublin, n.d. 1966?); H. Walsh, *Borris in Ossory: an Irish rural parish and its people* (Kilkenny, 1969). More specialised accounts include J. Grant, 'Some aspects of the Great Famine in Co. Armagh', *Seanchas Ard Mhaca*, viii, 2 (1977), 342–59; B. Mac Cnáimhsí, 'Arranmore Island in the Great Famine, 1846–8', *Donegal*

Annual, x, 3 (1973), 239–48; F. X. McCorry, 'The Famine of 1846', *Craigavon Hist. Soc. Jnl,* iii (1977), 11–17; G. Ó Dúghaill, 'Galway in the first Famine winter', *Saothar,* i (1975), 63–7; O. Devaney, 'Minutes of Longford Poor Law Guardians during the Great Famine', *Treabtha, Journal of the Longford Historical Society,* i, 4 (1978), 329–30; M. Farrell, *The Poor Law and the work house in Belfast 1838–1948* (Belfast, 1978); M. Quinn, 'Enniskillen Poor Law Union (1840–9)', *Clogher Record,* vii, 3 (1971–2), 498–513; R. J. Raymond, 'Pawnbrokers and pawnbroking in Dublin, 1830–1870', *Dub. Hist. Rec.,* xxxii, 1 (Dec. 1978), 15–26; 'Dublin: the Great Famine, 1845–1860', *ibid.,* xxxiii, 3 (June, 1980), 98–105. For perceptive general reflections on the Famine see M. A. G. Ó Tuathaigh, 'The Famine: further thoughts', *Quest,* 1 (1974), 11–20.

[85] J. Mokyr, 'The deadly fungus: an econometric investigation into the short term demographic impact of the Irish Famine, 1846–1851', *Research in population economics,* 2 (1980), 237–77.

[86] *ibid.,* 248–9.

[87] Among the first scholars to make effective use of the 1901 and/or 1911 census returns were D. G. Symes, 'Farm household and farm performance: a study of twentieth century changes in Ballyferriter, south west Ireland', *Ethnology,* xi (1972), 25–38; A. C. Hepburn, 'Catholics in the north of Ireland, 1850–1921: the urbanisation of a minority', in A. C. Hepburn (ed.), *Minorities in history* (London, 1978), 84–101; F. J. Carney, 'Household structure in two areas of Ireland, 1821 and 1911', paper presented at the Conference of Franco-Irish historians held in Dublin, 1977; C. Ó Grada, 'Primogeniture and ultimogeniture in rural Ireland', *Journal of Interdisciplinary History,* x, 3 (1980), 491–8; D. Fitzpatrick, 'The disappearance of the Irish agricultural labourer', *op. cit.*

[88] S. A. Royle, 'Irish manuscript census records: a neglected source of information', *Ir. Geog.,* xi (1978), 110–25, contains a list of all material known to survive at this stage.

[89] F. J. Carney, 'Pre-Famine Irish population: the evidence from the Trinity College estates', *Ir. Econ. Soc. Hist.,* ii (1975), 35–45; F. O'Ferrall, 'The population of a rural pre-Famine parish: Templebredin, Counties Limerick and Tipperary', *North Munster Antiquarian Journal,* xvii (1975), 91–102; P. de Brún, 'A census of the parish of Ferriter, January, 1835', *Kerry Arch. Soc. Jnl,* 7 (1974), 37–70.

[90] K. O'Neill, 'Family and farm in Ireland, 1780–1840' (Ph. D., Brown, 1979–80). See also G. Alwill, 'The 1841 census of Killeshandra parish', *Breifne,* v, 17 (1976), 7–36.

[91] F. J. Carney, 'Aspects of pre-Famine Irish household size; composi-

tion and differentials', in Cullen & Smout, *op. cit.*, 32–46; 'Household structure in two areas of Ireland, 1821 and 1911', *op. cit.;* 'Age of marriage in pre-Famine Ireland: the evidence from an 1821 sample', paper presented to the American Committee for Irish Studies, New England Regional Conference, Boston College, 1980.

[92] D. F. Hannan with N. Hardiman, 'Peasant proprietorship and changes in the Irish marriage rate in the late nineteenth century', Seminar paper, E.S.R.I., 1978; R. E. Kennedy, *The Irish: emigration, marriage and fertility* (London, 1973); D. Fitzpatrick, 'The study of Irish population, 1841–1921', presented to U.C.C. Historical Society, 1978; E. McKenna, 'Marriage and fertility in post-Famine Ireland: a multi-variant analysis', *American Journal of Sociology,* lxxx, 3 (1974), 688–705; 'Age, religion and marriage in post-Famine Ireland: an empirical examination', *Econ. Hist. Rev.*, 2nd ser., xxxi, 2 (1978), 238–56; G. S. L. Tucker, 'Irish fertility ratios before the Famine', *Econ. Hist. Rev.*, 2nd ser., xxiii, 2 (Aug. 1970), 267–84; B. M. Walsh, 'A perspective on Irish population patterns', *Éire–Ireland*, iv, 2 (Autumn 1969), 3–21; 'Marriage rates and population pressure: Ireland, 1871 and 1911', *Econ. Hist. Rev.*, 2nd ser., xxiii, 1 (1970), 148–62; 'An empirical study of the age structure of the Irish population', *Econ. Soc. Rev.*, i, 2 (Jan. 1970), 259–80; 'Some Irish population problems reconsidered, E.S.R.I., paper no. 42, (Dublin, 1968); 'Ireland's demographic transformation 1958–70', *Econ. Soc. Rev.*, iii, 2 (1972), 251–75.

[93] W. E. Vaughan & A. J. Fitzpatrick (eds.), *Irish historical statistics: population 1821–1971* (Dublin, 1978).

[94] 'Seasonal migration and post-Famine adjustment in the west of Ireland', *Studia Hibernica*, 13 (1973), 47–76; 'A note on nineteenth century Irish emigration statistics', *Population Studies,* xxix, 1 (1975), 143–50; 'Some aspects of nineteenth century emigration', in Cullen & Smout (eds.), *op. cit.*, 65–73; 'Seasonal migration and rural adjustment', paper presented at the conference of Franco-Irish historians in Dublin, 1977. For a wide-ranging survey of pre-famine emigration to Britain, see R. A. Harris, 'The nearest place that wasn't Ireland' (Ph.D., Tufts, 1980).

[95] D. Dickson, 'Irish population in the eighteenth century: some reconsiderations', *Bulletin of the Irish Committee of Historical Sciences*, 3rd ser., 1 (1974), 12–13. L. Clarkson, 'Eighteenth century population estimates', paper presented to the annual conference of the Irish Economic and Social History Society, Belfast, 1978.

[97] V. Morgan, 'The church of Ireland registers of

St Patrick's Coleraine, as a source for the study of a local pre-Famine population', *Ulster Folklife*, 19 (1973), 56–67; 'Mortality in Magherafelt, Co. Derry, in the early eighteenth century', *I.H.S.*, xix, 74 (Sept. 1974), 125–35; 'A case study of population change: Blaris, Lisburn, 1661–1848', *Ir. Econ. Soc. Hist.*, iii (1976), 5–16; D. Mac Cárthaigh, 'Marriage and birth rates for Knockainy parish 1822–1941', *Cork Hist. Arch. Soc. Jnl.*, xlvii, 165 (1942), 4–8.

[98] R. A. Butlin, *op. cit.*, 147; L. M. Cullen, *op. cit.*, 389. Cullen's estimates are derived from his paper 'Population trends in seventeenth century Ireland', *Econ. Soc. Rev.*, vi, 2 (1975), 149–65. N. Canny, 'Early modern Ireland: an appraisal appraised', *Ir. Econ. Soc. Hist.*, iv (1977), 63–5. T. C. Barnard, 'Sir William Petty, his Kerry estates and Irish population', *Ir. Econ. Soc. Hist.*, vi (1979), 64–9, casts considerable doubt on Petty as an authority. For comparable comments on eighteenth century estimates see J. Lee, 'Introduction', in *The population of Ireland before the nineteenth century* (Farnborough, 1973).

[99] J. Mokyr, *op. cit.* and 'Industrialisation and poverty in Ireland and the Netherlands, 1780–1845', *Journal of Interdisciplinary History*, x, 3 (1980), 429–58.

[100] P. Lynch & J. Vaizey, *Guinness's Brewery in the Irish economy* (Cambridge, 1960).

[101] Cullen, *Economic history, op. cit.*, 192; J. H. Johnson, 'The two "Irelands" at the beginning of the nineteenth century', in N. Stephens & R. E. Glasscock (eds.), *Irish geographical studies in honour of E. E. Evans*, 224–43; J. Lee, 'The dual economy in Ireland, 1800–50', in T. D. Williams (ed.), *Historical Studies*, viii (London, 1971), 191–201; W. H. Crawford, 'The case of John McNeelans of Shanoney, 1773', *Ulster Folklife*, 23 (1977), 92–6; C. Ó Grada, 'Supply responsiveness . . .', *op. cit.;* R. J. Raymond, 'The dual economy and the reinterpretation of Irish economic history, 1800–1850', *Kaw Valley Historical Review*, i, 3 (Jan. 1978).

[102] W. H. Crawford, *op. cit.*, 92. Note also the formulation by Mokyr, 'Industrialisation and poverty', *op. cit.*, 455, n. 39, 'rather than being a dual economy, Ireland was a continuum in which under-development gradually became more severe as one moved westward'.

[103] L. A. Clarkson, 'An anatomy of an Irish town: the economy of Armagh, 1770', *Ir. Econ. Soc. Hist.*, v (1978), 27–45; 'Household and family structure in Armagh city, 1770', *Local Population Studies*, 20 (1978), 14–31; 'Armagh 1770: portrait of an urban community', paper presented to the Irish Conference of Historians, Belfast, 1979.

104 Clarkson, 'Anatomy', *op. cit.*, 41.
105 *ibid.*, 44.
105a R. A. Butlin (ed.), *The development of the Irish town* (London, 1977) contains useful essays by Butlin and T. W. Freeman on the modern period, but they consolidate rather than advance existing knowledge. Among R. J. Hunter's contributions to the history of seventeenth century Ulster towns are 'Towns in the Ulster Plantation', *Studia Hibernica*, II (1971), 40–79; 'Sir William Cole and plantation Enniskillen', *Clogher Record*, ix, 3 (1978), 336–50; 'Ulster plantation towns, 1609–41', paper presented to the Irish Conference of Historians, Belfast, 1979.
106 J. C. Beckett & R. E. Glasscock (eds.), *Belfast: origin and growth of an industrial city* (London, 1967) remains the basic collection of essays on Belfast. Nothing comparable exists for any other Irish city. In addition, see R. W. M. Strain, *Belfast and its charitable society* (Oxford, 1961); S. E. Baker (S. Gribbon), 'Orange and green. Belfast, 1832–1912', in H. J. Dyos and M. Wolff (eds.), *The victorian city: images and realities* (2 vols, London, 1973), ii, 789–814; 'An Irish city: Belfast 1911', paper presented to the Irish Conference of Historians, Belfast, 1979; P. Froggatt, 'Industrialisation and health in Belfast in the early nineteenth century', *ibid.;* C. O'Leary, 'Belfast urban government in the age of reform' *ibid;* E. R. R. Green, 'Belfast enterpreneurship in the nineteenth century', paper presented to the conference of Franco–Irish historians in Bordeaux, 1978; N. E. Gamble, 'The business community and trade of Belfast, 1767–1800' (Ph.D., T.C.D., 1978), abstracted in *Ir. Econ. Soc. Hist.*, vii (1980), 93–4. On Cork see S. Daly, *Cork: a city in crisis 1870–72* (Cork, 1978); M. Murphy, 'The role of organised labour in the political and economic life of Cork city, 1820–1899' (Ph.D., Leicester, 1979); 'Fenianism, Parnellism and the Cork trades 1860–1900', *Saothar*, v (1979), 27–38; 'The economic and social structure of nineteenth century Cork', paper presented to the Irish Conference of Historians, Belfast, 1979; J. B. O'Brien, 'Agricultural prices and living costs in pre-Famine Cork', *Cork Hist. Arch. Soc. Jnl*, lxxxii (1977), 1–10; *The Catholic middle classes in pre-Famine Cork* (O'Donnell Lecture, N.U.I., 1980); S. F. Pettit, 'The royal Cork institution: a reflection of the cultural life of a city', *Cork Hist. Arch. Soc. Jnl*, lxxxi, 233 & 234 (1976), 70–90.
107 Dublin, 1978.
108 F. D'Arcy, 'The artisans of Dublin and Daniel O'Connell, 1830–47: an unquiet liaison', *I.H.S.*, xvii, 66 (Sept. 1970), 221–43; M. Craft, 'The development of Dublin: background to the housing problem', *Studies*, lix (Autumn 1970), 301–13; Mary Crowley, 'A social and economic study of

Dublin, 1860–1914' (M.A., N.U.I., 1972), abstracted in *Ir. Econ. Soc. Hist.*, 1 (1974), 63–5; 'Late nineteenth and early twentieth century Dublin', paper presented to the Irish Conference of Historians at Belfast, 1979; J. P. Haughton, 'The urban – rural fringe of Dublin', in Stephens and Glasscock, *op. cit.*, 360–72; P. Holohan, 'Daniel O'Connell and the Dublin trades: a collision 1837–8', *Saothar*, 1 (1975), 1–17; E. McParland, 'The wide street commissioners: their importance for Dublin architecture in the late eighteenth–early nineteenth century', *Quarterly Bulletin of the Irish Georgian Society*, xv, 1 (1972), 1–30; J. G. Simms, 'Dublin in 1776', *Dub. Hist. Rec.*, xxxi, 1 (1976), 2–13.

[109] P. Connell, 'The changing face of Navan in the nineteenth century', *Riocht na Midhe*, vi, 3 (1977), 38–59. See also J. K. Hourihan, 'Town growth in west Cork: Bantry 1600–1960', *Cork Hist. Arch. Soc. Jnl*, lxxxii, 236 (1977), 83–97.

[110] Connell, *ibid.*, 51.

[111] D. Hannan, 'Kinship, neighbourhood and social change in Irish rural communities', *Econ. Soc. Rev.*, iii, 2 (1972), 163–88; W. J. Smyth, 'Continuity and change in the territorial organisation of Irish rural communities', *Maynooth Review*, i, 1 (June 1975), 51–73; i, 2 (Nov. 1975), 52–101.

[112] H. F. Kearney, 'Father Matthew: apostle of modernisation', in A. Cosgrove and D. McCartney, *op. cit.*, 164–75.

[113] *Ibid.*, 175.

[114] A phrase first used, of course, with respect to Japanese responses to westernisation.

[115] K. Danaher, 'Irish vernacular architecture in relation to the Irish Sea', in D. Moore (ed.), *The Irish Sea province in archaeology and history* (Cardiff 1970), 98–107; P. Jenkins, 'Connections between the landed communities of Munster and South Wales, c. 1660–1780', *Cork Hist. Arch. Soc. Jnl.*, lxxxiv, 240 (1979), 95–101; D. McCourt, 'Innovation diffusion in Ireland: a historical case study', *P.R.I.A.*, 73, C (1973), 1–19. For a study of a more recent experience see T. Allen, 'Transferring technology to the firm: a study of the diffusion of technology in Irish manufacturing industry', *Journal of Irish business and administrative research*, i, 2 (Oct. 1979), 3–34.

[116] O. MacDonagh, 'Sea communications in the nineteenth century' in K. B. Nowlan (ed.), *Travel and transport in Ireland* (Dublin, 1973), 120–33; Miriam Daly, 'The return to the roads', *ibid.*, 134–49. Other relevant contributions in this volume include J. G. Barry, 'Transport and communication in medieval and Tudor Ireland', 32–46; J. L. McCracken,

'The age of the stage coach', 47–63; W. A. McCutcheon, 'The transport revolution: canals and river navigations', 64–81; Thomas P. O'Neill, 'Bianconi and his cars', 82–95; K. B. Nowlan, 'The transport revolution: the coming of the railways', 96–109; J. Lee, 'The Golden Age of Irish railways', 110–19; P. Lynch and G. Quinn, 'The latest phase in land transport', 150–69. Other studies include S. Ó Lúing, 'Richard Griffith and the roads of Kerry', *Kerry Arch. Soc. Jnl.*, 8 (1975), 89–113 and 9 (1976), 92–124; P. F. Wallace, 'The organisation of pre–railway public transport in counties Limerick and Clare', *North Munster Antiquarian Journal*, xv (1972), 34–58; R. Delaney, *The grand canal of Ireland* (Newton Abbott, 1973); P. Flanagan, *The Ballinamore and Ballyconnell Canal* (Newton Abbott, 1972); I. Murphy, 'Pre-famine passenger services on the lower Shannon', *North Munster Antiquarian Journal*, xvi (1973–74), 70–83; J. Leckey, 'The organisation and capital structure of the Irish north-western railway' (M.Sc. Econ., Q.U.B., 1974), abstracted in *Ir. Econ. Soc. Hist.*, iv (1977), 76–8. W. A. McCutcheon's monumental *The industrial archaeology of Northern Ireland* (Belfast, 1980) came to hand too late for appraisal, but includes extensive sections on the main forms of transport.

[117] A. A. Horner, 'Stability and change in the towns and villages west of Dublin' (Ph.D., T.C.D., 1974), abstracted in *Ir. Econ. Soc. Hist.*, iii (1976), 78–80; 'Planning the Irish transport network: parallels in nineteenth and twentieth century proposals', *Ir. Geog.*, x (1977), 44–57.

[118] P. G. Ollerenshaw, 'The rise of the Belfast banks, 1825–1900', *Moirae*, 5 (Trinity 1980), 132–48. Other contributions include G. L. Barrow, *the emergence of the Irish banking system, 1820–45* (Dublin, 1975); I. V. Jones, *The rise of a merchant bank* (Dublin, 1975); J. B. O'Brien, 'Sadleir's Bank, 1838–56', *Cork Hist. Arch. Soc. Jnl.*, lxxxii, 235, (1977), 33–8; N. S. Simpson, *The Belfast Bank, 1827–1970* (Belfast, 1975).

[118a] Studies of foreign trade include J. Bernard, 'The maritime intercourse between Bordeaux and Ireland c. 1450–c, 1520', *Ir. Econ. Soc. Hist.*, vii (1980), 7–21; L. M. Cullen, 'Merchant communities, the navigation acts and Irish and Scottish responses', in Cullen & Smout, *op. cit.*, 165–76; D. R. Hainsworth, 'Christopher Lowther's Canary adventure: a merchant venturer in Dublin, 1632–3', *Ir. Econ. Soc. Hist.*, ii (1975), 22–34; A. K. Longfield (Mrs. Leask), 'Irish linen for Spain and Portugal: James Archbold's letters 1771–79', *P.R.I.A.*, 76, C (1976), 13–22; P. M. Solar, 'The agricultural statistics in the Irish Railway Commissioners Report', *Ir. Econ. Soc. Hist.*, vi (1979), 24–40; T. M. Truxes, 'Con-

necticut in the Irish-American flaxseed trade', *Eire–Ireland*, xii, 2 (1977), 34–62; D. Woodward, 'The Anglo-Irish livestock trade in the seventeenth century', *I.H.S.* xviii, 72 (1973), 489–523; 'A comparative study of the Irish and Scottish livestock trades in the seventeenth century', in Cullen & Smout, *op. cit.*, 147–64; 'Sixteenth century shipping: the Charter–Party of the *Grace* of Neston, 1572', *Ir. Econ. Soc. Hist.*, v (1978), 64–9.

[119] A. Gailey, 'The Ballyhagan inventories, 1716–1740', *Folk Life*, xv (1977), 36–64. Other general inventories include V. M. Barry, 'House lists 1826–1838 of Lady Godfrey of Kilcoleman Abbey, Co. Kerry', *Irish Ancestor*, xi, 1 (1979), 30–44; C. C. Ellison, 'Setting up house – 1825 style', *ibid.*, viii, 2 (1976), 75–80; R. ffolliott, 'Household stuff', *ibid.*, i, 1 (1969), 43–51; 'Inventory of Killeen Castle in 1735–6', *ibid.*, ix, 2 (1977), 102–7; 'The inventory of John Mahon of Stokestown, Co. Roscommon, 1708', *ibid.*, x, 2 (1978), 77–80; O. Goodbody, 'Quaker inventories', *ibid.*, iii, 1 (1971), 52–62; 'Inventories of five Dublin Quaker merchants in the late seventeenth century', *ibid.*, x, 1 (1978), 38–48; J. C. Walton, 'The household effects of a Waterford merchant family in 1640', *Cork Hist. Arch. Soc. Jnl.*, lxxxiii, 238 (1978), 99–105. On clothing see R. ffolliott, 'Women's dress in Ireland 1680–1880', *Irish Ancestor*, iii, 2 (1971), 85–9; 'Men's clothes in Ireland, 1660–1850', *ibid.*, iv (1972), 89–93; L. Jones, 'Dress in nineteenth century Ireland: an approach to research', *Folklife*, xvi (1978), 42–53. On furniture see F. H. A. Aalen, 'Furnishings of traditional houses in the Wicklow hills', *Ulster Folklife*, xiii (1967), 61–7, R. ffolliott, 'The furnishings of a Palladian house in 1742–3; Barbaville, Co. Westmeath', *Irish Ancestor*, xi, 2 (1979), 86–95; A. Gailey, 'Kitchen furniture', *Ulster Folklife*, 12 (1966), 18–34. On housing see R. ffolliott, 'Houses in Ireland in the seventeenth century', *Irish Ancestor*, vi, 1 (1974), 16–21; 'Cottages and farmhouses', *ibid.*, iv, 1 (1972), 30–5; 'Houses in provincial towns', *ibid.*, vii, 2 (1975), 97–9; A. Gailey, 'The vernacular dwellings of Clogher diocese', *Clogher Record*, ix, 2 (1977), 187–231; 'The housing of the rural poor in nineteenth century Ulster', *Ulster Folklife*, 22 (1976), 34–58; P. Robinson, 'Vernacular housing in Ulster in the seventeenth century', *ibid.*, 25 (1979), 1–28. For a wide-ranging general survey see Timothy P. O'Neill, *Life and traditions in rural Ireland* (London, 1977).

[120] C.S.O., *Household budget enquiry 1951–52* (Dublin, 1954); C. E. Leser, *Demand relationships for Ireland,* E.S.R.I., paper no. 4 (Dublin, 1962); *A further analysis of Irish household budget data 1951–52,* E.S.R.I., paper no. 23 (Dublin, 1964); J. G. Hughes, 'The functional

distribution of income in Ireland, 1938–70', E.S.R.I. paper no. 65 (Dublin, 1971); P. Kaim-Caudle, *Housing in Ireland: some economic aspects,* E.S.R.I., paper no. 28 (Dublin, 1965); K. Kennedy, B. M. Walsh & L. P. Ebrill, 'The demand for beer and spirits in Ireland', *P.R.I.A.,* 73, C (1973), 669–711; J. L. Pratschke, *Income and expenditure relations in Ireland 1965–66,* E.S.R.I., paper no. 50 (Dublin, 1969); W. K. O'Riordan, 'The demand for food in Ireland 1947–1973', *Econ. Soc. Rev.,* vii, 4 (July 1976), 401–16.

121 J. Lee, 'Landlordism and economic development in modern Ireland', paper delivered at A.C.I.S. conference in Cortland, 1978. For some dimensions of poverty, see Timothy P. O'Neill, 'Poverty in Ireland, 1815–45', *Folk Life,* xi (1973), 22–33; 'Clare and Irish poverty, 1815–45', *Studia Hibernica,* 14 (1974), 7–27.

122 L. P. Curtis, 'Incumbered wealth: landed indebtedness in post-Famine Ireland', *A.H.R.,* lxxxv, 2 (April 1980), 332–67. M. O'Connell, 'Daniel O'Connell: income, expenditure and despair', *I.H.S.,* xvii, 66 (Sept. 1970), 200–20, recreates the glories of a distinguished consumer.

123 M. MacCurtain & D. Ó Corráin (eds.), *Women in Irish society* (Dublin, 1978), contains useful historical essays. It remains the only collection of its type. It does not, however, have much on women in working class Protestant Ireland, for which see W. Campbell, 'Down the Shankill', *Ulster Folklife,* 22 (1976), 1–33.

124 Relevant work on markets and entrepreneurs includes J. S. Donnelly, Jr., 'Cork market: its role in the nineteenth century butter trade', *Studia Hibernica,* 11 (1971), 130–63; L. Kennedy, 'The decline of the Cork butter market: a comment', *ibid.,* 16 (1976), 175–7; 'Traders in the Irish rural economy, 1880–1914', *Econ. Hist. Rev.,* xxxii, 2 (May 1979), 201–10; N. J. Farley, 'Determinants of establishment size in Irish manufacturing industries: some notes on the Irish case 1931–1972', *Econ. Soc. Rev.,* vi, 2 (Jan. 1975), 187–214. Papers presented to the conference of Franco-Irish historians in Bordeaux, 1978, include J. Mannion, 'Waterford merchants and the Irish-Newfoundland provisions trade, 1770–1820'; D. Dickson, 'The Cork merchant community in the eighteenth century: a regional perspective; L. M. Cullen, 'The Irish merchant communities of Bordeaux, La Rochelle and Cognac in the eighteenth century'; W. H. Crawford, 'Drapers and bleachers in the early Ulster linen industry'; E. R. R. Green, 'Belfast entrepreneurship in the nineteenth century'; J. Lee, 'Merchants and enterprise: the case of early Irish railways 1830–1855'.

125 N. J. J. Farley, 'Explanatory hypotheses for Irish trade in

manufactured goods in the mid-1960s', *Econ. Soc. Rev.,* iv, 1 (1972), 5–34; J. C. Stewart, 'Foreign direct investment and emergence of a dual economy', *ibid.,* vii, 2 (1976), 173–98; C. Cooper & N. Whelan, *Science, technology and industry in Ireland* (Dublin, 1973).

126 J. B. O'Brien, 'Business history', *Irish Archives Bulletin,* ii, 1 (1972), 50–7.

127 Studies of individual industries and/or firms include the following: W. H. Crawford, *Domestic industry in Ireland: the experience of the linen industry* (Dublin, 1972); 'The origins of the linen industry in northern Armagh and the Lagan valley', *Ulster Folklife,* 17 (1971), 42–51; W. H. Crawford & B. S. Trainor (eds.), *Aspects of Irish social history, 1750–1800* (Belfast, 1969); R. ffolliott, 'Some lists of mid-eighteenth century drapers in south east Ulster', *Irish Ancestor,* xi, 1 (1979), 9–14; D. G. Lockhart, 'Dunmanway, Co. Cork, 1746–9', *I.H.S.,* xx, 78 (Sept. 1976), 170–5; W. Hincks, 'Illustrations of the Irish linen industry in 1783', *Ulster Folklife,* 23 (1977), 1–32; W. J. Smyth, 'Location patterns and trends within the pre-Famine linen industry', *Ir. Geog.,* viii (1975), 97–110; D. Dickson, 'Aspects of the rise and decline of the Irish cotton industry', in Cullen & Smout, *op. cit.,* 100–15; E. B. McGuire, *Irish whiskey: a history of distilling, the spirit trade and excise controls in Ireland* (Dublin, 1973); R. Weir, 'The patent still distillers and the role of competition', in Cullen & Smout, *op. cit.,* 129–44; 'In and out of Ireland: the Distillers Company Ltd and the Irish whiskey trade 1900–39', *Ir. Econ. Soc. Hist.,* vii (1980), 45–65; P. Bolger, *The Irish cooperative movement* (Dublin, 1979); C. Ó Gráda, 'The beginnings of the Irish creamery system, 1880–1914', *Econ. Hist. Rev.,* 2nd ser., xxx, 2 (May 1977), 284–305; L. M. Cullen, 'Eighteenth century flour milling in Ireland', *Ir. Econ. Soc. Hist.,* iv (1977), 5–25; A. C. Davies, 'The first industrial exhibition: Cork, 1852', *ibid.,* ii (1975), 48–59; 'Roofing Belfast and Dublin 1896–8: American penetration of the Irish market for Welsh slate', *ibid.,* iv (1977), 26–35; D. S. Jacobson, 'The political economy of industrial location: the Ford motor company at Cork 1912–26', *ibid.,* 36–55; P. Flanagan, 'Some notes on Leitrim industry', *Breifne,* iv, 15 (1972), 406–25.

128 The following relevant articles appear in *Irish Archives Bulletin:* L. M. Cullen, 'Private sources for economic and social history', ii, 1 (1972), 5–25; Co. Cork: Two research experiences, D. Dickson 'The eighteenth century', and J. S. Donnelly, Jr., 'The nineteenth century', *ibid.,* 58–61, 61–6; N. Kissane, 'Business records and the archivist: a note', ii (Oct. 1972), 20–5; S. McMenamin, 'Board of Guardian Records: classifying

and cataloguing', i, 2 (Oct. 1971), 19–33; S. Healy, 'A note on a recent survey of the records held by Irish Distillers Limited in Cork', *ibid.*, 41–3; J. J. Leckey, 'A classification of Irish railway records', *ibid.*, iii, 2 (1973), 5–9; 'Survey of business records in Dublin', iii, 1 (1973), 10–13; W. MacAfee, 'Local historical studies of rural areas: methods and sources', 6 (1976), 1–31. Informative studies appearing elsewhere include P. Bottomley, *The Ulster textile industry: a catalogue of business rocords in P.R.O.N.I. relating principally to the linen industry in Ulster* (Belfast, 1978); J. J. Leckey and P. Rigney, *Archival collections of the Irish railway record society, D1–D10 (Dublin, 1975)*, T. Parkhill, 'Business records in County Kildare', *Kildare Arch. Hist. Soc. Jnl.*, xv, 3 (1973–4), 262–7.

[129] Exceptions to this generalisation include J. Lee, 'Railway labour in Ireland, 1833–1856', *Saothar*, 5 (1979), 9–26; K. A. Kennedy, *Productivity and industrial growth. The Irish experience* (Oxford, 1971); C. Mulvey and J. Trevithick, 'Wage inflation and wage leadership in Ireland, 1954–69', in A. A. Tait and J. A. Bristow (eds.), *Some problems of a developing economy* (Dublin, 1974), 204–34.

[130] For studies of trade union activity, and analyses of strikes, see: C. McCarthy, *A decade of upheaval. Irish trade unions in the 1960s* (Dublin, 1973); *Trade Unions in Ireland 1894–1960* (Dublin, 1977); 'A review of the objectives of national pay agreements 1970–77', *Administration*, xxv, i (Spring, 1977), 120–36; D. Nevin, (ed.), *Trade Unions and change in Irish society* (Dublin, 1980); D. O'Mahony, *Industrial relations in Ireland: the background*, E.S.R.I. paper no. 19 (Dublin, 1964); *Economic aspects of industrial relations*, E.S.R.I. paper no. 24 (Dublin, 1965); J. L. Pratschke, 'Business and labour in Irish society, 1945–70', in J. Lee (ed.), *Ireland 1945–70* (Dublin, 1979), 38–47; D. S. McLernon, 'Irish "Combinations" and economic activity in the latter half of the eighteenth century', *Journal of European Economic History*, v, 2 (Fall 1976), 401–6; E. Boyle, 'The linen strike of 1872', *Saothar*, 2 (1976), 12–22; J. J. Leckey, 'The railway servants' strike in County Cork 1898', *ibid.*, 39–45; J. Kemmy, 'The Limerick Soviet', *ibid.*, 45–52; M. Doyle, 'The Dublin guilds and journeymens' clubs', *Saothar*, 3 (1977), 6–13; D. Keogh, 'Michael O Lehane and the organisation of linen drapers assistants', *ibid.*, 33–43; A. Mitchell, 'William O'Brien, 1881–1968 and the Irish labour movement', *Studies*, 1x (1971), 311–31; D. Fitzpatrick, 'Strikes in Ireland, 1914–21', *Saothar*, 6 (1980), 26–39.

[131] See, for instance, E. Nevin, *Wages in Ireland, 1946–62*, E.S.R.I., paper no. 12 (Dublin, 1963); B. M. Walsh, *The structure of unemployment in Ireland, 1954–1972*, E.S.R.I. paper no. 77 (Dublin, 1975).

¹³² L. Kennedy, 'Retail markets in rural Ireland at the end of the nineteenth century', *Ir. Econ. Soc. Hist.*, v (1978), 46–63.

¹³³ *Ibid.*, 61.

¹³⁴ Welcome, if controversial, recent attempts to approach the question systematically are P. Bew, P. Gibbon and H. Patterson, *The state in Northern Ireland* (Manchester, 1977), and the contributions to Sociological Association of Ireland, *States in Ireland: power and conflict* (n. p. 1980). Oliver MacDonagh's *Ireland, op. cit.*, is an exception to this generalisation, as to most generalisations lamenting the lack of intellectual system in Irish historical writing.

¹³⁵ Studies which illuminate the role of ideology include T. C. Barnard, 'Planters and policies in Cromwellian Ireland' *Past & Present*, 61 (1973), 31–69; P. Bew and C. Norton, 'The Unionist state and the outdoor relief riots of 1932', *Econ. Soc. Rev.*, x, 3 (1979), 255–65; R. D. C. Black, 'The Irish experience in relation to the theory and policy of economic development', in A. J. Youngson (ed.), *Economic development in the long run* (London, 1972), 192–210; K. S. Bottigheimer, 'Kingdom and colony: Ireland and the Westward Enterprise, 1536–1660', in K. R. Andrews, N. P. Canny and P. E. H. Hair (eds.), *The Westward Enterprise* (Liverpool, 1978), 45–65; B. Bradshaw, 'Native reaction to the Westward Enterprise; a case study in Gaelic ideology', *ibid.*, 66–80; T. K. Daniel, 'Griffith on his noble head: the determinants of Cumann na nGaedheal's economic policy, 1922–32', *Ir. Econ. Soc. Hist.*, iii (1976), 55–65; C. A. Edie, 'The Irish Cattle Acts: a study in Restoration politics', *Amer. Phil. Soc. Trans.* n.s., lx, part ii (1970), 5–66; A. R. Griffiths, 'The Irish Board of Works in the Famine years', *Hist. Jnl.*, xiii (1970), 634–52; P. Kelly, 'The Irish woollen export prohibition act of 1699: Kearney revisited', *Ir. Econ. Soc. Hist.*, vii (1980), 22–44; G. M. T. Koot, 'Cliffe Leslie, Irish social reform and the origins of the English historical school of economics', *Hist. Pol. Econ.*, vii, 3 (1975), 312–36; J. Lee 'Aspects of corporatist thought in Ireland: the commission on vocational organisation, 1939–43', in Cosgrove and McCartney, *op. cit.*, 324–46; D. McAleese, 'Outward looking policies, manufactured exports and economic growth: the Irish experience', in M. J. Artis and A. R. Nobay (eds.), *Contemporary Economic Analysis* (London, 1977), 313–48; 'Political independence and economic performance – Ireland outside the U.K.', in E. Nevin (ed.), *The Economics of Devolution* (Cardiff, 1978), 130–46; J. W. Mason, 'The Duke of Argyll and the land question in late nineteenth century Britain', *Vict. Studies*, xxi, 2 (Winter 1978), 149–70.

¹³⁶ O. MacDonagh, 'The nineteenth-century revolution in govern-

ment: a reappraisal', *Hist. Jnl.,* i (1958), 52–67.

137 J. H. Andrews, 'Geography and government in Elizabethan Ireland', in Stephens & Glasscock, *op. cit.,* 178–91; 'The maps of the escheated counties of Ulster, 1609–10', *P.R.I.A.,* 74, C (1974), 133–70: *History in the ordnance map: an introduction for Irish readers* (Dublin, 1974).

138 Neither Grimshaw nor Coyne manage to find their way into the index of R. B. McDowell, *The Irish Administration 1801–1914* (London, 1964). For a pioneer of statistical services in the medical field see P. Froggatt, 'Sir William Wilde, 1815–70', P.R.I.A., 77, C (1977) 261–78.

139 A small selection of relevant studies includes T. Bartlett, 'Viscount Towshend and the Irish Revenue Board, 1767–75', *P.R.I.A.,* 79, C (1979), 153–75; D. Dickson, 'The Donegal revenue inspection of 1775', *Donegal Annual,* x, 2 (1972), 172–82; 'Edward Thompson's report on the management of customs and excise in Co. Kerry in 1735', *Kerry Arch. Soc. Jnl.,* 7 (1974), 12–21; H. D. Gribbon, 'The Irish Linen Board, 1771–1828', in Cullen & Smout, *op. cit.,* 77–87; L. Irwin, 'The role of the Presidency in the economic development of Munster, 1660–72', *Cork Hist. Arch. Soc. Jnl.,* lxxxii, 236 (1977), 102–14; R. Shipkey, 'Problems of alcoholic production and controls in early nineteenth century Ireland, *Hist. Jnl.,* xvi, 2 (1973), 293–302; V. Treadwell, 'The Irish customs administration of the sixteenth century', *I.H.S.,* xx, 80 (Sept. 1977), 384–417.

140 D. Hoctor, *The department's story: a history of the Department of Agriculture* (Dublin, 1971).

141 M. Moynihan, *Currency and central banking in Ireland, 1922–60* (Dublin, 1975).

142 J. Oliver, *Working at Stormont* (Dublin, 1978).

143 P. Buckland, *A factory of grievances* (Dublin, 1979).

144 R. Fanning, *The Irish Department of Finance, 1922–58* (Dublin, 1978).

145 R. M. Solow and P. Temin, 'Introduction: the inputs for growth', in P. Mathias and M. M. Postan (eds.), *The Cambridge Economic History of Europe,* vii, part 1 (Cambridge, 1978), 23.

146 E. D. Steele contends, for example, in a series of tightly argued and elegantly expressed contributions, that the refusal of the Irish to recognize the legitimacy of the property relations in land imposed by the state lay at the heart of the nineteenth century land question. See his *Irish land and British politics: tenant right and nationality, 1865–70* (London, 1974); 'Tenant-right and nationality in nineteenth century Ireland', *Proc. of the*

Leeds Phil. & Lit. Society, xv, part iv, (Dec. 1973), 75–111; 'Gladstone, Irish violence and conciliation', in Cosgrove & MacCartney, *op. cit.,* 257–78; 'Ireland for the Irish', *History,* lvii (June 1972), 240–2. See also C. Dewey, 'Celtic agrarian legislation and the Celtic revival: historicist implications of Gladstone's Irish and Scottish land acts, 1870–86', *Past & Pesent,* 64 (Aug. 1974), 30–70.

[147] The following is a list of studies, not mentioned elsewhere in this chapter, selected to illustrate the range of themes and approaches which the economic historian may find relevant for particular prupoises. The categories chosen are religion, education, family and community, law and order, politics, and general. S. J. Connolly, 'Catholicism and social discipline in pre-Famine Ireland' (D. Phil., N.U.U., 1977), abstracted in *Ir. Econ. Soc. Hist.,* iv (1977), 74–6; 'Illigitimacy and pre-nuptial pregnancy in Ireland before 1864: the evidence of some Catholic parish registers', *ibid.,* vi (1979), 5–23; R. Harris, *Prejudice and Tolerance in Ulster* (Manchester, 1970); L. Kennedy, 'The early response of the Irish catholic clergy to the cooperative movement', *I.H.S.,* xxi, 81 (Mar. 1978), 55–74; E. Larkin, *The historical dimensions of Irish Catholicism* (New York, 1976); D. W. Miller, 'Irish catholicism and the Great Famine', *Jnl. Social Hist.,* ix (1975), 81–98; 'Presbyterianism and 'modernisation' in Ulster', *Past & Present,* 80 (1978), 66–90; P. O'Farrell, *Ireland's English Question* (London, 1971); 'Millenialism, messianism and utopianism in Irish history', *Anglo-Irish Studies,* ii (1976), 45–68; Mary Daly, 'The development of the national school system, 1831–40', in Cosgrove and MacCartney, *op. cit.,* 150–63; J. M. Goldstrom, *The social content of education, 1808–70* (Shannon, 1972); K. T. Hoppen, *The common scientist in the seventeenth century* (London, 1970 (See also T. C. Barnard, 'The Hartlib circle and the origins of the Dublin Philosophical Society;', *I.H.S.,* xix, 73, (Mar. 1974), 56–71, and K. T. Hoppen's reply, *I.H.S.,* xx, 77, (Mar. 1976), 40–8); K. Flanagan, 'The rise and fall of the Celtic ineligible: competitive examinations for the Irish and Indian civil services in relation, to the educational and occupational structure of Ireland 1853–1921' (Ph.D. Sussex, 1978), abstracted in *Ir. Econ. Soc. Hist.,* vii (1980), 74–7. D. H. Akenson, *Between two revolutions–Islandmagee, Co. Antrim, 1798–1926* (Hamden. Conn., 1979); D. J. Casey and R. E. Rhodes (eds.), *Views of the Irish peasantry, 1800–1966* (Hamden, Conn. 1977); T. M. Gabriel, 'An anthropological perspective on land in western Ireland', *Anglo-Irish Studies,* iii (1977), 71–84; D. F. Hannan and L. Katsiaouni, *Traditional families? From culturally prescribed to negotiated roles in farm families,* E.S.R.I. paper no. 87 (Dublin, 1977);

D. F. Hannan, 'Patterns of spousal accommodation and conflict in traditional and modern farm families', *Econ. Soc. Rev.*, x, 1 (1978), 61–84; E. MacThomáis, *The 'Labour' and the Royal* (Dublin, 1979); B. Messenger, *Picking up the linen threads: a study in industrial folklore* (Austin, 1978); C. O'Danachair, 'Some marriage customs and their regional distribution', *Béaloides,* xlii–xliv (1974–6), 135–75; C. Ó Gráda, 'The Owenite community at Ralahine, County Clare, 1831–33: a reassessment', *Ir. Econ. Soc. Hist.*, i (1974), 36–48; G. Broeker, *Rural disorder and police reform in Ireland, 1812–36* (London, 1970); A. McClelland, 'Potato riots in County Down', *Ulster Folk and Transport Museum Year Book, 1975–6* (1977), 14–17; M. A. G. Ó'Tuathaigh, *Thomas Drummond and the government of Ireland* (N.U.I. O'Donnell Lecture, 1979); S. H. Palmer, 'The Irish police experiment: the beginning of modern police in the British Isles', *Social Science Quarterly,* 56 (1975), 410–24; K. T. Hoppen, 'Landlords, society and electoral politics in mid-nineteenth century Ireland', *Past & Present,* 75 (May 1977), 62–93; 'National politics and local realities in mid-nineteenth century Ireland', in Cosgrove and MacCartney, *op. cit.,* 190–227; F. O'Ferrall, 'The growth of national consciousness in Ireland, 1824–1848' (Ph.D., T.C.D., 1978), abstracted in *Ir. Econ Soc. Hist.,* vi (1979), 70–1; T. Powell, 'An economic factor in the Wexford rebellion of 1798', *Studia Hibernica,* 16 (1976), 140–57; C. Townshend, 'The Irish railway strike of 1920: industrial action and civil resistance in the struggle for independence', I.H.S., xxi, 83 (Mar. 1979), 265–82; K. Danaher, *The year in Ireland: a calendar* (Cork, 1972); E. E. Evans, *The personality of Ireland. Habitat, heritage and history* (Cambridge, 1973); O. MacDonagh, *The nineteenth century novel and Irish social history: some aspects* (N.U.I., O'Donnell Lecture, 1971).

[148] B. Hutchinson, 'The study of non-economic factors in Irish economic development', *Econ. Soc. Rev.,* 1 (July, 1970), 509–29.

[149] For two converging perspectives see P. Jenkins, 'Witches and fairies: supernatural aggression and deviance among the Irish peasantry', *Ulster Folklife,* 23 (1977), 33–56, and J. Lee, 'Continuity and change in Ireland, 1945–70', in J. Lee (ed.), *op. cit.* 166–77.

[150] N. P. Canny, *The Elizabethan conquest of Ireland: a pattern established 1565–76* (Hassocks, Sussex, 1976); 'The permissive frontier: social control in English settlements in Ireland and Virginia, 1550–1650', in K. R. Andrews, N. P. Canny and P. E. H. Hair, op. cit., 17–44; 'Dominant minorities: English settlers in Ireland and Virginia, 1550–1650', in A. C. Hepburn (ed.), *Minorities in History* (London, 1978), 51–69; W. J. Smyth, 'The western isle of Ireland and the eastern

seaboard of America–England's first frontiers', *Ir. Geog.,* xi (1978), 1–22.

[151] D. McAleese, 'Industrial specialisation and trade: Northern Ireland and the Republic', *Econ. Soc. Rev.,* vii, 2 (Jan. 1976), 143–60; D. S. Johnson, *op. cit.,* and 'Cattle smuggling on the Irish border 1932–38', *Ir. Econ. Soc. Hist.* vi (1979), 41–63. Other studies which employ a comparative approach include G. Fitzgerald, *Towards a new Ireland* (London, 1972); N. J. Gibson and J. E. Spencer (eds.), *Economic activity in Ireland: a study of two open economies* (Dublin, 1977); L. Symes, 'Rural land utilisation in Ireland', in Stephens and Glasscock, *op. cit.,* 259–73.

[152] It may be hoped that studies comparable to Mokyr, 'Industrialisation and poverty in Ireland and the Netherlands', *op. cit.,* will multiply during the coming decade.

[153] For the early history of the society cf. L. M. Cullen, 'Hon. Secretary's Report', *Ir. Econ. Soc. Hist.,* i (1974), 71–4.

[154] F. M. L. Thompson, Review of *Irish Economic and Social History, i–iv', I.H.S.,* xx, 80 (Sept. 1977), 495–6.

[155] An index to the first ten volumes can be found in the *Economic and Social Review,* special tenth anniversary issue, Jan., 1980.

[156] R. ffolliott, 'Our tenth birthday', *Irish Ancestor,* xi, i (1979), I.

[157] Speakers at the early conferences of the society included E. A. Wrigley, 'The significance of new demographic methods in historical demography', D. E. C. Eversley, 'The demography of Irish and English Quakers: some preliminary observations', and Phyllis Deane, 'National income accounting: methodological problems'. See L. M. Cullen, 'Hon. Secretary's Report', *op. cit.,* 72–3.

[158] This was held in Trinity College Dublin. The proceedings were published in Cullen & Smout, *op. cit.*

[159] The 1977 conference was held in Dublin and the 1978 conference in Bordeaux. The proceedings of both conferences are scheduled for publication. It should be noted that David Dickson also played a very active role in organising these conferences.

[160] See R. Samuel, 'Dublin history workshop, 10–12 March 1978', *History Workshop,* 6 (Autumn, 1978), 215–7.

[161] Interesting reviews and review articles include N. Canny, 'Early modern Ireland: an appraisal appraised', *Ir. Econ. Soc. Hist.,* iv (1977), 56–65; F. Carney, Review of R. E. Kennedy, Jr., *The Irish: emigration, marriage and fertility, ibid.,* i (1974), 81–3; D. Dickson, Review of J. S. Donnelly, Jr., *The land and the people of nineteenth century Cork, Econ Soc. Rev.,* vii, 4 (July 1976), 427–9; J. S. Donnelly Jr., Review of J. Lee,

The modernisation of Irish society, 1848–1918, I.H.S., xx, 78 (Sept. 1976), 206–12; P. Froggatt, Review of Peter Razzell, *The conquest of small-pox, I.H.S.*, xxi, 82 (Sept. 1978), 230–2; S. Gribbon, 'The social origins of Ulster unionism', *Ir. Econ. Soc. Hist.*, iv (1977), 66–72; L. Irwin, Review of T. C. Barnard, *Cromwellian Ireland, Cork Hist. Arch. Soc. Jnl*, lxxxiv, 239 (1979), 60–2; M. Murphy, Review of Sean Daly, *Cork: a city in crisis, ibid.*, 53–5; J. B. O'Brien, Review of J. S. Donnelly, Jr., *The Land and the people of nineteenth century Cork, Cork. Hist. Arch. Soc. Jnl.*, lxxx, 232 (1975), 95–101. M. A. G. Ó Tuathaigh, Review of A. P. W. Malcomson, *John Foster: the politics of the Anglo-Irish ascendancy, Ir. Econ. Soc. Hist*, vi (1979), 99–101; P. Roebuck, Review of F. M. L. Thompson & D. Tierney (eds), *General report on the Gosford estates in Co. Armagh, 1821 by William Greig, I.H.S.*, xx, 80 (Sept. 1977), 512–4.

[162] In addition to the publications on business history listed in n. 128 above, see S. Cullen, 'Sources of Cavan local history', *Breifne*, v, 18 (1977–8), 185–205; W. MacAfee, 'Local historical studies of rural areas: methods and sources', *Irish Archives Bulletin*, vi (1976), 1–31; W. Nolan, *Sources for local studies* (Dublin, n.d. 1978?); P. Roebuck, 'The Irish registry of deeds: a comparative study', I.H.S., xviii, 69 (March, 1972), 61–73.

[163] See, for instance, John Swift, 'The bakers' records', *Saothar*, 3 (1977), 1–5; P. Rigney, 'Some records of the Irish Transport and General Workers' Union in the National Library of Ireland', *ibid.*, 14–15; and the sections devoted specifically to 'Sources' in *Saothar*, 5 (1979) and 6 (1980).

[164] R. D. Edwards, 'An agenda for Irish history, 1978–2018', *I.H.S.*, xxi, 81 (Mar. 1978), 18.

[165] L. M. Clarkson, 'The writing of Irish economic and social history since 1968', *op. cit.*, 100.

[166] Anon., 'Kenneth H. Connell 1917–1973', *Econ. Soc. Rev.*, vi, 1 (Oct. 1974), 1.

[167] *ibid.*, 1–4; K. M. Drake, 'Professor K. H. Connell', *I.H.S.*, xix, 73 (Mar. 1974), 83–5; R. M. Hartwell, 'Kenneth H. Connell – an appreciation', *Ir. Econ. Soc. Hist.*, i (1974), 7–13.

[168] M. Wall, 'The Whiteboys', *op. cit.;* 'Catholics in economic life', in L. M. Cullen (ed.), *The formation of the Irish economy* (Cork, 1969), 37–52. See the obituaries by Seán Mac Loingsigh, 'In memoriam: Maureen Wall', *Donegal Annual*, x, 3 (1973), 335–6; U.C.D., *Report of the president, 1971–2, Academic*, 100–1 (I am grateful to Professor R. D.

Edwards for drawing my attention to, and providing me with a copy of, this obituary).

[169] For obituaries of Miriam Daly see Harry Gribbon and Joseph Leckey, *Ir. Econ. Soc. Hist.*, vii (1980), 5–6; John Swift, in *Saothar*, 6 (1980), 6; Sean Hutton, in *History Workshop,* 10 (Autumn 1980), 234.

[170] See D. C. North's comments in 'Discussion' on D. N. McCloskey, 'The achievements of the cliometric school', *Journal of Economic History,* xxxviii, 1 (Mar. 1978), 77–80 and 13–28 respectively. See also R. Cameron, 'Economic history, pure and applied', *ibid.,* xxxvi, 1 (Mar. 1976), 3–27.

[171] D. C. North, 'Structue and performance: the task of economic history', *Journal of Economic Literature, xvi (Sept. 1978), 974.*

[172] For a perceptive analysis of the preconditions for the triumph of the cliometricians in America see A. W. Coats, 'The historical context of the "new" economic history', *Journal of European Economic History,* ix, 1 (Spring 1980), 185–208.

[173] The contributions of the *Annales* school towards total history would be even more impressive if its imaginative power was reinforced by more rigorous application of economic theory. See R. Forster, 'Achievements of the Annales School', *Journal of Economic History,* xxxviii, 1 (Mar. 1978), 58–76.

ADDENDA

The proceedings of three conferences mentioned above have come to hand since completion of the text.

L. M. Cullen & P. Butel (eds.), *Négoce et industrie en France et en Irlande aux xviiie et xixe siècles* (C.N.R.S., Paris, 1980).

Distributed through Eason's, O'Connell Street, Dublin, at IR £8.25.

L. M. Cullen & F. Furet (eds.), *Ireland and France–Towards a comparative study of rural history* (Paris, 1981).

David Harkness and Mary O'Hara (eds.), *The town in Ireland* (Belfast, 1981). Published by Appletree Press, at £8.95 sterling.

Bulletin of the Irish Committee of Historical Sciences, 1939–74

LIST AND GUIDE TO CONTENTS

J. I. Mc Guire

The *Bulletin of the Irish Committee of Historical Sciences* was first issued in December, 1939. Its purpose was to keep members and associates of the Irish Historical Society and Ulster Society for Irish Historical Studies informed of work in progress. It provided notes and news of Irish historical interest and abstracts of papers read before both societies. A similar bulletin had already been issued by the Ulster Society for Irish Historical Studies between February and May and in October, 1939. In December this pioneer bulletin was incorporated in the new I.C.H.S. *Bulletin*.

While some of the papers summarised in the *Bulletin* later appeared in full in *Irish Historical Studies* or some other journal, most did not and so the *Bulletin* remains an invaluable source for work in Irish, occasionally European, history over more than two decades. In addition papers read before the Irish Conference of Historians or the Dublin Historical Association were occasionally summarised, as were contributions to symposia organised by the two originating societies.

The *Bulletin* appeared regularly from its inception in 1939 until the end of 1948. However, owing to the last illness and death of the editor, F. J. O'Kelly, no further issues appeared until 1952 when it was revived under Dr H. F. Kearney's editorship. Regular publication was again maintained until the early 1960s. An attempt to revive the *Bulletin* was made in 1974, when the Ulster Society for Irish Historical Studies, with the assistance of the Public Record Office of Northern Ireland and the Ulster Folk Museum, issued what was intended to be the first number of the *Bulletin's* third series, containing abstracts of papers read before the U.S.I.H.S. and the Irish Historical Society. Unfortunately no further issues appeared. A quite separate development has been the publication in 1979 of a new style *Bulletin* containing thesis abstracts.

A. Issues of the *Bulletin* with dates and serial numbers.

First series 1939-48
1939 : 1 (Dec.)
1940 : 2 (Jan.), 3 (Feb.), 4 (Mar.), 5 (Apr.), 6 (May), 7 (Nov.), 8 (Dec.)
1941 : 9 (Jan.), 10 (Feb.), 11 (Mar.), 12 (Apr.), 13 (May), 14 (Nov.), 15 (Dec.)
1942 : 16 (Jan.), 17 (Feb.), 18 (Mar.), 19 (Apr), 20 (May), 21 (Nov.), 22 (Dec.)
1943 : 23 (Jan.), 24 (Feb.), 25 (Mar.), 26 (Apr.), 27 (May), 28 (Dec.)
1944 : 29 (Jan.), 30 (Feb.), 31 (Mar.), 32 (Apr.), 33 (May), 34 (Nov.), 35 (Dec.)
1945 : 36 (Feb.), 37 (Mar.), 38 (Apr.), 39 (May), 40 (Nov.), 41 (Dec.)
1946 : 42 (Jan.), 43 (Feb.), 44 (Mar.), 45 (Apr.), 46 (May), 47 (June), 48 (Dec.)
1947 : 49 (Jan.), 50 (Mar.), 51 (Apr.), 52 (May), 53 (Dec.)
1948 : 54 (Jan.), 55 (Feb.), 56 (Mar.), 57 (Apr.), 58 (May), 59 (Dec.)
Nos 6, 8 and 9 were re-issued in a second edition.

Second series 1952-66
(The individual enumeration of each issue was continued from the first series).
1952 : 60 (Jan.), 61 (Apr.), 62 (Sept.), 63 (Dec.)
1953 : 64 (Mar.), 65 (June), 66 (Nov.)
1954 : 67 (Feb.), 68 (Apr.), 69 (June), 70 (Oct.)
1955 : 71 (Jan.), 72 (May), 73 (Oct.)
1956 : 74 (Jan.), 75 (Apr.), 76 (Oct.), 77 (Dec.)
1957 : 78 (Mar.), 79 (June), 80 (Nov.)
1958 : 81 (Feb.), 82 (Apr.), 83 (July), 84 (Nov.)
1959 : 85 (Feb.), 86 (May), 87 (Oct.)
1960 : 88 (Jan.), 89 (Apr.), 90 (winter)
1961 : 91 (spring), 92 (summer), 93 (autumn), 94 (winter)
1962 : 95 (spring), 96 – 97 (summer – autumn)
1962 – 63 : 98 (winter – spring).
1965 – 66 : 99

Third series 1974
1974 : 1

B. *Editors 1939 — 66*

J. F. O'Doherty,	1939 – 44
F. J. O'Kelly,	1944 – 48
H. F. Kearney,	1952 – 60
J. B. Morrall,	1961 – 62
K. B. Nowlan,	1962 – 66

C. *Bulletin* contents: guide to abstracts of papers and discussions arranged according to content (numbers in brackets refer to issues of the *Bulletin*).

i. *General* (covering longer periods of time).

E. Estyn Evans,	The continuity of Irish rural life (18)
E. Estyn Evans,	The site and growth of Belfast (32)
J. P. Haughton	Historical geography of Dublin (50)
George Kelly,	The historical significance of some Ulster placenames (43)
John O'Loan,	Agricultural history of the parish of Dromiskin (88)
D. G. Andrews,	The origins of local government in Ireland (99)
Síle Ní Chinnéide,	The Gaelic contribution to Irish nationalism (88)
M. J. Boyd,	The study of Latin and Greek in Ulster, from the seventeenth to the nineteenth centuries (36)
N. D. Emerson,	The presbyterian factor in Irish history (91)
H. D. Gribbon,	Industrial use of water power in Ulster (99)
M. G. Doyle,	The Dublin guilds and journeymen's clubs (3rd ser., 1)
J. J. Monaghan,	The rise and fall of the Belfast cotton trade (8)
Henry Mangan,	Irish historical portraits (65)
R. A. S. Macalister,	The origin and nature of the Irish books of annals (12)

ii. *Early medieval*

Ludwig Bieler,	Silva Focluti (22)
Nicolai Tolstoy,	Germanus, Cunedda, and Palladius: the origins of Irish christianity (93).
	Symposium on fifth century sources (79). Participants: Seán Mac Airt, F. Henry, Ludwig Bieler, Con Ó Cléirigh, James Carney, Eoin Mac White, T. Ó Raifeartaigh.
Ludwig Bieler,	Irish manuscripts in medieval Germania (77)
Kathleen Hughes,	The cult of St. Finnian of Clonard from the eight to the eleventh century (67)
John Hennig,	The Irish monastic tradition in eastern Europe (23)
Fergus Barrett,	Uí Fidgente: a kingdom of the Eoghanachta (24)
M. E. Dobbs,	The Dál Fiatach of County Down (38)
J. B. Andrews,	Early Irish law (62)
M. Ó Dubhghaill,	The political career of Cearbhall, king of Ossory, 844 – 88 (13).
John Ryan,	The historical content of the Caithréim Ceallacháin Chaisil (14).
Aubrey Gwynn,	Some Irish ecclesiastical titles in the tenth and eleventh centuries (17).
R. B. Knox,	Decline of early Irish monasticism (39).
Aubrey Gwynn,	Ireland and the continent in the eleventh century (63).
Felim Ó Briain,	The expansion of Irish christianity to 1200 : an historical survey (19).
Paul Walsh,	The dating of the Irish annals (11).
J. E. Caerwyn Williams,	The contribution of Ireland to medieval vision literature (33).
Aubrey Gwynn,	Some notes on the history of the Book of Kells (70).

iii. *Medieval*

C. Doherty,	The unreformed church in Ireland in the twelfth century (3rd ser., 1).
M. T. Flanagan,	Irish royal charters of the twelfth century (3rd ser., 1).

W. L. Warren,	Ireland in the twelfth century (96 – 97).
J. G. Grey,	Roman canon law in England; an historical controversy re-examined (78).
P. J. Dunning,	Norman clerical aggression in Irish south-eastern dioceses, 1198 – 1216 (52).
P. J. Dunning,	Pope Innocent III and Ireland : some unnoticed letters (36).
Aubrey Gwynn,	Archbishop David Mac Cearbhaill and the petition for the grant of English law to the Irish, 1277 – 83 (77).
James Lydon,	The Irish exchequer in the thirteenth century (81).
M. Richter,	Medieval nationalism – the case of Wales (3rd ser., 1).
J. Otway-Ruthven,	The native Irish and English law in medieval Ireland (59).
Jocelyn Otway-Ruthven,	Anglo-Irish local government in the late thirteenth century (41).
Ranald Nicholson,	Ireland and the Scottish wars of independence (96 – 97).
J. Watt,	Pope John XXII, King Edward II and Ireland (74).
M. D. O'Sullivan,	Revenue and expenditure in a medieval Irish town (16).
G. O. Sayles,	Who was the parson of Strabannon in 1351 ? (57).
Séamus Henchy,	Fosterage in medieval Ireland (44).
O. Davies,	Types and distribution of Ulster churches (15).
G. A. Hayes-McCoy,	Strategy and tactics in later medieval Ireland : a general survey (20).

iv. *Fifteenth to eighteenth centuries*

Urban G. Flanagan,	The church in Ireland in the mid-fifteenth century (62).
A. F. Scott Pearson,	British puritanism in the 15th and 16th centuries (47). Discussed by J. F. O'Doherty and R. B. McDowell.

A. G. Donaldson,	Methods of applying English legislation in Ireland 1495 – 1783 (69).
David B. Quinn,	Henry VIII and Ireland, 1509 – 34 (87).
B. Bradshaw,	Vested interests and the dissolution of the religious orders in Ireland, 1536 – 47 (3rd Ser., 1).
T. Desmond Williams,	The German nunciature of Giovanni Morone 1536 – 42 (69).
N. D. Atkinson,	The fall of the O'Carroll chieftainship in the sixteenth century (85).
Seán Ó Domhnaill,	Some aspects of sixteenth century Irish warfare (35).
W. S. Ferguson,	Church control over the grammar schools in Ireland, c. 1540 – 1714 (47).
W. S. Ferguson,	The beginnings of grammar schools in Ireland (21).
Dean White,	The reign of Edward VI in Ireland; some political, social and economic aspects (89).
B. Rowan,	Settlers and natives in the Leix-Offaly plantation (15).
T. Ó Laidhin,	Sir Henry Sidney's first lord deputyship (80).
Penry Williams,	The Council in Munster in the late sixteenth century (94).
T. O. Ranger,	The making of an Irish fortune : the early career of Richard Boyle, 1588 – 1614 (74).
J. Smyth,	The Monaghan land settlement of 1591 (25).
G. A. Hayes-McCoy,	Strategy and tactics in Irish warfare, 1593 – 1601.
F. M. Jones	Pope Clement VIII (1592 – 1605) and Hugh O'Neill (65).
N. P. Canny,	The emergence of the old English in late sixteenth century Ireland (3rd ser., 1).
Eileen McCracken,	Woodlands of Ulster in the early seventeenth century (41).
Eileen McCracken,	The Irish woodlands in the seventeenth century (82).
Gilbert Waterhouse,	Fynes Moryson: traveller (36).
A. F. Scott Pearson,	The origins of presbyterianism in Co. Antrim, 1600 – 60 (57).
J. Carty,	Contemporary accounts of the battle of Kinsale, 1601 (6).

Brendan Jennings,	The career of Hugh, son of Rory O'Donnell, earl of Tirconnel, in the Low Countries, 1607 – 42 (8).
Cajetan Finegan,	Coarbs and erenaghs in north-west Ulster in the seventeenth century (56).
H. F. Kearney,	Ecclesiastical politics and the counter-reformation in Ireland, 1620 – 48 (85).
Thomas J. O'Donnell,	Don Philip O'Sullivan Beare, historian (27).
W. V. Treadwell,	The origins of the Irish Commission of 1622 (70).
F. X. Martin,	An Irish Capuchin missionary in politics : Francis Nugent negotiates with James I, 1623 – 4 (90).
H. F. Kearney,	Wentworth and Ireland 1629 – 33 (71).
M. Benvenuta Curtin,	Dominic O'Daly and the counter-reformation (99).
J. R. McCormick,	English politics and Irish land (71).
Donal F. Cregan,	Machinery of government in the Confederation of Kilkenny (57).
Seán Doyle,	The Confederation of Kilkenny and catholic Europe (79).
John A. Murphy,	The vacillitating politics of Inchiquin, 1643 – 9 (64).
John Lowe,	Some factors in the negotiations between Charles I and the Confederation of Kilkenny (94).
J. Lowe,	The Glamorgan episode : a reassessment (86).
Patrick J. Corish,	Nicholas French, bishop of Ferns, and the peace with Ormond, 1649 (49).
P. J. Corish,	John Lynch, a historian of the confederate period (63).
R. B. McDowell,	Problem of dissent in Ireland, 1660 – 1740 (40).
B. Mulrean,	Peter Walsh and the remonstrance (46).
Benignus Millett,	The affaire Taaffe, 1666 – 68 : the extraordinary mission of Fr. James Taaffe, O.F.M. (95).
W. H. C. Smith,	The removal of the duke of Ormond from the government of Ireland, 1669 (61).

H. Carmichael,	The 'protestant interest' under the earl of Essex, 1672 – 7 (87).
Maurice Twomey,	Charles II, Lord Ranelagh and the Irish finances (89).
D. A. Chart,	The account book of the Rev. Andrew Rowan, rector of Dunaghy, Co. Antrim (5).
Bian Ó Cuív,	James Cotter : a seventeenth century agent of the crown (76).
Homer L. Calkin,	Anglo-Irish relations in 1689 (44). Discussed by Kevin B. Nowlan.
J. C. Beckett,	William King as bishop of Derry, 1691 – 1703 (20).
J. C. Beckett,	Church and state in Ireland in the eighteenth century (2).
D. Dickson,	Irish population in the eighteenth century: some reconsiderations (3rd ser., 1).
Kenneth Milne,	The borough as the organ of administration in eighteenth century Ireland (98)
F. G. James,	Irish smuggling in the eighteenth century (92).
John Ainsworth,	Some aspects of 18th century Irish land tenure (87).
Albert Carré,	Louis Crommelin (7).
G. W. Shummacher,	Settlement of Palatines in Ireland, 1709 – 15 (58).
Sean Moloney,	Irish parliament and Wood's halfpence (34).
J. L. McCracken,	Parliamentary elections 1727 – 68 (47).
J. J. Graneek,	Southwell charity, Downpatrick 1733 – 1948 (58).
J. J. Campbell,	David Manson, schoolmaster in Belfast (60)
David Kennedy,	Joseph Black, M.D., 1728 – 1799 (60)
M. McGeehin,	The opposition of catholic townsmen to quarterage in eighteenth century Ireland (61).
Maureen Wall,	Catholic wealth in eighteenth century Ireland (81).
Maureen MacGeehin,	The catholic committee and the Kenmare secession (53).
(Charles) O'Conor Don,	The beginnings of Irish catholic organisation in the eighteent century (26).
David Kennedy,	The journal of John Black of Belfast, merchant, 1751 – 66 (93).

J. L. McCracken,	The revenue bill dispute of 1753 (16).
J. J. Auchmuty,	Francois Thurot (3).
Edith Johnston,	The career and correspondence of Thomas Allen 1767 – 85 (75).
Edith Johnston,	The Irish administration 1767 – 85 (75).
Éamonn Ó Riagáin,	Analyses of the personnel of the Irish commons, 1769 – 76 (47).
Walter Love,	Charles O'Conor of Belanagare and Thomas Leland's 'philosophical' history of Ireland (90).
Eilish Clune,	The Irish parliament, 1776 – 83 : a general survey (32).
Robert Allen,	William Steel Dickson, 1774 – 1824 (50).
James Fitzsimons,	The mathematical tradition in popular education, 1780 – 1870 (26).
James A. MacCauley,	Peep o' Day Boys and Defenders, 1784 – 95 (58).
David Kennedy,	Ulster academies and the teaching of science, 1785 – 1835 (11).
John Hall Stewart,	The fall of the Bastille on the Dublin stage (64).
R. B. McDowell,	The United Irishmen of Dublin, 1791 – 4 (1).
R. B. McDowell,	Irish radical thought at the end of the eighteenth century (6).
R. B. McDowell,	The Irish parliament, 1790 – 7 : a general survey (18).
A. T. Q. Stewart,	Presbyterian radicalism in the north of Ireland, 1792 – 3 (76).
R. G. Morton,	The Ulster insurrection of 1798 (65).
G. A. Hayes-McCoy,	Miles Byrne's yeomanry corps in 1798 (54).
G. A. Hayes-McCoy,	The Irish pike (21).
Henry McAnally,	French invasion of Connacht, 1798 : some problems in numbers (37).
Barbara M. Kerr,	Irish emigration to England, 1798 – 1838 (4).
T. A. Burke,	Irish catholics and the legislative union, 1800 (33).
Francis O'Kelley,	Survey of newspapers printed in Ireland before 1801 (7).
Francis O'Kelley,	Ulster journalism to 1850 : contrasts and parallels (27). Deals with eighteenth century in part.

v. *Nineteenth and twentieth centuries*

K. B. Nowlan,	South-east Baltic land and national questions 1800 – 1905 (72).
J. B. Morrall,	Lamennais as an interpreter of history (72).
Kennedy F. Roche,	O'Connell as a utilitarian (98).
Donal McCartney,	The writing of history in Ireland, 1800 – 30 (75).
R. D. Collison Black,	The classical economists and the Irish problem (62).
G. D. P. Allt,	Irish society as seen in the novels of Edgeworth and Lever (10).
J. J. Monaghan,	The Belfast theatre about 1800 (42).
R. B. McDowell,	Relations between the viceroy and the chief secretary of Ireland from the union to 1921 (69).
Cathaldus Giblin,	Richard Hayes, O.F.M., and the veto question, 1815 – 24 (86).
Robert Allen,	Henry Montgomery, ecclesiastic and politician (30). 1820s.
John Jamiesan,	Reverend Henry Cooke as a politician (78). 1820s.
Deirdré Clancy,	Archbishop John MacHale in Irish politics 1830 – 50 (84).
R. J. Rodgers,	The contribution of James Carlile to national education in Ireland (3rd ser., 1). From 1831.
J. L. Lord,	The early political activity of Isaac Butt (59). 1830s.
J. H. Whyte,	Daniel O'Connell and the Repeal Party (83). 1832.
D. Large,	The house of lords and Ireland in the age of Peel, 1832 – 1847 (73).
Brian A. Kennedy,	Sharman Crawford, O'Connell and the tithe question, 1834 – 8 (15).
Timothy F. Kelly,	Thomas Drummond and Irish administrative reform (31). 1830s.
David Kennedy,	Captain Pitt Kennedy's plan for Irish agriculture, 1835 – 45 (32).
Max Berger,	Irish settlement in the United States, 1836 – 50 (29).
Nessan Shaw,	The problem of intemperance in Ireland, 1838 – 56 (39).

Kevin B. Nowlan,	Sir James Graham and Ireland, 1841 – 46 (76).
J. Maher,	The repeal movement and the land question (61).
J. R. Hill,	Aspects of the role of Dublin in the Irish national movement of the 1840s (3rd ser., 1).
Brian A. Kennedy,	William Sharman Crawford and domestic legislation for Ireland (52). 1840s.
T. Jones Hughes,	The mid-nineteenth century Irish landscape (95).
Brian A. Kennedy,	Tenant-right agitation in Ulster, 1845 – 50 (34).
J. Grant,	The great famine and the province of Ulster with especial reference to County Armagh (3rd ser., 1).
T. P. O'Neill,	The scientific investigation of the failure of the potato crop, 1845 – 6 (45).
Oliver MacDonagh,	The attitude of the Irish catholic clergy towards emigration, during the great famine (51). 1845 – 52.
T. P. O'Neill	Sources for a history of Young Ireland (47).
Kevin B. Nowlan,	Young Ireland centenary publications (47).
D. C. Linehan,	The Irish executive and the crisis of 1848 (71).
Brian A. Kennedy,	John Martin's diary, 'Journal of voyage from Ireland in the convict ship Mountstuart Elphinstone (1849)' (73).
J. C. Beckett,	Queen's College, Belfast : a survey of the early years (37).
G. Woledge,	The organisation of Irish university education in the mid-nineteenth century (29).
C. L. Wilson,	Thomas Andrews (63). Chemist, university administrator, liberal thinker, Queen's University, Belfast c. 1849.
Solomon F. Bloom,	Ireland's destiny as it appeared to Karl Marx (46). Post 1850. Discussed by R. B. McDowell.
E. R. R. Green,	The founding of the Fenian Brotherhood (83). 1850s.
Desmond Ryan,	The historians and Fenianism (79).
E. D. Steele,	Cardinal Cullen and Irish nationality (3rd ser., 1).
J. L. Montrose,	The Landlord and Tenant Act of 1860 (1).

J. J. Auchmuty,	Irish public opinion and the Roman question, 1860 (30).
Hugh Shearman,	British statesmen and the Irish church question (45) 1860s.
Canon Breene,	Church law and the disestablishment of the Church of Ireland (22)
Hugh Shearman,	State-aided tenant purchase under the Irish Church Act (28).
David Thornley,	The attitude of Irish conservatives to home rule from the Disestablishment Act to the National Conference of 1873 (82).
D. Lindsay Keir,	Froude and Lecky on eighteenth century Ireland (14).
Donal McCartney,	Lecky's *Leaders of public opinion in Ireland* (99).
T. W. Moody,	Michael Davitt in Dartmoor (9). 1870.
T. W. Moody,	Michael Davitt and the 'pen' letter (38). 1870.
Lawrence J. McCaffrey,	The general election of 1874 in Ireland (67).
C. Cruise O'Brien,	The Irish parliamentary party machine 1874 – 85 (42).
R. Dudley Edwards,	Parnell and the second Irish-American national challenge (80).
T. N. Brówn,	The new departure, 1879 – 80 (82).
C. H. D. Howard,	Joseph Chamberlain, Parnell and the Irish 'Central Board' scheme (63). 1884 – 5.
C. Cruise O'Brien,	The Galway election of 1886 (70).
James A. MacCauley,	Ulster and the first Home Rule Bill (48). 1886.
Kennedy Lindsay,	The liberal split of 1886 in the commons (71).
R. P. Davis,	Sinn Fein and the Irish Parliamentary Party, 1890 – 1908 (86).
F. J. Whitford,	Joseph Devlin and the Catholic Representation Association of Belfast 1895 – 1905 (78).
G. R. C. Keep,	The underworld of Irish emigration in the later nineteenth century (65).
F. S. L. Lyons,	The Irish Unionist Party and the devolution crisis of 1904 – 5 (55)
J. C. Beckett,	The Irish Universities Act, 1908 (61).
H. Patterson,	The shipyard and engineering workers' strike in Belfast 1919 (3rd ser., 1).
T. Desmond Williams,	Negotiations leading up to the announcement of an Anglo-Polish agreement on 31 March 1939 (72).

vi. ARCHIVES AND SOURCES

R. J. Hayes,	The National Library and the historian (12).
Samuel Weir,	The Registry of Deeds, Ireland (26).
Henry Mangan,	Reflections on the Irish Manuscripts Commission (40). Reply by Aubrey Gwynn.
D. A. Chart,	The National Register of Archives (55).
Margaret C. Griffith,	The history of the Public Record Office of Ireland (55).
R. J. Hayes,	The future organisation of Irish public archives (57). Discussed by R. C. Simington and T. W. Moody.
R. L. Atkinson,	The United Kingdom Historical Manuscripts Commission : its work and development (60).
W. D. Coates,	The working of the register (60). Deals with National Register of Archives.
B. Mac Giolla Coille,	Register of archives for Eire (60).
E. Heatly, K. Darwin and B. Trainor	Register of archives for Northern Ireland (68).
Kenneth Darwin,	Locating manuscripts in Northern Ireland (92).
Homer L. Calkin,	The United States government and the Irish bibliographical study of research materials in the National Archives (66).
J. E. Nolan,	Reproduction of ancient manuscripts (6).
R. Dudley Edwards,	Local history and An Tóstal (68).

vii. *TEACHING HISTORY : SYMPOSIA*
The teaching of Irish history (17). Participants: Dr Monaghan, J. C. Beckett, J. L. McCracken, D. B. Quinn and D. A. Chart.
The new secondary school programme in history (25). Participants: Miss Davitt, Fr Cregan, Mr O'Rourke, Fr Bodkin, Mr Parker, Mr F. W. Ryan, Fr Gwynn, Dr R. Dudley Edwards.

Problems in the teaching of history : 1, primary schools (44) Participants: Éamonn Riagáin, M. Ó Dubhghaill and others.

Problems in the teaching of history : 2, secondary schools (47). Participants : Eileen Davitt, D. F. Cregan, T. A. O'Rourke, and E. Aughney.

viii. *AREAS FOR FURTHER WORK*
Things to be done in Irish history:
i, early period (2). John Ryan.
ii, ecclesiastical history (2). Dr O'Doherty
iii, historical maps of Ireland (2). T. W. Moody, T. W. Freeman, T. Corcoran.
iv, modern period (12). R. Dudley Edwards and T. W. Moody.
v, eighteenth century (21). R. B. McDowell, Dr Kirkpatrick and Mr Ó Dubhghaill.
vi, nineteenth century (28). T. W. Moody and others.
[vii], genealogical history (45). Gerard Slevin, James A. MacCauley and others.

The future of Irish history (24). Participants: D. B. Quinn, Mr Woledge, Dr Monaghan, Dr Fizsimons, J. C. Beckett, D. A. Chart, E. R. R. Green.
R. J. McHugh   Irish folklore and the Irish historian (9).

Problems of the study of local history (10). D. A. Chart and Dr Monaghan.
D. F. Gleeson,   A scheme for local history (19).

Problems in the study of local history (47). Participants; John Brady, Dermot F. Gleeson, Patrick Brophy and Edward MacLysaght.
Dermot F. Gleeson,   Problems of Irish ecclesiastical history for the local worker (62).
J. R. Greeves,   The study of family history (68).

*Dublin University Press Limited
has 200 years experience in Printing
for Universities in Ireland.*

DUBLIN UNIVERSITY PRESS LTD.
17 GILFORD ROAD,
SANDYMOUNT,
DUBLIN 4.

Tel. 01-694422

CORK UNIVERSITY PRESS
RECENT PUBLICATIONS

THE ROMAN CATHOLIC CHURCH AND THE PLAN OF CAMPAIGN IN IRELAND 1886 - 1888
The first phase of the Consolidation of the Modern Irish State
by
Professor Emmet Larkin
Department of History, The University of Chicago

Published: 1979　　　　　　　　　　Price: IR £9.00 Hardback

* * * * * *

PROTESTANT SOCIETY AND POLITICS IN CORK 1812 - 1844
by
Dr. Ian d'Alton

Ready: May, 1981　　　　　　　　　Price: IR £13.25 Hardback

* * * * * *

CATHOLIC MISSIONARIES AND LIBERIA
A study of Christian Enterprise in West Africa 1842 - 1949
by
Fr. Edmund M. Hogan

Ready: May, 1981　　　　　　　　　Price IR £12.00

ORDER THROUGH BOOKSELLERS OR DIRECT FROM THE PUBLISHERS

CORK UNIVERSITY PRESS
UNIVERSITY COLLEGE, CORK

IRELAND AND FRANCE
17th – 20th centuries

TOWARDS A COMPARATIVE STUDY OF RURAL HISTORY

Proceedings of the First
Franco-Irish Symposium on Social and Economic History – Dublin

edited by

L. M. CULLEN & F. FURET

ÉDITIONS DE L'ÉCOLE DES HAUTES ÉTUDES
EN SCIENCES SOCIALES

The first attempt at a comparative study of Franco-Irish rural history has brought together the best specialists in two countries where history has long remained deeply linked to the life of peasant communities, solid, numerous, unyielding and as unamenable to control by landlords as they were obedient to the Catholic Church. Both these European peasant societies, while being similarly subject to the constraints of available space or arable land did not evolve either at the same rate or in the same way. In comparing overall population, the type and size of farms, the modes of social reproduction and inheritance, the historical tissue of two societies with long standing peasant backgrounds has been brought forth. Thus two countries with two agricultures show different answers to problems that are often the same.

Avaliable from Eason's, O'Connell Street, Dublin 1   IR £7.60

THE TOWN in Ireland

**Edited by David Harkness
and Mary O'Dowd**

HISTORICAL STUDIES XIII
Papers read before the Irish
Conference of Historians

BELFAST
30 May–2 June, 1979

G. MacNIOCAILL   G. H. MARTIN
R. J. HUNTER   L. CLARKSON
M. MURPHY   P. J. JUPP
P. FROGGATT   C. O'LEARY
S. GRIBBON   M. DALY

APPLETREE PRESS

CORK UNIVERSITY PRESS

Recent Publication

The Roman Catholic Church and the Plan of Campaign in Ireland 1886 – 1888

by
Professor Emmet Larkin
Dept. of History, The University of Chicago.

This story is primarily concerned with how the governing consensus of Leader, Party and Bishops, which had evolved in Ireland by 1886, was transformed into a constitutional system by the impact of the Plan of Campaign on that consensus.

"Valuable contribution to our understanding of this seminal and formative period in modern Irish history" – *Studies*.

"Rich, thoughtfully written volume" – *John V. Kelleher*.

"Larkin tells the story with admirable skill, placing in a highly readable narrative, an otherwise tangled and confusing skein of events" *Donald H. Akenson, Victorian Studies*.

"This book enhance Professor Larkins existing reputation as the accepted expert on church affairs in 19th Century and one congratulates Cork University Press for making it available" – *Cork Examiner*.

"A masterly account of the Plan which will not be surpassed for many a year" – *Irish Independent*.

Published: 1979   Price IR £9.00 Hardback.

CORK UNIVERSITY PRESS

Recent Publication

Catholic Missionaries and Liberia

A study of Christian Enterprise in West Africa
1842 – 1949

by
Fr. Edmund Hogan

"Catholic missionaries and Liberia" tells the story of the church's repeated efforts to establish itself in Liberia. It describes in vivid detail the course of three ill-fated 19th Century expeditions and the manner in which 20th Century missionaries from Alsace, Ireland and America set down roots.

Published, May, 1981

Price IR £12.00 to 31 Dec. '81 – thereafter IR £16.00